alongtheway.libripublishing

The accompanying website of this Revised Edition features colour photographs and an assessment of novels about the Camino *that are introduced in Chapter 9 "Inventing Santiago."*

Finisterre — San Paio — Arzúa — Ligonde-Ereixe
Santiago de Compostela — Melide — Portomarín
Barbadelo — Triacastela — O Cebreiro
Trabadelo — Cacabelos — Villar de Mazarife
Rabanal del Camino — León
El Acebo — Astorga — Hospital de Órbigo — Mansi de M

ALONG THE WAY

ALONG THE WAY

PILGRIMAGE SCENES FROM THE CAMINO
FRANCÉS TO SANTIAGO DE COMPOSTELA

ROBERT LAWRENCE FRANCE

Front cover image: Carving of apostle originally from the Compostela cathedral, now in Harvard University's Fogg Museum (see pages 115-116). Back cover: Left: Sunrise over the *meseta* just after near disaster of the broken backpack (see pages 62-63). Centre: Saint James in a fifteenth-century stained-glass window of St. Neot's on Bodmin Moor, Cornwall. Right: Close-up of monument to celebrate the 1993 visit of the Pope to Monte del Gozo overlooking Compostela (see pages 109-110). Title page spread: Cape Cod in Massachusetts. This image is representative of the fact that the true camino is only really finished upon returning home (see page 142).

First published in 2014 by Libri Publishing ■ Revised edition published in 2021 by Libri Publishing ■ Copyright © Robert L France ■ ISBN: Paperback 978 1 911450 83 2 ■ All rights reserved. No part of this publication may be reproduced, stored in any retrieval system or transmitted in any form or by any means, electronic, mechanical, photocopying, recording or otherwise, without the prior written permission of the copyright holder for which application should be addressed in the first instance to the publishers. No liability shall be attached to the author, the copyright holder or the publishers for loss or damage of any nature suffered as a result of reliance on the reproduction of any of the contents of this publication or any errors or omissions in its contents. ■ A CIP catalogue record for this book is available from The British Library ■ Design by Helen Taylor ■ Libri Publishing, Brunel House, Volunteer Way, Faringdon, Oxfordshire SN7 7YR ■ Tel: +44 (0)845 873 3837 ■ www.libripublishing.co.uk

*Reflections on Landscape, Literature, and Longing
of Europe's First Cultural Itinerary Route
and a United Nations World Heritage Site*

– A WEB-ENHANCED BOOK –

All the way to Heaven, is Heaven.
Saint Catherine of Siena

Heaven is under our feet as well as over our heads.
Henry David Thoreau

Well I know that as you go *along the way*
You plan to tell tales...
Geoffrey Chaucer

Dedication

TO MY FELLOW WAYFARERS AMADOR, ELIDAE, LAURENT, MARIA, SANDRA, SIMONE, AND TONY, AMONG OTHERS, AND TO JEAN-OLIVIER, EMMANUELLE, AND ESPECIALLY PASQUALE IN PARTICULAR. THOUGH WE MAY NEVER MEET AGAIN AND YOU ARE UNLIKELY TO EVER READ THIS IN YOUR NON-NATIVE LANGUAGES, I WILL HOLD DEAR THE MEMORY OF OUR CONFRATERNITY…ALWAYS. MY SINCEREST THANKS FOR WELCOMING ME INTO THAT SHARED FELLOWSHIP OF LAUGHTER, TEARS, SPIRIT, AND ACCOMPLISHMENT. AND FINALLY, IN LOVING MEMORY OF MY PARENTS, MARILYN AND BARRY FRANCE, FOR THEIR OWN RECENTLY COMPLETED EARTHLY PILGRIMAGES.

CONTENTS

xii	LIST OF PHOTOGRAPH IDENTIFICATIONS
xvi	**PREFACE**
	Ultreia: The Santiago Pilgrimage 101
1	**INTRODUCTION**
	Camino Triptych: Literary →Personal →Cultural
9	**PART I READING THE WAY**
11	**Pre-script**
	On Contemplation...
17	**Chapter 1**
	"Give Me My Scallop-Shell of Quiet"
18	History
21	Humanity
22	Spirituality
24	Pilgrimage
	On Adventure...
29	**Chapter 2**
	"My Staff of Faith to Walk Upon"
30	Weather
30	Wayfinding
32	Danger
33	Hardship
	On Joy...
37	**Chapter 3**
	"My Scrip of Joy, Immortal Diet"
38	Excitement
39	Relaxation
40	Playfulness
40	Happiness
	On Contact...
43	**Chapter 4**
	"And Thus I'll Make My Pilgrimage"
44	Walking
45	Landscape
47	Places
49	People

55 **PART II WALKING THE WAY**

56 **Pre-amble**

On Landscape....

59 **Chapter 5**
Over the Hills and Far Away
60 Fields
65 Hills
71 Communities
75 Woods
79 Coasts

On Architecture...

85 **Chapter 6**
The Presumed Eternity of Stone
86 Structures
90 Bridges
94 Sculpture
98 Churches
108 Monuments

On Memories...

113 **Chapter 7**
Parallel Roads
114 The Road Most Travailed
119 Roads to Romantic Ruin
125 The Road to Heaven
131 The Road Within
137 Rocky Roads

On Pilgrimage....

143 **Chapter 8**
Communitas
144 Routines
149 Pilgrims
155 Meals
158 Beds
164 Locals

171 **PART III   BECOMING THE WAY**

173 **Pro-logue**

On Literary...

177 **Chapter 9**
     Inventing Santiago
178 Mystery
183 History
189 Esoteric/New Age
194 Contemporary
203 Poetry and Inspiration

On Visual and Auditory...

207 **Chapter 10**
     Capturing Compostela
208 Photography and Art
215 Films
222 Documentaries
228 Electronic
232 Music

On Confraternity...

241 **Chapter 11**
     Bulletin Bonhomie
242 Purpose and Methods
244 Incidents and Anecdotes
246 Depth and Breadth
247 Practicalities and Reciprocity
248 Rants and Reviews

On Zeitgeist...

253 **Chapter 12**
     Shell Shocked and Star Struck
254 Slouching Towards Santiago
258 Anthropology, Ethnography, and Geography
262 Building a Camino Reference Library
270 The Pilgrimage Disease: Diagnosis Caminophilia!
273 The Modern Cultural Phenomenon of Pilgrimage

281 BIBLIOGRAPHY

LIST OF PHOTOGRAPH IDENTIFICATIONS

On Landscape...

CHAPTER 5
OVER THE HILLS AND FAR AWAY

Fields

Page 60 Fields between Obanos and Puneta la Reina.

Page 61 Fields between Cañas and Santo Domingo de la Calzada.

Page 62 The Way crossing the border between La Rioja and Old Castile.

Page 63 The Way traversing hamlet and hill on the *meseta*.

Page 65 Heavenly display observed outside of Sahagún.

Hills

Page 66 (upper) Rolling hills near Villamayor de Monjardin.

Page 66 (lower) Edge of the Barranco Mataburros canyon on approach to Viana.

Page 67 Labyrinth of pilgrim stones atop the Sierra de Atapuerca.

Page 68 Grasses dancing in the wind in the hills near El Acebo.

Page 70 View backward from O'Cebreiro of cloud-filled valley

Communities

Page 71 Ramshackle porches on homes in village of Pieros.

Page 72 Distant view of Iglesia de San Francisco in Villafranca del Bierzo.

Page 73 (upper) Ancient *palloza* buildings in O'Cebreiro.

Page 73 (lower) Juxtaposition of old

and new buildings on the outskirts of Sarria.

Page 74 Last scallop shell insignia of the Camino in Compostela's Plaza de Obradorio.

Woods

Page 76 The Way through the woods before Sarria.

Page 77 (upper) A tree-bordered field after Gonzar.

Page 77 (lower) Copses of trees along the way to Finisterre.

Page 78 Eucalyptus forests near the Galician coast.

Coasts

Page 79 The Muxia peninsula.

Page 80 The Muxia lighthouse.

Page 81 (upper) Celebratory *coquille St. Jacques* dinner in Finisterre.

Page 81 (lower) Finisterre beach.

Page 83 'Rebirthing' waves and last steps at Finisterre.

On Architecture...

CHAPTER 6
THE PRESUMED ETERNITY OF STONE

Structures

Page 86 Gateway in Obanos at start of pilgrimage walk.

Page 87 Estella's Palacio de los Reyes de Navarra.

Page 88 The Monasterio de las Huelgas on the outskirts of Burgos.

Page 89 Skeletal arches of the San Anton hospice near Castrojeriz.

Page 90 The Templar castle in Ponferrada.

Bridges

Page 91 The pilgrim bridge in Puente la Reina at the start of the Camino Francés.

Page 92 (upper) Approaching the Roman bridge on the Via Traiana after Cirauqui.

Page 92 (lower) The Roman causeway crossing the flood-plain after Castrojeriz.

Page 93 La Puente del Passo Honoroso leading into Hospital de Órbigo.

Sculpture

Page 94 Capitals in the cloister of San Pedro de la Rúa in Estella.

Page 95 Carvings on the coffin of the Abbess of monastery of Santa Maria de Cañas.

Page 96 Column and archivolt carvings on the façade of the Iglesia de Santiago in Carrión de los Condes.

Page 97 Bas-relief scallop shells decorating the façade of the San Marcos church in León.

Page 98 The Annunciation portrayed on the tympanum of the church of San Nicholás in Portomarín.

Churches

Page 99 Romanesque north portal of the Iglesia de San Miguel in Estella.

Page 100 San Martin church in Frómista.

Page 101 Gothic front of the cathedral in León.

Page 102 Romanesque interior of the Basilica de San Isidoro in León.

Page 104 The Renaissance front of the cathedral of Santiago de Compostela.

Page 105 The Romanesque Puerta de las Platerias of the Compostela cathedral.

Page 106 Carvings on the tympanum of the Puerta de las Platerias.

Monuments

Page 108 Traffic fatality monument to a Canadian cyclist.

Page 109 Modern statue of Way-weary pilgrim in front of the San Marcos hospice in León.

Page 110 Monument celebrating Pope's mass on the Monte del Gozo overlooking Compostela.

Page 111 Statue honouring Galician emigration in Negreira.

Page 112 Pilgrim boot statue at Cabo Fisterra.

On Memories…

CHAPTER 7
PARALLEL ROADS

The Road Most Travailed

Page 114 Church of Saint James in Cambridge, Massachusetts where pilgrim blessing was received.

Page 116 Capital carvings in Harvard University's Fogg Museum visited on walk to Boston airport.

Page 117 Cathedral of Santiago de Compostela.

Page 118 Landscape architecture in Muxia.

Page 119 Boulder where burning ritual was performed at Cabo Fisterra.

Roads to Romantic Ruin

Page 120 Alabaster sarcophagus in the Burgos cathedral.

Page 121 Bar poster in Castrojeriz.

Page 122 Sarcophagus in the monastery-hotel of San Zoilo in Carrión.

Page 123 Modern pilgrim statue in Samos.

Page 124 Statue in the Santiago de Compostela museum.

The Road to Heaven

Page 125 Pilgrim crosses in a fence between Logrono and Navarrete.

Page 126 Santiago *Matamoros* statue in Burgos cathedral.

Page 127 Capital in the monastery-hotel of San Zoilo in Carrión.

Page 130 Entrance to the Apostle's putative tomb.

The Road Within

Page 132 Home living-room in Cambridge, Massachusetts.

Page 133 Modern statue to ancient hominids found in Atapuerca.

Page 134 Mural in hamlet before Burgos.
Page 135 Death carvings in Castrojeriz.
Page 136 Roadside sign near Mansila de las Mulas.

Rocky Roads

Page 137 Ruins of dwellings in Bethsaida in Upper Galilee.
Page 139 Stone pile at the base of the Cruz de Ferro.
Page 141 Hills near Tricastela.
Page 142 Beach at Plum Island, Massachusetts.

On Pilgrimage…

CHAPTER 8
COMMUNITAS

Routines

Page 145 (upper) Street sign in Navarrete.
Page 145 (lower) Road sign near Carrión de los Condes.
Page 146 Tower of San Lorenzo church in Sahagún.
Page 148 Fieldstone buildings in village of Rabanal.

Pilgrims

Page 149 Pilgrims crossing the *meseta* after Castrojeriz.
Page 151 Pilgrim resting on Way through the forest before Portomarin.
Page 152 Traditional pilgrim washing site in the Rio Lavacolla before Compostela.
Page 154 Country lane beside Monte Aro on the way to Finisterre.

Meals

Page 157 Meal in restaurant in Astorga.

Beds

Page 158 Pilgrim hostel in Puenta la Reina at start of the Camino Francés.
Page 159 Rustic pilgrim hostel attached to church in Azofra.
Page 160 Grounds of modern pilgrim hostel in Tricastela.
Page 162 Pilgrim dormitory beds in the modern hostel in Gonzar.
Page 163 Cloister in the historic Hotel de los Reyes Católicos in Compostela.

Locals

Page 167 The Way beside the Rio Ucieza approaching Carrión de los Condes.
Page 168 Historic buildings beside the Compostela cathedral.
Page 170 Rustic buildings in village of Olveiro on the way to the Galician coast.

PREFACE

Ultreia: The Santiago Pilgrimage 101*

For over one thousand years, the collective imagination and footsteps of millions of people has been captured by the pilgrimage to Santiago de Compostela. At the height of its popularity in the eleventh and twelfth centuries, hundreds of thousands of individuals from all of Christian Europe are thought to have made the pilgrimage. Though numbers decreased sharply from the eighteenth to the twentieth century, there has recently been a great resurgence with tens of thousands now completing the pilgrimage each year. Indeed, the stream of pilgrims sauntering through the fields across France and northern Spain today is such that parts of the route can be almost unbearably crowded in mid-summer. Recently, in recognition that the pilgrimage routes functioned as much as conceptual conduits for establishing medieval culture as they did physical pathways for wandering travellers, the Way of St. James has been designated a European cultural itinerary.

The physical objective of the pilgrimage was to reach Santiago de Compostela in north-western Spain, said to be the final resting place of the remains of Saint James. Legend has it that Saint James travelled to Spain as an evangelist before returning to Jerusalem where he became the first Apostle to be martyred when beheaded by Herod in about 44 AD. His followers are then said to have placed his body on a ship which, with heavenly help, made landfall on the Galician coast not far from present-day Santiago de Compostela.

The pilgrimage to Compostela increased in popularity after Jerusalem fell to the Muslims at the end of the twelfth century. The fact that there is little likelihood that Saint James ever set foot in Spain was in no way a deterrent. Nor did the thinly veiled, unsavoury aspects associated with the Church's endorsement of the pilgrimage dissuade the faithful.

For the Church, the pilgrimage represented both an opportunity for amassing great wealth and a way to keep the Muslims in southern Spain in check during the Christian Reconquest. In terms of the latter, Saint James the Gospel-toting Apostle became transmuted into Saint James the sword-yielding Moor slayer.

Even the origin of the pilgrimage's destination name is in question, some believing Compostela to be derived from the Latin *Campus Stellae* or 'field of stars,' while others – supported by archaeological excavations made in the middle of the twentieth century – think it comes from the Latin word *Compostum*, signifying, much less romantically, 'cemetery' at best, or 'compost pile' at worst!

But still they came…and came…in the tens of thousands, year after year, throughout the long centuries of strife, disease, and hardship that characterised much of the European Middle Ages.

Medieval pilgrims undertook the journey for a variety of reasons: as a profession of faith, as atonement for realised or imagined sins, as a way to venerate the saints whose relics were contained in many shrines that dotted the route, as a form of prescribed punishment for committed crimes, as a way of obtaining indulgences and so reducing time spent in Purgatory, as a means for empowering prayers to alleviate suffering from illness, and finally, simply as a reprieve from the drudgery of life – a grand adventure to see exciting new places and meet interesting new people.

Popes, royalty, nobility, and those who would later be beatified, all undertook the pilgrimage to Santiago de Compostela. The vast majority of pilgrims, however, were simple lay-folk who every spring would rendezvous in half a dozen meeting places in France and then head off together on foot for the long trip, hoping to return home before the following winter. And, for those that did return, what marvellous stories they could tell of their experiences!

Celebrities upon returning to their native villages, some pilgrims would assume the surnames 'King,' 'Roy,' or 'Köing' if they had been the fortunate individual in their group who, upon cresting the last hill before the bustling city of Compostela, were the first to have glimpsed the Romanesque towers of the cathedral housing the Apostle's sacred remains. And every successful pilgrim for the rest of his or her days would advertise the pride of their accomplishment by wearing a scallop shell from Finisterre on the Galician coast near Compostela – literally the end of the known medieval world. Evidence from exhumed graves in northern Europe revealed that some pilgrims would even be buried with their shells – their most cherished possession from the most noted accomplishment or adventure of their lives.

Pilgrims from the fifteenth century onwards left accounts of their travels. And in what is regarded as the world's first travel guide – the twelfth-century *Codex Calixtinus* attributed to the French cleric Aymery Picaud – practical notes are provided on travel routes, vernacular architecture, foreign customs, and the like; in a sense, not dissimilar to the many contemporary guidebooks for El Camino de Santiago, as the pilgrimage route has become known.

Present-day pilgrims undertake the journey for reasons that range from the spiritual to the sportive. For some, the pilgrimage still represents the soulful cleansing sought by their religious medieval ancestors and possibly reinterpreted through a veneer of modern New Age mysticism; for others, it is a once-in-a-lifetime opportunity to intimately connect with the landscape, architecture, and culture of a foreign location; and for yet others, it represents perhaps nothing more than an athletic challenge, a sort of horizontal Mt. Everest.

PREFACE TO REVISED EDITION

Since *Along the Way* was published in 2014, the number of pilgrims traversing the Camino Francés has continued to increase substantially. A friend of mine, a long-distance walker who is a former chair of the Confraternity of Pilgrims to Rome and the author of two engaging pilgrimage books, tells of a walk he undertook several years ago in Spain, wherein he had to wait until the westerly flow of pilgrim traffic for Compostela had cleared before he could cross the intersection and proceed northward on his own, non-Camino, route.

Along the Way, seven years on, continues to be the most comprehensive book published for a lay audience about the popular culture of the Camino. By including over a hundred photographs, the book remains one of the most detailed illustrated records in an inexpensive, non-coffee-table format. And through opting for a novel thematic organization rather than a straightforward temporal narrative, the book is still part of a select few that manage to break free of the traditional, and by now, hackneyed, description of the pilgrimage experience. In consequence, this Revised Edition does not alter the original book but is based on providing additional material presented on two new websites that have been specifically created. Covers of dozens of books and CDs that comprise the catholic scholarship in *Along the Way* are now presented in the overview website **www.bestcaminobook.com**. A second, book-enhanced website **alongtheway.libripublishing.co.uk** contains new colour photographs and, in response to queries received from readers, a new rank-assessment of the novels written about the Camino. And so, with respect to your own continued parallel journeys of both paces and pages…*Ultreia!*

★ Adapted from *Ultreia! Onward! Progress of the Pilgrim* (France, R., Green Frigate Books, 2007)

INTRODUCTION

Camino Triptych: Literary → Personal → Cultural
– Centre Fold –

Deus aia nos! (God help us!) was the rejoinder to the chant of *E Ultreia! E suseia!* (Onward! Upward!) used as encouragement by medieval pilgrims struggling toward Santiago de Compostela. Today it might also be cried out in mock dismay of yet *another* Camino book being published. For the pilgrimage along the Way or the 'Camino' to the shrine of Saint James (*San Iago*) in northern Spain has become incredibly popular with tens of thousands completing the walk each and every year. And of those, many have felt compelled to leave behind a written record of their experiences and travails for posterity, something aided of late by the easy and inexpensive access to various means for self-publication. In this respect, the Camino of today is rather like Venice of the eighteenth and nineteenth centuries in that foreign travellers to both, marvelling at how different things are from their lives and landscapes back at home, feel that they have to capture these insights in text for homebound friends, family, and sometimes the general public. As a result, the number of Camino books appearing on the market is growing exponentially, with more being published in the last five years than in the preceding decade, which in turn had produced more books than in the four decades before that. Indeed, it could be argued with respect to writings about the Camino, that we are rapidly approaching that oft-stated condition that has been ascribed to Venice for at least fifty years, namely that "everything including this statement has been said before". This poses a particular challenge to pilgrim authors from academe who by definition must, or at least shall we say *should,* be attempting to produce something of distinct scholarship. Fortunately, this is not all that difficult to accomplish as there is an incredible sameness that characterises the bulk of Camino books

Having read most of the of English-language pilgrimage accounts, I am familiar with the strengths of these memoirs as well as their all-too-common weaknesses. Almost all begin and end their journal memoirs in the same places and contain the same day-to-day itinerary of events as well as describe the same, standard historic happenings or sights. Indeed, though the writing quality does certainly vary, it is safe to say that one could very well begin reading one book with its cover removed – and sometimes you don't even have to do that – and have it surreptitiously switched several times as you repeatedly leave the room to refill your glass with Spanish wine, returning to the reading being none the wiser. The present pilgrimage account, Part II, is different from the majority that have been published in a handful of significant ways: structure of the text, subject matter covered, prevalence of photographs, seasonal timing and ultimate destination of the walk, and finally, age of the pilgrim.

Firstly, the present book dispenses with the traditional day-to-day journal account and instead follows the lead of several that have been published recently in presenting the pilgrimage experience thematically rather than chronologically (although as a concession for those who feel they simply *must* read everything through a temporal linearity, I have included a pictorial chronology on the affiliated website to enable this). Therefore, instead of a complete account of all experiences along the Way, both the profound and the mundane, the present account focuses instead upon what might be called my one hundred Camino highlights: those luminous snapshots from the pilgrimage that have lingered and been incorporated into who I am and what I might become. Doing so, and thereby avoiding historical regurgitations and boring anecdotes, allowed me to move beyond the superficial overview to elaborating upon the particular minutiae. In this I was influenced foremost by the insightful pilgrim accounts of Rudolph (2004) and especially Sing (1981), as well as by the non-traditional biography of Saint Francis by Martin (2001). For these works, as well as that of Mahoney (2003), I was struck by how readers were left with a feeling of completeness despite the near surgical precision with which the authors selectively excerpted and described but a few of the many moments of the pilgrimage or life journey.

Secondly, the subject matter covered in these pages strays from the conventional in several ways. I have included material, for example, about both the pre-trip and post-trip experiences and have avoided recounting detailed conversations with locals or fellow pilgrims, the former being occasionally presented in the literature whereas the latter often forming the staple in many recent pilgrimage accounts. What is most different about the present work is the attention paid to architectural detail. This is in marked contrast to many if not most Camino authors who either go out of their way to purposely mention that they were only interested in the spiritual, social, or physical side of pilgrimage or to those who simply couldn't care less about what they saw along the Way, as for example, demonstrated in the following egregious example: "After washing our socks we went out to spend a few minutes looking at the cathedral which was supposed to be one of the best around." Period. End of description. And this was about the cathedral of León, truly one of the most magnificent ecclesiastical buildings in Europe. Finally, given that all pilgrim accounts go over the same old ground, what really makes one book stand out from another are the glimpses provided into the back-life of the writer. Indeed, for some worthy accounts this is the major lasting memory of the book. The present work follows the lead of several other Camino narratives by academics wherein a balance is sought between descriptions reflective of both the outer and inner journeys which make up any thoughtful person's pilgrimage.

The third element of obvious difference between the present work and that of the bulk of the other Camino books is the space provided here for a photographic record of the pilgrimage. It is remarkable given the obvious "sight and sensibility" of the Camino experience, that the majority of pilgrimage accounts provide little or even no visualisation to accompany their texts. The harsh reality is that it is a rare writer indeed whose skill at constructing word pictures of her or his surroundings is such as to make photographs superfluous. For the rest of us, it is useful to present text that can be closely associated with images. As such, this book and its accompanying website contain more photographs of the Camino than other pilgrim accounts (with the exception of a few expensive coffee-table books). And it is for this reason that the subtitle "Pilgrimage *Scenes* from the Camino Francés to Santiago de Compostela" is apt. The present photographs, which were selected from many through their ability to elucidate what is described in the accompanying text, are therefore a very important part of the overall book. And as mentioned above, the different emphasis in subject matter of the present account means that a good number of these images are of sights that have rarely if ever been presented in other books.

A fourth and very unusual feature of the present account is that it describes a pilgrimage undertaken in the early winter to the Galician seacoast, the then known western edge of the medieval world. Over three-quarters of pilgrims who reach Compostela do so in the summer months of June, July, and August. Adding in the two neighbouring months on either side increases that total to over ninety percent. The published narratives of pilgrims of course reflect this seasonal bias. Until recently only a few hardy pilgrims undertook a winter pilgrimage, although this will almost certainly increase given the increasingly unbearable saturation of the Camino during the peak summer season. Almost nothing can influence one's pilgrimage experience more than the decision of what time of year to do the walk. If one is interested in only the social and physical externalities of pilgrimage, then the boisterous crowds of summer's dog days are for you; if, however, one wishes a more contemplative inner pilgrimage with a handful of close encounters with fellow wayfarers, then there is no alternative these days but to seek out the stillness and solitude of winter's depths. The present book therefore provides some insight into the particular differences and occasional difficulties involved in following through on this latter decision. Then there is the question of the pilgrimage destination. Despite evidence suggesting a pre-Christian pilgrimage route to the Galician seacoast, the cult of Saint James has all but obscured this earlier palimpsest tracing. As a result, fewer than five percent of pilgrims walking to Compostela continue on in like fashion to reach Finisterre or Muxia on the coast. The present work is therefore one of a few to describe elements of that, I would argue, *essential,* capstone experience.

Finally, examining the demographics of modern pilgrims indicates that those walking the complete or near-complete length of Camino are for the most part contained within two groups who have the luxury of extended time to undertake such a trip: the retired elderly and the university-student young. It is the former who, upon returning home, most often set about capturing their impressions in book form whereas the latter are too busy to do so, instead throwing themselves into their next big enterprise. This fact has greatly influenced (and biased) the literature of the Camino. For the retired, the Camino pilgrimage is often the grand adventure of their frequently sedentary lives and their accounts are loaded with hyperbole about how unprepared their ageing bodies often were for the hardships of the Way; whereas for the students, this is just one more European experience, and a pretty tame one at that for anyone enjoying the robust vigour and confidence of youth. And in their mind, why anyone would take the time to write about such a mundane act of walking a completely way-marked and smoothed trail across the mostly flat fields of Spain is bizarre to say the least. In between, there have been relatively few Camino narratives from the middle-aged, those who might have also undertaken the pilgrimage, as for example did I, as a way to mark their fiftieth birthday, balanced on that auspicious cusp of being sufficiently old enough to have faced both life's benefits and disappointments upon which to reflect and yet still young enough to be able to possibly take advantage of whatever long-lasting, life-altering insights might be offered by the Camino experience as its hype promises.

If one approaches the Camino as a passionate pilgrim with eyes, and especially heart, wide open, the ensuing benefits can be manifold. Theologian Matthew Fox knows this well, for as he wrote in the Foreword to *Ultreia!*

Onward!: Progress of the Pilgrim, my compilation of quotations from modern pilgrims, "While we still have feet, we ought to walk. While we still have eyes, we ought to observe. While we still have ears, we ought to listen. While we have existence on the earth, we ought to be fully present here." It is my sincere hope that these few scenes from the Camino, these glimpses through Blake's sensual gateways to the soul, presented herein with an unapologetic passion though hopefully shy of a too florid nature, will serve as both a provocation for those having completed the Camino to reflect back on their own similar highlights as well as especially for those potential future pilgrims deliberating about whether to embark on their own walk across northern Spain. And for the latter, I hope these scenes will encourage you to undertake that walk during the solitary days of winter when, although the outer temperatures may plummet, the inner warmth can soar from savouring the richness found in the unhurried sight and sensibility offered by a Camino pilgrimage fully engaged in, far from the madding crowd.

Left Fold –

I finished writing my pilgrimage narrative on my fifty-first birthday, exactly one year after plunging into the ocean on completion of the journey. For an academic used to writing technical papers in third-person prose for professional journals, it was uncomfortable to see all those "I's" scattered about the manuscript pages. That, and of course the personal nature of the subject matter covered, left a feeling of emotional vulnerability that was unsettling. As for a gothic cathedral with stained glass windows letting in the light, I too felt a narrative of such personal transparency needed buttressing, in this case of a scholarly form, for support. And so to this end, and in between working on other writing projects, I spent the next four years researching and producing the two sections that bookend the personal narrative.

Like their medieval predecessors, contemporary pilgrims often feel motivated to leave behind written records of their journey for prosperity. Several readers have been critical of the recently published deluge of pilgrimage narratives. For example, historian Michael Jacobs (2002) dismissed most such accounts which in his opinion "tend to be tediously sentimental and filled with not especially profound spiritual reflections." Travel blogger "Amawalker" (2011) notes that while some of the hundreds of pilgrimage accounts are good, "many, however, read as though they have followed a 'write-by-numbers' template – clones of the same story-teller." An example of such formulaic redundancy and a prescription on how this can be avoided is offered by this critic:

> *'I felt 'called' to the camino. I started at St. Jean/Roncesvalles/Pamplona etc. I slept in crowded refuges with snoring pilgrims. I ate humble pilgrim menus and bocadillos. Day after day – I walked in the rain, sun, wind and cold – I walked, arrived, showered, ate, slept. Ditto. Ditto. Ditto. Blah, blah, blah. I arrived in Santiago. Although I am not religious, it was such a spiritual experience that I am a changed person. Amen.'*
>
> ZZZZZZZzzzzzzzzz ….. boring!
>
> No snippets of history, no traditions, no fauna or flora, no folklore, no art or architecture to spice things up in what is, essentially, a travel book with soul. If you are thinking of writing a book about your camino PLEASE find an original angle or focus. Hundreds of thousands of people walk a camino every year and all have similar experiences, passing through the same physical and spiritual landscape. And, they all want to share their experience. You don't have to walk with a donkey or with your elderly parent, you don't have to visit your previous lives (Shirley MacLaine) or wrestle with your Master (Paulo Coehlo) but some new insight, something fresh, something that your reader hasn't already read a dozen times would be nice.

While it is true that many pilgrimage accounts can veer embarrassingly towards the trite and pedestrian as I found when reviewing the literature for my volume of motivational quotations (France 2007), in every offering one can still find gems of insight. Part I demonstrates this by examining a representative subsample of the Camino literature. Other scholars have commented upon the Camino experience through lenses of pilgrims interviewed while en route or excerpts of unpublished diaries. To my knowledge, my efforts here are the first time the published literature has been mined in a search for shared commonalities of the modern pilgrimage experience.

– Right Fold

The city of Santiago de Compostela and the pilgrimage routes through France and Spain have been designated as (a) international sites of cultural patrimony for humanity, (b) a world heritage site, (c) a European city of culture, and (d) the continent's first cultural itinerary route. None of this would surprise Goethe who stated more than two centuries ago that "the idea of Europe was born along the road to Santiago." The lofty idea, or perhaps more accurately, *ideal,* behind these modern designations lies in the belief that the medieval pilgrimage provided a unifying centre in pluralistic Europe, resulting in the development of tolerance, understanding, and solidarity among peoples. Less provocative and perhaps more realistic is the belief that the medieval pilgrimage routes were just as important for the flow of art and architecture, science and song, poetry and philosophy, and engineering and egalitarianism, as they were for the to-and-fro shuffling of pilgrims. Through its considerable influence on developments in arts, sciences, literature, and philosophy, pilgrimage, the Nolans (1989) write, "is as much a part of the ongoing drama of European history as are wars, revolutions, the rise and fall of empires, industrialization, and urbanization."

Since medieval times, a lively debate has reigned regarding the motivations of pilgrims, the devout for example being critical of the curious. When considered as polar opposites, pilgrims, Cohen (1992) states, journey to the ordered centre of their world, whereas tourists escape from that ordered centre toward the periphery. In reality, there is, Cohen continues, no sharp demarcation between spiritual and secular motivations. Modern tourism is often thought to have its roots in pilgrimage. Indeed, the medieval text about the Santiago pilgrimage, the *Codex Calixtinus,* is frequently cited as being the world's first tourist guide. And let us not forget that the word 'holiday' is itself derived from holy or sacred days. If, as noted pilgrimage scholar Victor Turner (1978) has stated, a tourist is half a pilgrim, then it stands to reason that a pilgrim is half a tourist. And being a tourist, or even a half-tourist, means partaking in a culture.

The Camino has become a modern cultural icon. In many respects, today's secular Camino has outgrown its medieval precursor, at least in terms of the breadth of its zeitgeist, as described in Part III. In fact, many different caminos can be traversed. Novelists, poets, musicians, film-makers, painters, video-gamers, and sculptors have all invented caminos of their own imaginings. As the numbers of pilgrims travelling to Compostela increase year after year, these individuals find solidarity in organisations of like-minded folk and search out information and share ideas in newsletters, websites, and reference books, all the while being studied by anthropologists and sociologists. Some individuals become obsessed with all things related to the Camino. Others use their Camino experience as a springboard into the world of pilgrimage writ large. To my knowledge, the present book is the first to examine and critically review all these manifold elements of the wider Camino culture.

PART I

Reading the Way

"The pathway to Santiago is always there, waiting…"

– Georgiana Goddard King, *The Way of Saint James*

PRE-SCRIPT

"And this is Man's whole life a Pilgrimage."

– Samuel Purchas, *Purchas His Pilgrimes (Hakluytus Posthumus)*

Long before one ever takes one's first footsteps on the Camino another pilgrimage has often been traversed in the comfort of one's home. This is a pilgrimage of pages, navigated over the period of years, sometimes decades, through the background literature and personal narratives of the Way to Santiago de Compostela. And for every pilgrim, there is a unique route, never waymarked, transitioning from pages to pavement.

It is fascinating to reflect back through the cluttered cobwebs of time to that precise instance when one meets with an individual or an idea that, often unrecognised at the moment, will transform one's life. So it is with me and my relationship with the pilgrimage to Saint James' shrine. On my thirteenth birthday, five days before Christmas in 1970, I opened my monthly mailing of the *School Bulletin* from the National Geographic Society. This little (usually sixteen or so pages in length) bulletin was a monthly publication from the parent organisation that distilled articles from the well-known magazine and published books, appropriately rewritten for inquisitive grade-school children. And issue number 14, the "Special Christmas Issue" that I held in my hand, was an introduction to the Middle Ages.

The cover displayed a close-up of a panel of stained glass from the window of Notre Dame Cathedral in Paris, a location I recognised through having recently watched, in serial form on Canadian television, the 1939 version of the Hunchback of Notre Dame. Written with simplicity and an exaggerated floridity, the text guided young readers through a thousand years of monarchy and peasantry, war and faith, plague and artistry, all accompanied by wonderful photographs cribbed from the signature magazine. The final brief article was entitled "Beacon of Faith Led Medieval Travelers". I was drawn in from the very first words: "To the pilgrim [that was the first time I ever remembered having seen that word], faith could overcome fear of hardships, sickness far from home, or even fear of death. Pilgrims drew strength from their nearly endless treks." A few paragraphs further on I was introduced to Saint James for the first time, realising with a shock that the Winnipeg municipality of that very name, located just across the river from where I lived, was in fact named after this Apostle (we had not been a frequent church-going household and so I was unaware of hagiography). The text continued:

> Despite bad food and water, thieves, cold, and heat, French pilgrims streamed southward to Spain's Province of Galicia and the shrine of St. James in the cathedral at Santiago de Compostela. A song lightened their footsteps:
>
> > *James, thy very own Galicia,*
> > *Famous for its path of glory*
> > *Trod by weary-footed throngs*
>
> The words appeared in the *Codex Calixtinus*, a 12th-century guidebook whose pages warn of dangers and joys on the way to Santiago.
>
> One medieval monk describes faces he saw in a pilgrim procession. 'The maidens and the young men,' he wrote, '…said verse and song; even the old started singing again: All have a look of joy!'

The two photographs related to the Spanish pilgrimage that accompanied the text certainly gave credence to what the medieval monk had written centuries before. One showed several young [and very beautiful, as I now look at the image more than four decades later] schoolgirls kneeling in the cathedral shrine of Santo Domingo de la Calzada.

The other showed a pilgrim embracing the famous gilded and bejewelled statue of Saint James in his eponymous cathedral in Compostela.

I was hooked. My mother was pleased that I was expressing an interest in her Catholic religion, and my father, a former Church of England attendee as a child, was only too glad to share his love of cartography as we located the two mentioned Spanish cities in our family world atlas.

Half a year later, three large National Geographic books arrived, ordered by my mother, a further needless expense for our struggling middle-class family my father thought in the months leading up to his departure. Nights when I should have been doing homework were spent in the shadow of my parents' disintegrating marriage, geographically and temporally escaping into the worlds offered in *Everyday Life in Bible Times*, *Greece and Rome: Builders of Our World*, and *The Age of Chivalry*. More than the other two, it was this latter book that drew me in the quickest and the deepest. Sections therein dealt with the worlds of Charlemagne, William the Conqueror, Richard the Lionheart, Jacques Coeur, and Bernard of Clairvaux. And in the latter, was the chapter "Pilgrimage to Compostela" from which the photographs had been culled for the *School Bulletin* that had so captured my interest the preceding year. Here, for the first time, I learnt of the history, traditions, and sites along *"El Camino de Santiago"* as told through the first-person account of the writer who had travelled by automobile from Le Puy to Galicia. I was mesmerised by the photographs: the surrealistic volcanic landscape of Le Puy, the golden-visaged reliquary of Saint Foy at Conques, the graceful Pont Valentré arching over the river in Cahors, the rolling hills of sun-ripened grain near Santo Domingo de la Calzada, the impressive gate of Santa Maria in Burgos, monks swinging the massive incense burner in the cathedral of Santiago, and the fireworks over the cathedral on the Saint's feast day of July 25th.

What most captured my thirteen-year-old, adventure-thirsty imagination was the knowledge, as witnessed from the photographs and described in the text, that the pilgrimage was not just a memory from the past but was rather something that was still alive at the present time. Near Compostela, the writer met a priest who had walked from Poitiers in the footsteps of *Codex* writer Aymery Picaud and who recounted "I cannot express, monsieur, the joy this has given me, this journey of faith and tradition. I have been freezing and sunstruck, exhausted, hungry – all those extremes from which today we are protected. I have been given kindness and hospitality everywhere. For me these 29 days have been a march through history and brotherhood that I shall never forget."

It was several pages in the chapter that initiated my long-lasting love affair with the Camino. One showed a roughly drawn map of the four pilgrimage routes traversing France to a union just before and then just after crossing the Pyrenees, thumbnail illustrations of significant churches and cathedrals near their geographic locations shown beside the tracings. Holding up my own juvenile right hand beside the map, palm outward, in my fertile imagination the pattern seemed like a demonstration of the hand of God: index finger – the route from Tours, middle finger – the route from Vézelay, ring finger – the route from Le Puy, little finger – the route from Arles, the thumb – the main route in Spain. And then there was the page on which the image of the Castilian plain was shown, beneath which the caption began with the following words: "Balm of a bountiful landscape cheered pilgrims on the Camino Francés..." What was this? The "Camino *Francés*". My very own namesake road! I immediately vowed that someday I would have to walk its length.

I know of two scholarly studies of contemporary pilgrim accounts. Post (1998) selected six published narratives from Dutch pilgrims, four pertaining to Compostela, two to Rome, and one to Assisi, two of which had been privately published. The major topics were found to be the daily ritual, departure and arrival, encounters, digressions about the meaning of pilgrimage, Nature, and the past. Post categorised the writing into three levels: daily descriptions of experiences of the linear journey; contemplative sections framing or interpreting the perception of the journey; and meditations on the ultimate meaning of the pilgrimage.

Gossen (2012) reviewed hundreds of unpublished pilgrim diaries in the Confraternity of Saint James library in London. The emphasis in most accounts was on relationships with other pilgrims, and the adventures and storylines shared. The subjects of most importance were camaraderie on the road, the kindness of strangers, emotional feelings upon arrival, a sense of history, contact with nature, and the opportunity for quiet reflection. She elaborated on Post's scheme by noting that the sequence from level-one daily experiences to level-two contemplations on perception, to level-three reflections on the big picture represent three levels of self-categorisation, moving from the personal "I" to the social "we", to the "we humans" collective species. The bulk of diary writing was found to deal with the first and second, personal and social levels. The first level of writing concerned the commonplace elements in intimate text, describing the immediate impressions and feelings about the daily life of the pilgrim: sleeping, rising, walking, getting lost, meeting people, weather, towns, the landscape, sustenance, and nightly accommodation. As Post also found, a big emphasis in the writing was on how different the pilgrim's life was from that back at home. An interesting finding was that the cathedral of Saint James was of secondary importance to pilgrims compared to the city itself, or in particular, the plaza in front of the cathedral where pilgrims gather and meet. It is no surprise then that most journal writers considered the pilgrimage to Compostela to be a secular rather than a sacred undertaking. Contemplative digressions in the second level of writing concerned comparing the present Camino with knowledge of past pilgrimages, questioning of personal motives, and perceived changes in the pilgrim's behaviour and attitudes along the Way. The third level of writing concerned end-of-day insights and occasional epiphanies.

My own analysis of the Camino literature in this section uses a phenomenological framework I developed previously to describe writings by noted American environmentalist Henry David Thoreau and authors inspired by him, concerning their experiences of water, as well as Thoreau's writings about how cats experience the world (France 2003a,b; Chat 2012). These experiential categories were 'Adventure', 'Joy', 'Contact', and 'Contemplation'. All three of Post and Gossen's levels of pilgrimage writing (i.e. personal, social, and humankind dimensions) can easily be expressed within the present framework.

I restricted my review of the Camino literature to accounts by Canadian pilgrims: Atman's (2008) *Walking in Grace;* Arthur Paul Boers' (2007) *The Way is Made by Walking*; Jane Christmas' (2007) *What the Psychic Told the Pilgrim*; Laurie Dennett's (1987) *A Hug for the Apostle*; Lesley D. Harman's (2009) *We Are Never Alone: Healing Lessons From the Camino*; Sue Kenney's (2004) *My Camino*; Julie Kirkpatrick's (2010) *The Camino Letters: 26 Tasks on the Way to Finisterre*; Marilyn Melville's (2002) *Peregrina: A Woman's Journey on the Camino*; Paul Myers' (2009) *Rooster in the Cathedral; Reflections of a Pilgrim While Walking to Santiago*; Guy Thatcher's (2008) *A Journey of Days*; Mary Victoria Wallis' (2003) *Among the Pilgrims: Journeys to Santiago de Compostela*; and Robert Ward's (2007) *All the Good Pilgrims: Tales of the Camino de Santiago*. To round out the number of books to thirteen, for no better reason than to be reflective of the number of stages Aymery Picaud suggested the journey should take on horseback in his medieval guidebook, I added expat American Lee Hoinacki's (1997) *El Camino: Walking to Santiago de Compostela*, which was the first pilgrim narrative I purchased.

This subsample of the more than seventy-five published English language accounts currently available is considered to be representative of the larger literature. Publication dates range from the late 1980s before the modern resurgence in the pilgrimage to those which have come out within the last five years. Four of the thirteen books were self published, four were published in well-established, international presses, with the remainder being published by regionally or thematically specialised houses. The authors consist of professional writers, past and present academics, those involved with religious teaching or preaching, New Age or self-help practitioners, and both working and retired individuals. Most authors are middle-aged; several are elderly. The majority of authors are first-time pilgrims; several integrate repeat journeys into their accounts. The bulk of the accounts follow the straightforward linear narrative of travelling the Camino; several, however, deconstruct the temporal sequence by being thematically didactic or experimental in scope. The only obvious bias in this subsample compared to the larger literature is that only five of the thirteen authors are male. In terms of originality and reading enjoyment, several of the books are among the very best Camino accounts that have been published, whereas others are among the bottom third of the corpus in this regard. Almost all the accounts are well-written. Like Post and

Gossen's analyses, most of the writing consists of the "I" and "we" levels of personal and social descriptions and reflections. When dealing with level-one personal descriptions, sometimes the intensity of self-examination is remarkably moving in its stark honesty; at other times, however, it may stray toward being self-indulgent. In some cases, the depth of insight exhibited by the authors into level-two digressions about the nature of pilgrimage and level-three contemplations about humanity writ large can be truly humbling.

Chapter titles derive from lines in Sir Walter Raleigh's famous pilgrimage poem, arranged sequentially as they occur in that text.

On Contemplation…

CHAPTER 1

"GIVE ME MY SCALLOP-SHELL OF QUIET"

History

WALKING THE CAMINO IS SOMEWHAT CONFUCIAN in spirit in that it provides, for those of European descent, a feeling of connectivity with one's ancestors who may have traversed the Way before. The contemplative lesson from the Camino for Dennett is that we are not entirely separated from those worthy lives of the past. While on Monte del Gozo, Ward feels likewise: "I stand like a child, not knowing how to put one foot in front of the other. And then I think of them, all the pilgrims who have passed this way. They tell me, 'You're not alone. We're here with you. We've been here all along.'" For Wallis, scrambling up the accumulated pile of stones deposited by thousands of previous pilgrims at the Cruz de Fierro is to participate in an inspiring tradition: "You have done exactly what centuries of pilgrims have also done: stopped at the top of a long hill, listened to your heart thumping into the road, looked up with relief at an old thin cross and wondered about something to drink."

Saint James himself is generally ill regarded by modern-day, secular pilgrims. First, there is the thorny issue of whether the body in the tomb at Compostela really belongs to him or is that of the heretical Bishop Priscillian. "Should not the bones be DNA tested and is not the human race a tad too old for such religious fairy tales?" Christmas asks before continuing with the shocking "The Camino suddenly seemed like a massive joke." Her iconoclastic attitude toward Saint James continues elsewhere in her narrative when she calls him a loudmouth brown-noser and likens him and his equally annoying brother Apostle to being the Beavis and Butt-head of the group. The miraculous discovery of his remains just when it was most politically convenient is dismissed irreverently by Christmas as "Before you could say 'Holy souvenirs!' the site was proclaimed sacred." And second, there is the disturbing manner in which Spain warped the Apostle to suit its own needs during the *Reconquista*. Therefore, despite the historically challenged modern romantics who effuse on and on about how the Camino was built on sweat, tears and faith, Ward is clear that it was also constructed on rivalries, lies, greed, ambition, bigotry, and blood. Wallis also states that the Camino was born in blood, reminding us that the very first pilgrim to arrive from France, Charlemagne, actually fought his way across northern Spain. Would the Camino even exist at all, Ward wonders, had it not been for the transformation of Saint James into the character of *Matamoros*, the killer of Moors, a character who Wallis aptly likens to the equally fictitious Obi-Wan Kenobi. When she obtains her *compostela* (certificate) at the completion of her pilgrimage, Wallis notices that the document has an image of the Saint as a pilgrim whereas those in the past had been emblazoned with Santiago *Matamoros*. This leaves her bothered by the convenient white-washing of history. It is important to remember, she writes in one of the most perfect descriptions of the historicity of the pilgrimage to Compostela that the Camino "is a concoction of rabble-rousing propaganda, nationalistic fetishes, falsifications and forgeries, well-meaning moral tales, and religious hoaxes."

One couldn't find two pilgrims more diametrically opposed in their contemplations on the relative merits of history to the Camino experience than Wallis and Hoinacki. Although he frequently quotes from the accounts of late-medieval pilgrims, Hoinacki goes out of his way to avoid all contact with historical buildings or structures along the Way. Indeed, he actually walks right past the Pórtico de la Gloria, accredited to be an apogee of Romanesque sculpture, refusing to even look at it! And he celebrates his anti-intellectualism, proud that he has read only a few lines from St. Isidore's *Etimologias*, regarded by many to be one of the most important books of the Middle Ages. He seems to struggle with his contempt of those interested in the historical art and architecture of the Camino. "Would gawking at his [St. Isidore's] tomb," Hoinacki asks, "be anything more than morose curiosity?" The designation of the Camino Francés as Europe's first Cultural Itinerary Route is absurd, he believes, since culture "means anything and nothing" and there was certainly no uniform European identity at the time when early pilgrims were walking the Camino. "I see no way to relate today's pretentious signs to those wandering walkers of old," he concludes. How can faith be boiled down to a facile cultural attribute like Romanesque architecture, he asks. He continues his impassioned diatribe:

> I was saddened by what appeared to be an invasion of the *camino* by these latter-day Philistines – modern carpetbaggers. How many of them have crossed its mountains? How many of them have sought to lean its secrets, not in elegant salons, but out there in its rich solitude? How many of them have arrived at a *refugio* wet, cold, wracked by pain and exhaustion, yet buoyantly happy to be there, to have accompanied the pilgrims of old for a few more kilos, to have walked into the darkness of the *camino*, through the *naturaleza*, yes, but reaching beyond? It appears that the academic and political opportunities of the *camino* are increasing. Perhaps next I'll read that the *camino* is now necessary for the ecological salvation of Europe. After all, it worked so well in the past for the religion, social, and political salvation of Spain. I was reminded of the official mascot, the updated

Mickey Mouse pilgrim seen all over Spain this year – the trivialization of the hopes of so many, of those who sought Santiago, and of those who sought to rob innocent pilgrims.

And then there is the silly attempt by historians, Hoinacki contends, who "tend to write as if there is *one camino, one* pilgrim, *one* experience", as they attempt to create a bizarre unitary truth. "But this is to collapse," he emphatically states, "the fears, the dreams, the ambitions, the heterogeneity, the innumerable persons stretched at over twenty centuries into one ideal type. This can't be."

In contrast, Wallis devotes more space to the history of the Camino in her narrative than that found in almost all other pilgrim accounts. Simply put, for her, "the Camino is history alive." And it is, most wonderful of all to Wallis, a deep palimpsest landscape in which she can revel in the legends, myths, and artifacts of ancient humans, Iberians, Romans, Carthaginians, Visigoths, Moors, the French, etc., such that her pilgrimage is "a walk through the floating tissue" of time. Unlike Hoinacki, she visits every historical site on the Camino and occasionally even leaves the established route to see other locations of similar import. Reflections are offered about the Romanesque mindset of battling demons and angels, and the cult of physically incorruptible relics and the debasement of morally corruptible indulgences that respectively created and then destroyed the pilgrimage. The analogy made by Wallis of relics operating as spiritual synapses between earthly sinners and God on his heavenly throne is particularly appealing, as is her perceptive interlinking of Christian pilgrims travelling to the shrine in Galicia with those ancient humans entering the painted caves and dolmens in nearby Cantabria, both being inspired by a desire to glimpse something of the other world. Be heartened then, Wallis writes, as you slog toward Compostela, by looking northward to the coastal mountains and recognising that there is a continuity of your own pilgrimage endeavour with that of the deepest reservoirs of sacredness in the human past. Both share the same ritualistic form: "a journey through a charged landscape to a sanctuary where visible mementos offer the life-giving power of those who live now on the other side of death's door." And in a little display of the kind of kismet that seems so pervasive on the Camino, is it any accident that Saint James' remains were rediscovered in 1879, the very same year that the first Palaeolithic cave paintings were found at Altamira?

Humanity

RECREATIONAL RUNNERS KNOW THAT AT SLIGHTLY more than twenty-six miles, marathons are *just* the precise distance for fostering personal development. No human being, no matter how well trained, can run for that distance without breaking down muscle tissue for energy. And it is the physical hitting of this 'wall,' and the mental willpower needed to cross over it and keep going for the last few miles, that underlies the reason why running a marathon can be such a life-altering experience. The physical environment of the Camino is likewise its greatest attribute for transformative change. As extended walks go, the Camino is for the most part dead easy, the landscape offering little in the way of physical challenge other than that of distance. This then is the most critical reason as to why the Camino has approached its exalted, cult-like status. Frequently free of the need to focus on where to place the next step, and in the absence of an overabundance of dramatic and distracting scenery, and with the luxury of uninterrupted time, the mind can wander every which way, dancing and alighting upon, and sorting through, contextualising, and contemplating a cacophony of themes.

Reflections in published pilgrimage journals address an incredible diversity of topics of personal and societal concern: waste generation, organisational consultants, family disintegration, home architecture and isolated modern lives, George Bush's Bible-thumping militarism, "frantic, frenetic and frazzled" restless lifestyles, a car-obsessed culture that is suspicious of pedestrians, life deformation caused by an over-reliance on technology and a worship of rampant consumerism, and the need for localism (Boers); modern Christianity, middle-age, women's over-dependence on husbands or Oprah, and female reasoning skills and attitudes to others of their gender (Christmas); feminine energy and the importance of dreams (Melville); motherhood, familial deaths, yoga, travel, witches, energy fields, world peace, menstruation, and childbirth (Kirkpatrick); drugs, energy fields, modern medicine, love, animal rights, vegetarianism, and nationality (Atman); loneliness, female fear, living in the moment, teaching, and distinctions between wisdom and intelligence (Harmon); tribalism, ageing, love, and too-rigid thinking (Myers); overwork, stress, emotional turmoil, farming, and multi-generational social mixing (Dennett); and landscape desecration by pollution, the English Romantic movement, the importance of solitude, lifestyles focused on little else besides comfort, and the "volatile and dangerous mixture of religious faith and political ambition" as showcased by the Spanish Civil War (Hoinacki).

Spirituality

It is the opportunity – sometimes the *expectation* – to search for and be rewarded by a glimpse of the Divine that is, at its core, what fundamentally separates the Camino from other long-distance, secularly inspired hikes. Pilgrimage is after all touted to be a form of physical prayer, the repeated planting of left foot, walking staff, right foot, being symbolic of the Holy Trinity. Not surprisingly given the many varied motivations voiced by those undertaking the pilgrimage to Compostela, there is considerable individuality of expression of that spirituality.

International pilgrims most commonly experience spiritual feelings when outside of Spanish churches. Wallis reviews the history of the Church's triumph over paganism along with the consequent death of how we once viewed natural wonders. Myer catches a glimpse of a pantheistic 'Providence' in a pool of water from which he has just emerged. In his account of spiritual awakening, Hoinacki refers to Spinoza, the Romantics, and the Transcendentalists. Entitling his book *The Way is Made by Walking*, and beginning it with the quip "I once walked five hundred miles to attend church", Boers thinks all church-goers would benefit by actually walking to service every Sunday. He stresses that the Bible is basically an outdoor book, Christ's ministry being one of the road, and that our relationship with God may actually be hampered by staying inside buildings. Is this not the lesson of Saint Francis? Hoinacki agrees, stating that all ecclesiastical buildings should be given away since they have nothing to do with modern faith. The physical act of undertaking a walking pilgrimage is the particular reason he is there: "The *camino* will take me to the place I must reach before I die, will make me the person I must be when I die, a man of faith." That, he believes, will be the lasting gift of the Camino, and the way to accomplish this is through learning how to pray while walking, using as an aid the rosary from his long-departed father.

The Camino, however, can be difficult at times for those of undemonstrable or uncertain faith. Hoinacki, who momentarily stops praying with slight embarrassment each time he encounters other people, longs for the overt faith of past pilgrims. "Is there some contact," he wonders, "between them and me, between their faith and mine? Can I rid myself enough of distractions to walk into their world?" Wallis recounts a tender scene in a church while she watches an elderly couple a few pews ahead who seem so at ease with one another and so perfectly assured in their religion: "I watched their bodies and the way their heads sat straight and parallel. It was a kind of communion I would probably never know. For a few moments, I wished I could believe." Despite her surname, seemingly secular Christmas also reverts to prayer on one occasion, wonderfully joking "If you were praying to God on May 12, 2004, it is unlikely that God heard you. He was too busy with me. Sorry – I sucked up a lot of God that day."

What is remarkable too is how little Saint James really matters to any of this. Relative to other historic figures and especially to modern-day caregivers met along the Way, the bellicose Apostle remains completely remote to Wallis. Disabuse yourselves that the Camino is a path leading to Saint James, Hoinacki instructs, for it is really a Way to reach Christ "if one can learn how to walk on it." For did not Christ, he reminds us, quoting from John 14:6, tell us that He "is the Way?" Collapsed one day by the side of the path, Christmas takes out frustration at her weakened state by ranting against the Camino as being a big Vatican-engineered hoax based on luring naïve pilgrims to the tomb of a dead saint with a promise of salvation…for a price.

It is easy to be critical about modern religion. Myers writes of the shortcomings of contemporary Churches which often focus on the insignificant. Boers thinks a solution is for the Church to dwell more on matters of spirit and less on power, politics, and self-interest. The unpleasant history of egregious religious hubris that characterises Spain, Hoinacki reminds, is very different from that of all other European nations. And Wallis comments upon the loss of Catholic mystery in Protestant rationalism.

Sometimes epiphanies are unforthcoming, introspection failing to foster inspiration. Thatcher, near the start of his pilgrimage, announces in a mixture of disappointment and optimism that "so far, no blinding light from the heavens or psychological insights, just tired legs and feet, but it is early yet." By the end of his walk he tallies things up as "Epiphanies and spiritual breakthroughs: zero." Ward, too, admits to no earth-shattering epiphanies, concluding that "in the end it's all just a long walk." Christmas is taken back when handed her *compostela* by the absence of any questions about whether she had grasped the holy lessons of the Camino and had been a true pilgrim. By not being forced on the spot by authorities to address such deep questions, one is left with the impression that she somehow feels cheated.

But if one looks beyond traditional church-based spirituality, the Camino does to have much to offer to those who are searching. For Myers, the physicality of pilgrimage is the key: "our bodies help us to taste God, to smell God, and to see God." Ward agrees, believing that spirituality comes through the senses when one feels gratefulness when discomfort is eased. Thatcher finds holiness in a small *albergue* that was an ancient hospital. "If there is a God," he writes, "it is in places like this that one can sense the divine." At the end of her pilgrimage, Wallis reflects that faith may simply be about knowing that no matter how wayward you feel, "something" always knows where you are. Boers would agree, offering the insightful comment that "if Catherine of Siena is right that 'all the way to heaven is heaven,' then surely anything that is now part of our faithful pilgrimage will already be richly rewarding and evoke glimpses of heaven for us."

New Age esoterism seems at times to have replaced traditional Christianity as the dominant 'religion' of the Camino. Kenney walks the Way picking up, carrying, and then laying down various stones that she believes absorb some of her or her loved ones' sorrow. Harmon feels that the Camino is "alive" with radiating energy fields that enable her to heal quicker while she appreciates the universal consciousness of all creation and is visited by animal totem sprits and protective angels.

Boers is one of the few to take issue with the recent phenomena of personalising and even divinising the Camino [as I write that, I cannot but wonder how he would feel about my capitalising the word itself as I've done throughout these pages]. If the modern Church took the lessons of pilgrimage more seriously, he believes, it could still connect with "people of good faith who still want and long to meet God" and thus avoid them having to search for solutions in repackaged New Age esoterism.

PILGRIMAGE

PILGRIMAGE PROVIDES PARTICIPANTS WITH considerable time to contemplate the nature of what such a journey represents. Whether secular, sacred, or sportive, pilgrims, with few exceptions, struggle with ascribing meaning to their singular or collective actions.

Dennett thinks that we should keep in mind that pilgrimage is now, as it always has been, as much about joy as it is about faith. It is also very much a cultural construct, transcending the barriers of language, linking together nations, and offering a shared feeling of goodwill.

Hoinacki hopes that the rewards of his increased attentiveness while on pilgrimage – walking with all his senses wide open and in receiving mode – will lead him "toward the *mysterium* that lies at the end of this journey." Being one of the first modern pilgrims to write of his Camino experiences, he becomes preoccupied with concerns about authenticity: "I have heard that some see the origins of modern tourism in the pilgrimage to Compostela. If there is any truth to that, is the securalisation of such a journey, in fact, a perversion? The prostitution of foreign and exotic places and people in order to entertain the affluent is surely a despicable use of the other. I fall asleep, troubled. Am I, too, a tourist?"

Melville reflects that the "healing grace" of the Camino often seems to provide what is least expected but perhaps most needed. Not wishing to offend the benevolent guardian angel of the Camino, she becomes upset by her lack of stamina that forces frequent "cheating" by travelling in buses and taxis.

Wallis offers the apt synopsis that pilgrimage is a negotiation between mechanics and will during a trip from one's own small mind into a larger reality. Pilgrimage then requires "a submission to the moment, a release of illusion and a movement of body and soul, in trust, into the world as it was. As it is." The most important element is to go out doubtlessly and to above all look around and bear witness to being part of a collective journey in time. Judging authenticity is a difficult task, Wallis cautions, for which of the following are more worthy of the appellation of 'pilgrim': bus-transported believers or walk-weary non-believers? She concludes her narrative with the insightful caution against succumbing to what I refer to, in the penultimate section in the present book, as the pilgrimage disease of 'Caminophilia'. Reminding us that pilgrimage is about letting go of things – worldly pretensions, greed, one's ego, etc. – Wallis considers that the last great task of the Santiago pilgrimage is letting go of the Camino itself. But this is often a difficult task to embrace, she admits: "It's hard. Despite ourselves, we have romanticised it, identified with it, clung to it as the expression of who we are or want to be."

Kenney announces her lofty pilgrimage goals as being nothing less than discovering a new state of awareness to be brought about by "establishing a relationship with Mother Earth, the stars, planets, trees and the universe itself." Doing so will enable her to distil her lifetime of knowledge and "create a vision that would define the depth of my wisdom, so I could manifest it in my life." By surrendering to "the Camino's spiritual quest", she expects to become a more authentic person. The end-of-journey platitude that "when the Camino ends, the journey begins" is offered, in her mind, as support that all her goals have been or are on the way to being achieved.

Boers contends that pilgrimage is about integrating body and soul, feet and faith, on a path made hallowed by centuries of foot traffic of the many. Pilgrimage is a process that forces confrontations with memories jarred loose along the Way. And one reason for its growing popularity is that it presents alternative choices for how best to learn from those memories and continue with one's life back at home, which is the really ultimate testing ground for any pilgrimage. That said, the procedure of exiting a pilgrimage and regaining or recreating one's life can be trying. Boers recounts, for example, meeting one pilgrim who was treated so rudely in the cathedral office in Compostela when they disbelieved he had walked the entire way, that he actually burnt his *credential*, a document of acquired stamps generally cherished and often wall-mounted at home by many pilgrims.

Ward admits to beginning with a romanticised idea of pilgrimage as a solitary, monkish journey of pure spirit before coming to recognise that people are there for a vast spectrum of different reasons. Also, the relative merits of a pilgrim cannot easily be assessed by such superficial measures as pack weight, distance travelled, time started, or even whether or not that person had walked at all. The paradox of the pilgrim, Ward posits, is that s/he travels to a foreign land to find his or her spirit's home. Therefore, whether a pilgrim is 'authentic' or not need not be any more complicated than simply identifying whether or not that individual is actively looking for something. This reasoning leads Ward to be critical of those who skip over the *meseta* – the vast empty plains of north-central Spain – because there is nothing to see without realising that that is the entire point of that particular piece of "spiritual geography." Like many modern-day pilgrims, Ward can neither resist the temptation to trot out the hackneyed 'life is a pilgrimage/the road of life' trope, nor to anthropomorphise the "trickster Camino" as something capable of discerning and responding to one's needs, testing and rewarding individuals, and giving and taking away. Ward does make a very interesting and novel observation about changing wayside statuary on the Camino over the years. In medieval times, these statues were of the Holy family, Saint James, or other saints. "But the old heroes have retreated to the churches and the heavens," he explains, "The hero of the Camino today – or so the statues suggest – is the pilgrim himself, the pilgrim of old, pictured always humble, stoic, pure of heart, trusting, possessed of an unclouded faith that today's pilgrims can never hope to equal." Then there is the disjuncture about what is deemed essential for a pilgrimage and what is the reality. Once on a wall in an *albergue*, Ward reads the attributes that a Spanish priest considered to be needed for the Santiago pilgrimage: silence, slowness, solitude, effort, sobriety, gifts freely taken, and the Romanesque arch. The big problem, however, according to Ward, is that the Spanish treat the Camino as a Mediterranean form of *romeria*: a communal walk in the country to strengthen familial or friendship bonds with much laughter, food, and drink.

Christmas becomes aware that pilgrimage is not about punishment but "about an intentional decision to look at the world with fresh awareness and to consider your place in it." Pilgrims live an artificial existence of poverty, pain, and shared purpose, where the importance of the material world gradually disappears. In its place, the simplification of needs such as clean beds, warm smiles, and hot water can produce feelings of "near-orgasmic pleasure." The presence of so many sad and damaged people along the Way leads Christmas to coin the apt expression "the weight of the Camino." In her case, she decides that the vagabond lifestyle of a pilgrim is a perfect metaphor for her own life of spiritual waywardness "at the periphery of belonging." And she becomes critical upon discovering that the Camino "had morphed into a highly competitive sport" in direct opposition to the original idea that pilgrimages were supposed to teach one to "stop, observe, and reflect."

Thatcher believes that one of the most important things missing from our modern lives is having the gift of time in which to ponder. Walking the Camino at the pace through which most of human history has moved forces us to find that time. Admitting to becoming possessive of the term 'pilgrim,' Thatcher refuses to refer to those who only walk the last hundred kilometres to Compostela, their bags carried for them in an accompanying van, as anything other than 'tourists.'

Myers anthropomorphises the Camino as an entity always on the lookout for the unprepared and capable of retributively exacting a toll on those behaving inappropriately. The Camino, for her, imposes a purging of the unnecessary and an opening to that which is essential. In this respect, the reduction of daily activities is liberating, not incarcerating. Myers likens the Camino to a common fountain from which all pilgrims, past, present and future, obtain nourishment. The greatest adversary faced by any pilgrim is the misconception that s/he has finally arrived and that no further travelling is needed.

Harmon considers that one of the major attributes of the Camino is its paradox of community and isolation. By forcing her to honestly confront her life as if staring back into a mirror of time, the Camino teaches Harmon that from self-acceptance comes self-love, which leads to the realisation that one is never alone (reflected by the title she chose for her book).

And finally, Kirkpatrick succinctly boils it all down, concluding that there are really only two emotions displayed by pilgrims walking the Way: fear and love.

On Adventure…

CHAPTER 2

"MY STAFF OF FAITH TO WALK UPON"

Weather

These days, mortalities resulting from extreme weather on the Camino are rare. For most pilgrims, therefore, the elements represent little more than a nuisance. In the summer, it is the intense heat that is debilitating. In such circumstances, Ward states his "survival strategy" is to move slowly with head down and hope the sun doesn't notice him. While being baked on the *meseta*, Myers refers to the sun as the "executioner, silently meting out judgment, silently killing us." At other times, it is the famous falling rain on Spain's plains that cause discomfort. Hoinacki vividly describes a situation in which he desperately struggles in "near panic" to arrange his rain poncho over his pack in a deluge. Having the bad luck to be walking through one of the wettest and coldest springs on record, Dennett is in constant battle with the elements, finding it hard to believe that there can be so much water in the universe as that falling upon her head, and sad that she cannot enjoy the scenery with the wind whipping the rain into her eyes. One morning she is actually so cold that she returns to her hotel room to put her nightgown on and double it up underneath her armpits to give herself two more layers.

The imagined personal malevolence of the weather is a much-used trope in pilgrim narratives. Wallis warns of the fickle nature of the elements turning against you at any moment. Once when feeling sorry for herself, Christmas writes: "The wind slapped my face. Even God was cross with me." Reduced to tears, Dennett tries to control her building anger: "I resent the reduction of the walk to a test of simple endurance. Somehow it seems unjust that the elements should hound me so unceasingly. Rationally I know they are independent of my concerns, but when I am wet and cold, reduced to a kind of dumb, animal misery, I am aware of the childish tendency to take it all personally, despite my effort to pull myself together."

Encounters with weather need not always be stressful. Wind without rain and cold can be enjoyed. Atop a mountain, Myers feels like a piece of paper being tossed about. And while on the *meseta*, Dennett enjoys a reprieve from the rain by rejecting the compulsion to wear extra clothes in case the weather changes: "I want nothing between me and the air," she writes. "I spread my arms wide to catch the breeze."

Wayfinding

Given the proliferation of yellow arrows in recent years, one might be surprised that anyone can become disorientated and lost while walking the

Camino. But it does happen. Free of having to constantly take stock of one's whereabouts, many develop a reliance on waymarking to such an extent that they fret on those rare occasions when clarity of direction is unclear. Boers admits to being fearful when he doesn't spot another mark for a prolonged time after earlier finding an arrow that had pointed perplexingly in two directions. In the same spirit, Hoinacki writes "When I think I should see another arrow, and I do not, an inner tension starts to build up, increasing with each step. Am I walking farther out of my way with this step? Will I have to return? And then, finally, each time the arrows appear again – all the tension flows out – dumped by the side of the path. I can continue with a light heart."

Wayfinding assistance can come from human sources. On one occasion, Hoinacki is somewhat surprised to regain the route after asking directions from an obviously mad woman. Worried about not having seen another person or waymarker for hours, and thinking that a new perspective might help, Kenney turns around to look back over the way she had walked: "Immediately my eyes were drawn to a grouping of stones on the path. Looking more closely I could see they were placed in the shape of an arrow and it was pointing toward me. I smiled, relieved there was a sign after all. The direction of the arrow confirmed I was walking the right way. With humble gratitude I thanked the considerate pilgrims who went before me and placed that stone arrow." Other pilgrims believe help arrives through divine intervention. Myers is rescued by a shepherd whom he considers to be a sure sign from Providence. And whenever momentarily confused about direction, Atman asks for spiritual guidance before proceeding confidently along what she informs readers is always the correct route.

Sometimes pilgrims can actually become stuck on a wrong path. Harman finds herself sealed off from a highway by a tall wire fence. "*TRAPPED!*" she writes in italicised capitals, before becoming more frantic:

> I couldn't get out! So I kept walking along the highway, thinking that eventually there would be a break in the fence. It came in the form of a culvert running underneath the highway, taking a stream with it. *TRAPPED AGAIN!* I searched for a way to cross the stream, but the incline was so great that I would have risked spraining my ankle. So I walked along the stream through a whole field of thistles that ate up my legs. *TRAPPED AGAIN!* After another kilometre of this, I realized that my only option was to return in the direction from which I had come.

On one occasion, Christmas walks four kilometres along a rising road only to find it end at a garbage dump, which with characteristic humour she considers to be a perfect metaphor for her life. The absolute silence of the location at first spooks her but then she is tantalised by the fact that she might be able to disappear since not a soul in the world would know where to begin looking for her. But then worries intercede about a lonely death from an accident or getting ill and she retreats back to the waymarked Camino.

Danger

Most of the dozen or so deaths that occur every year on the Camino are due to heart attacks. But accidents always can and occasionally do happen. For example, during an early morning start Hoinacki slips in the dark and rain and the heavy pack pulls him down onto an already bad knee, "It smacks the concrete," he writes, continuing, "Pain shoots up and runs all through me. I think I shall faint right here on the sidewalk. It's awful. The knee has been troubling me almost every day, all day...One scene alone appears before my eyes: This is the end of my pilgrimage." Kirkpatrick picks up and drinks from her water pouch which had lain in the grass beside her during a rest stop and finds her tongue and throat suddenly going numb, terrifying her that she might have poisoned herself from a toxic plant.

Sometimes it is the perceived threat of danger which can be worrying. Hoinacki is nervous while walking on a road beneath overhanging cliffs as he navigates his way around a landslide "large enough to bury a dozen pilgrims." And Christmas is spooked by a snake that slithers across the path, suddenly panicking her about what other nasty wildlife might be lurking in the fringeing bushes.

It is a sad fact of life that female pilgrims, just as females everywhere, need to be as vigilant as birds to avoid misfortune. Atman tells of one pilgrim being groped by an old man in a *refugio* kitchen and Kenney warns of a dirty-minded hotel owner who tries to lure young females to his establishment. One day when walking alone, Melville becomes fearful by her over-active imagination which has baddies leaping out of the bushes. And Dennett recounts a very real and very terrifying encounter in a remote forest when a motorcycle stops in front of her, the driver encased within a helmet and visor. He says nothing and Dennett steps around him and keeps walking. Hearing the engine behind her, she knows that he is following but fights the impulse to turn around and confront him. After a hundred metres she hears the crunch of gravel indicating the motorcycle has turned around. But then, ten minutes later, she again hears the engine and knows he has returned to stalk her. Continuing to stride forward, Dennett debates on whether to flee into the woods or to stay on the road and fight. Then a car approaches which she flags down and asks the female driver to take her to the next village.

Hardship

It is no surprise that the act of walking hundreds of kilometres over a period of weeks with a heavy backpack can exact a toll upon middle-aged or elderly bodies. This is especially the case with an absence of prior long-distance hiking experience or a compensatory rigorous training regime. Adventures are stories well told back in the safety of comfortable surroundings, and journeys without hardship are not really adventures. As a result, pilgrimage accounts pitched as grand adventures are filled with descriptions about the plethora of hardships bravely confronted and heroically surmounted by the intrepid storytellers.

Like many setting out from St.-Jean-Pied-de-Port, Hoinacki's pilgrimage begins in great discomfort: "I start to feel tired, and the pain, too, begins, first in my feet, then in my legs, reaching my back and shoulders until my entire body aches. Curiously, I am able to distinguish two distinct but 'complementary' feelings – pain and exhaustion." A former theologian, he begrudgingly accepts the hardship as a penitential experience: "The pain and exhaustion will be measured out to me in accord with what I need to bring a balance back in my life." At the end of that first day, Hoinacki lies in his sleeping bag wracked with terrible chills and violent trembling. He considers alerting others for help but eventually succumbs to sleep. Weeks later and still in great pain he is given a glucose pill by Spanish pilgrims at a roadside break. But despite their belief in the curative properties of the pill, Hoinacki is soon in pain again, leading him to reflect that one would have to travel far on the road of drugs to ease the discomfort of the Camino. But if so, he asks, would it still be the Camino?

A long day spent walking along a sharply angled roadside verge produces pain in Dennett's twisted hips and down-slope toes. She is brought to the edge of tears when encountering a sign stating that her intended destination is a further four kilometres, and struggles onward, trying to keep her mind from dwelling on her body's pain by counting trees, birds, and even the number of steps. Finally, as near to exhaustion as she has ever been in her life, Dennett enters her hotel room and upon removing her boots finds she can barely put her damaged feet on the floor. Weeks later, while walking on a stone-surfaced trail, every step is agony: "Hips, knees, ankles all received their share of jolts, through the soles of my shoes, which had withstood any amount of uneven ground until now, jagged rocks gouged and bruised my arches." And during a particularly difficult climb, Dennett writes: "After a hundred metres I was gasping. At twice that, I thought I would explode with the heat. My face blazed like a fever patient's, and the pack suddenly seemed to weigh as much as a sarcophagus."

With language to make even the hardiest pilgrim cringe in empathy, Myers dramatically refers to his erupting blisters as blending into "a sickening mush." Once he helps carry a fellow pilgrim's pack and reflects "To see a pilgrim whose body would go no further and whose will is broken is to remember one's own fragility and one's own failures. Most of us have known it – when no amount of sweating or praying saved us." One of the hardest lessons of the Camino for some to come to terms with, Myers contends, is to be able to accept and understand failure.

Injuries cause Thatcher to be wracked by worry and self-doubt: "My left foot is swollen, hard, shining, red, really painful to touch, and it is painful to articulate my foot up or down. How on earth will I go on? I cannot walk without pain and I know that my further walking will only prolong and likely aggravate the inflammation." And Atman encounters similar travails: "I feel as if every step I take I put bones on asphalt. I feel as if there is no flesh left on my feet, nor can I feel my boots. I feel bone on asphalt. I am in such pain I can't comprehend how it is possible that I am walking." As also does Kenney: "The balls of my feet ached, then became an excruciating pain eventually forcing me to stop. I sat down and took off my boots to relieve my entire foot from the pressure. My enthusiasm had dwindled and left me in a miserable mood." Later she worries that all she may have to show for her efforts at the end of the Camino, should she get there, "would be a catalogue of sundry stories" about her manifest injuries. Boers refers to his own "bagel-sized blood blister" that needs medical treatment and how he feels part of the mass of the walking wounded by sharing their aliments of bandaged feet, damaged hips, and limps from tendonitis. "I pondered the irony," he writes, "that in medieval times folks often made pilgrimages to shrines to receive healing but I experienced physical deterioration instead."

Free of debilitating troubles himself, Ward offers some insightful commentary on the hardships, realised or imaginary, of the pilgrimage experience. He makes the cute quip that unlike their medieval predecessors, the torments of most of today's pilgrims have less to do about souls and more to do about soles. And he offers the following bit of myth-busting: "The climbing of O Cebreiro is the Camino's biggest fish story, a morning walk up a big hill that rumour has turned into an assault on Everest." Ward is also mindful of the slightly hypocritical, presumed penitential aspirations of modern pilgrims compared to those in medieval times: "Suffering is a thing we almost play at on the Camino these days – walking an extra kilometre on our blistered feet, braving the wind and rain – knowing full well that at the end of the day we will have a dry place to sleep and a hot meal."

Melville's account is interesting in that it describes the harrowing misfortune of a couple woefully unsuited for undertaking the pilgrimage walk, and who, as a resort, have to make frequent use of taxis and buses. As also described in other accounts, Melville too faces painful blisters out of which brown liquid oozes. It is her husband's health, however, which concerns her most. Early on, he becomes so exhausted that she is left wondering about how to arrange to have his body shipped home. Later he is so crippled by infected blisters that she has to walk ahead to a village to try to find a taxi and when that fails, to return to him and flag down a passing car to transport him to a clinic. Then he develops a perpetual cough and during one attack while she is running about trying to find a taxi, he writes his will in the hotel room. It is hard not to sympathise with Melville when she writes: "I am fed up with walking, refugios and snoring. I wish this stupid camino was over."

Christmas brings a wonderful sense of black humour to the discussion of hardships experienced along the Way. Like so many others, she too struggles over the Pyrenees, describing the process as "torture" or "Hell under sunny skies", and wishing for a car to stop and offer her a lift: "Had Jeffrey Dahmer been behind the wheel, I would have climbed in and willingly offered him my left arm as a snack." Other members of her group are similarly minded. One regards the first day from St.-Jean as being the worst in her life, and another writes in her journal that evening: "Only thirty-one more days left of this goddam trip." Days later and much stressed, Christmas questions her own sanity for deciding to walk the Camino and offers a heart-felt description of homesickness experienced by many: "Tears squirted from my eyes. I suddenly missed my children – their hugs and their screaming matches – and missed my home, missed scrubbing toilets, driving the kids to band practice, dragging the trash to the curb every Sunday night." At another time, she weeps for her aching legs, the separation from all that was familiar, and for her loneliness and fear. Once when frustrated by her injuries, she opinions the succinct indictment "*Buen* fucking Camino, indeed." At another time she is woken up in the middle of the night by bells ringing forty-two times and ponders her options: "Go back to bed. Start walking. Quit this stupid pilgrimage and go home." But it is the "blood sport" of securing a bed for the night and the behaviour of her fellow pilgrims that are the biggest hardships Christmas endures along the Way. Her reflections on how to deal with an obnoxious snorer have been shared but seldom so honestly admitted by many pilgrims: "All night long, I had been kept awake by the woman in the next bunk. She snored. All. Friggin'. Night…She was still issuing loud bodily emissions from both ends when, in the too-early hours of the morning, I swung my pack into position and groped in the darkness for my walking stick. I considered whacking her with it, but had I started I would not have been able to stop."

On Joy…

Chapter 3

"MY SCRIPT OF JOY, IMMORTAL DIET"

Excitement

Published narratives describe the excitement felt at all stages of the pilgrimage experience. Before even the first steps are taken, Ward confesses to longing for undertaking an adventure on foot "like the ones in books" and Melville expresses excitement about the possibility of a new life being born out of the Camino. Later, while upon the Way, Melville feels exhilarated as he crests over a large hill, remarking: "I have never felt so free and unfettered." Likewise, on her first day of walking, Wallis states: "A shimmer of freedom cycled through me. A gift. All I needed, I had in my pack. Under its weight, I felt my shoulders relax. I felt relief." Both pilgrims revel in the shedding of the restrictive cocoons of their previous lives. For Hoinacki, it is the first sighting of a genuine pilgrim that inspires him at the start of his journey: "All the pictures of European pilgrim iconography show nothing compared to the excited feel of encountering the real thing, in the early morning light, right before my eyes." And at the end of his pilgrimage, Boers waits excitedly and then beams in joy upon hearing his name being read out in the cathedral mass as being the sole Canadian arriving that day from St.-Jean-Pied-de-Port. "And that was me. It was true. I was here," he reflects before catching the eyes of other pilgrims and acknowledging their accomplishments in a tsunami of shared euphoria.

While along the Way, the anticipation of what the next day might bring is regularly commented upon. Ward remarks on "the tremor of excitement" running through a *refugio* bunk room filled with a hundred people who can't wait for the morrow. Struggling to fall asleep while awash with excitement, Hoinacki has to reign in his eagerness to get underway again, whereas in similar circumstances Kenney is nervous about the next day's offerings.

Expressions of excitement are of course idiosyncratic. For Kirkpatrick, it is her near disbelief that the wonderful day just experienced really did happen. For Dennett, it is anticipating and planning out her arrival in Compostela with the many press interviews she will have to give. For Wallis and a fellow pilgrim with a shared love of history, it is jubilance felt when encountering an ancient Roman road and bridge. And for Hoinacki, it is "the joy of surprise" that comes about from his purposeful decision not to carry a detailed guidebook filled with maps, photos, and descriptions.

Relaxation

THE PLEASURE OF A RELAXING AND THERAPEUTIC shower after a hard day of walking the Camino is something eagerly sought for and enjoyed by many pilgrims. Hoinacki "abandons" himself to the comfort of such "an incredible luxury." Atman goes even further in her praise: "Nothing ever before gave me such relief. My whole body is thanking me for this hot water washing away tension and pain. I, in turn, am grateful to my body for what it is putting up with for me. It is a moment of sacred union. It is a communion." Refreshment through food and drink are also a huge part of the pilgrimage experience. Hoinacki believes his meals along the Way to be among the best in his entire life and savours the "glorious, sensual luxury" of his first coffee in a week, Thatcher refers to a big, cold glass of beer as being a bit of "paradise", Atman becomes blissful when eating a piece of chocolate, and Myers describes eating fresh cherries as "an interlude with ecstasy." Christmas hits the mark in her summary that "there is no happier pilgrim than one who is clean, pressed, rested, and stuffed."

Relaxation is of course perhaps best experienced by simply doing nothing at all. Often the joy of pilgrimage is most heartfelt in those cherished moments of contrast between movement and meditation. Dennett enjoys rest breaks along the Way that allow her to hear the sounds she most enjoys, that of wind in the leaves of trees and of the rush of a stream over stones. At such times, she stretches out on the ground, head on pack, and watches the clouds pass and the busy lives of insects around her. Kenney is like-minded in savouring such joyful ephemera: "When we finished eating, I lay down resting my head on my backpack and looked beyond the treetops to the blue sky, watching the leaves gently fall to the ground. At no other time in my life have I felt as completely part of the universe; something bigger than the world I entered when I was born."

Evening relaxation is often a special time and an important component of one's inner pilgrimage. Kenney, lying down on her mattress, achieves peace by simply becoming lost daydreaming about the day's events, leaving her "with a contented grin" on her face during the reminiscence. Dennett, having the misfortune to be walking at a time of some of the worst spring weather recorded in a century, temporarily escapes the hardships by immersing herself in various novels or music and in studying the cityscape from her hotel window: "The view of the tiled roofs to the tower was lit by the waning moon, a cool, sharp light that flooded into the room. Night scents drifted up from the garden below – lilacs, roses, and damp grass. Everything visible and audible touched a chord of wonder."

Playfulness

Pilgrimage, if we are to believe the pundits, is supposed to be a serious affair. Journal travelogues, frequently filled with doom, gloom, misery, and despair, seem to support this contention. Occasionally, however, authors do engage in joyful activities or thoughts, discovering as they do, the long-repressed, playful child within. Shocked by the gaudy colour scheme in her hotel room, Dennett sneaks about to empty rooms to turn down the covers on beds just to see how the sheets match the over-the-top wallpaper. Melville is shamefacedly filled with delight by a fantasy in which she smothers an annoying snorer with a pillow. When visiting a castle, Kenny and a companion chase "each other up and down the stairs with youthful laughter." Upon stumbling onto a village fair, Wallis and her companion drop their packs and join in the dancing, jiving and twisting about in the hot, moist air, causing her to break out in laughter. When approaching the cathedral in Compostela, Myers admits to feeling more cheerful than pious, wishing as he does for a celebratory tickertape greeting to mark his meritorious arrival. And when leisurely approaching the beach at Finisterre, Kirkpatrick suddenly notices the changing light, which leads her to run, as she had never done before, to catch the sunset, laughing all the way.

Happiness

Pilgrims are no different from the general public in finding happiness from a wide diversity of sources. For some, it is the joy of slowly moving through a sublime landscape. Melville feels "a deep sense of happiness" as she walks down a country road between hills filled with grass. Hoinacki rejoices in the simple pleasure of the heat penetrating deep into his body from the warm sun as he crests a mountain. "As I get closer to Compostela," he writes, "each day is more lovely, more filled with charm, more resplendent with wonder." Despite pain from blisters, Atman so relishes the lovely and loving scenery it brings her to rears. "I am so happy to be alive," she writes, "I am grateful to be alive and experience and participate in this beauty." It is the physical act of walking itself that registers with Kenney: "I walked with my shoulders pulled back standing tall, smiling inwardly as I discovered this joyful expression within my being." Dennett is happy to be able to walk all day, occasionally even needing to force herself to slow down to keep from running, yet still have enough energy to go out after a brief rest for local sightseeing. Once, she remarks "What was going through my mind was the realisation of how happy I was, unencumbered by anything more than I needed, my energies directed solely to the accomplishments of today's purpose." Kirkpatrick is happy about conquering her anxiety about every little imagined danger and in pushing herself to new limits of physical and mental capabilities. Other pilgrims find joy inside buildings. Melville is made blissful by listening to Bach fugues from the practising organist wash over her while sitting alone in a church. Early on his pilgrimage, Myers is deeply moved by interpreting the message of a choir as "Joy will coax us. Joy will strengthen us for the hard journey. Joy will prevail." And at the end of her pilgrimage, Kenney's eyes "overflowed with tears of joy" upon hearing "Canada" announced at the pilgrim mass in the Santiago cathedral and knowing that it referred to her. Happiness is also found in the company and companionship of others. Hoinacki draws strength from the people who preceded him on the route each day and sleep beside him each night which leads him to be enveloped by a great peacefulness. The most cherished memory Thatcher has at the end of his pilgrimage is the "real, intense joy [of] really loving and being loved."

Occasionally the happiness may be so great as to leave pilgrims laughing in joy. Seeking refuge from the cold rain, Dennett savours the smell of beeswax polish and burning apple wood from an enormous hearth: "I stood electrified with pleasure, breathing deeply, until I began to laugh." Badly dubbed or translated old American television shows and store signs provoke laughter from both Dennett and Atman. At one point during an evening meal, Thatcher and a fellow pilgrim share a big laugh when neither can remember what town they are presently in. When reliving their shared experiences with laughter following the pilgrim mass in the Compostela cathedral, Myers and his companions are shooed outside. "We only wanted the joy to stay," he writes defensively.

At other times, the happiness can be expressed in song. For Dennett, this occurred as the mist evaporated from a beautiful, bird-filled wood she was walking through one perfect morning. Myers feels compelled to sing when strolling about over the "restorative floors" of old churches in his socks. The closer she gets to Finisterre the more frequently Harmon finds herself remembering and singing the words to old songs as the pain in her heart is progressively alleviated. After recovering from a bad fall with cessation of pain, Hoinacki feels like singing in the rain and blessing all the creatures about him. Myers has to force himself from a café: "It is time to resume walking. But I hesitate here, where I am filled, where the complexities of the journey, are made simple, and where, on a round metal table beside a bowl of jam, a song note sits within me." Overjoyed at the freedom she feels when walking the Camino, when a companion begins to sing *Mr. Tambourine Man*, Wallis states that "Suddenly, it seemed impossible to be happier."

Such intense feelings of happiness are a common feature in Camino narratives. Many pilgrims find themselves gradually or suddenly waking up to the realisation that their time along the Way may be the happiest they have ever felt in their lives. At one point, for example, Thatcher simply states his belief that he not only is he the happiest he has ever been, he must also surely be "the happiest man alive." After only his second day, Hoinacki marvels that all the cost, trouble, and pain are nothing compared to his being introduced to experiences the existence of which he never would have suspected or dreamed. "To imagine," he marvels, "I might have died without knowing this." And at Finisterre while watching the setting sun, Kirkpatrick feels like bursting: "I have never had such a feeling of joy and confirmation and grace," she confesses.

On Contact…

Chapter 4

"AND THUS I'LL MAKE MY PILGRIMAGE"

Walking

FOR MANY, THE PILGRIMAGE ALONG the Camino Francés to Santiago de Compostela is first and foremost about walking. Everything else derives from this basic fact. Not surprisingly, given all the attention paid to and all the time spent engaged in walking, pilgrims are effusive in their opinions about its multitudinous merits. For some, it is the direct physicality of the contact that most resonates. For others, it is the ensuing indirect benefits, by no means ancillary, that are most cherished.

The slow pace of walking is deemed essential by many for fostering feelings of connectivity to the landscape. Hoinacki believes that the attentiveness that comes from slowly progressing through the world has to it an elemental quality. On his second day, he comes to a metaphorical realisation that he has never before been able to feel his entire body move from one place to another, occupying each in succession, in a way unlike anything that can be experienced in motorised transport wherein all one does is to move *through* space, rather than become part of it. Savouring the irregularity of uneven natural surfaces felt through his boots, Hoinacki also appreciates "the power of contact" of the earth entering his feet as measured by their soreness. Wallis tries at times when she is free of pain and worry to feel the route through individual steps. Dennett expresses similar emotions felt when life is boiled down to nothing more than a reality of the open road, the weather, and her own body: "Sometimes I simply revel in the physical sensation of moving along, the feel of varied surfaces under my feet, the strength in my legs that flows when I am in full stride, right through me like a current."

Dennett continues the quote above with the following: "Invigorating though it is, walking seems to have a particularly calming effect on the mind." That walking somehow allows us to think more clearly or more profoundly has been recognised by many pilgrims. Myers, who uses the expression "the catharsis of walking", and entitled a chapter in his book "The Earth is Singing Into My Feet", likens the act to triggering an internal light-bulb. He reminds readers that Saint Augustine coined the wonderful phrase "*solvitur ambulando*", roughly "it is solved by walking." Dennett uses the walk to review her friendships, focusing on individuals through time. Boers thinks his watch may actually move more slowly when he is on foot. "Walking," he discovers, "affects not just space and distance but also time itself."

For some, walking is a spiritual practice. Harmon calls it "a moving meditation." Kenney thinks it exposes "the inner rhythm of [her] divine soul." And for theologian Boers, it is a direct way to communicate with God's lessons that only seem to be able to get through to us at the speed of walking. For him, the major gift of the Camino is its way of linking walking on earth to feelings of the Divine: "Never in my life have I felt so strongly that connection. Celtic Christians once spoke of 'thin places,' where the veil separating the present and eternity was flimsier than usual. Is the Camino a thin place? Or has it just become so, worn to translucence by the persistent pressure of many pilgrims? Which came first, the thin place or the pilgrim?" No accident that Boers titles his book *The Way is Made By Walking* and reminds us of Christ's statement that He is the Way.

Opinions differ on whether pilgrimage walking should be undertaken as a solo or collective endeavour. Hoinacki is adamant that his decision to walk alone was necessary to allow him to "explore the secrets of the *camino*" by enabling him to mingle across time with those who had walked before under the same sky and over top of the same soil. Kirkpatrick, too, expresses her "sheer relief of being alone, being able to reflect on my own little history, being able to think and feel and be totally and completely alone in it", something she insists can never happen on a short walk since "it takes many, many steps and many, many thoughts." Atman emphatically states that she wants to walk alone free from distracting conversation which would impede her sense of connectivity to the ground. Christmas, however, believes the opposite, considering walking to be a combination of exercise and therapy in which two things are released: endorphins and conversation. "Words, thoughts, and ideas bubble up from the depth of your soul," she writes, and "there's something about walking and talking side by side that makes conversations more candid than they would be face-to-face. What you have to say isn't influenced by your walking partner's facial reactions."

LANDSCAPE

SPENDING MORE THAN THREE HUNDRED hours slowly moving through varied landscapes can leave strong impressions upon sensitive pilgrims. Hoinacki refers to the beauty always "sweetly pressing" itself upon him. Dennett savours the visual quality of an harmonious land "long tamed, but treated lovingly by its inhabitants", and on one occasion feels "almost wrung out with emotion" after walking through kilometres of blooming flowers that leave her in ecstasy. Atman calls the scents, sounds, and sights a "constant feast" for her heart. And Kenney considers a mountaintop view so sublime it produces an "overall feeling of peace" such as she had never hitherto experienced.

The most characteristic landscape feature of the Camino is the vast *meseta*.

It is not uncommon, however, for pilgrims to take a bus to avoid walking across the high plains which they imagine to be no more than a boring experience of traversing a featureless waste. Those who do walk the *meseta*, in contrast, cannot fathom the ignorance or negligence of others in missing what they regard being as the most important part of the entire Camino. Dennett appreciates the arid, austere beauty of the plains. Ward enjoys the roundness of the world touching the sky. Kirkpatrick find herself stopping and listening to the sound of the fields of wheat rustling in the wind. Sometimes pilgrims become rhapsodic about the *meseta*. Wallis believes the landscape to be the perfect intoxicant for those craving the aesthetic and the sublime and feels inspired by its vastness: "I stared across the plain. I was a visitor from the other side of the planet, almost from the other side of the millennium, a lone spectator in this theatre of time now bereft of its players and inhumanly quiet in the bright sun." Harmon recognises the "gift" of the *meseta* that allows her to walk alone all day free of all distractions while finding comfort in the emptiness about her: "As I became more and more accustomed to the silence and solitude in my walking, I looked for the longer distances between pilgrims and destinations. For there I knew I would find what I was looking for, and it would find me."

Occasionally pilgrims can experience a deep feeling of contact with the enveloping landscape. "On the *camino*," Hoinacki writes, "I've come to an intimate awareness of the earth, the air, and water. The soil powerfully presses itself into me with every step; the air fills my lungs with fresh life in every breath; the pure, sparkling water of the springs continually revives my spirit." He comes to realise that neither destinations nor grand vistas really matter; only that he is in the immediate present and can feel the landscape: "There is only the earth that I touch in so many ways, and the promise of a new earth, a new soil, under, around me, in the next step." After watching the sunset and subsequent moonrise at Finisterre, Kirkpatrick runs into the water: "I was alone, with waves crashing, for a long time. I cried to the ocean and I felt larger than life, far beyond the edges of my own body." Kenney, too, experiences such a transcendent harmony: "Hours of rain acted like a mantra arousing my senses and elevating the level of conscious awareness I was experiencing. Soon my skin began to take on the aroma of nature, absorbing the fresh scent of the rain soaked forest. I was becoming the Camino." While witnessing a mountain sunrise, which she refers to as "the heartbeat of a new day", Christmas spreads her arms in welcome to let the heat enter and energise her. Reflecting on her entire journey, she writes: "I had crossed a landscape like no other. It was a landscape I could smell and feel, one that permeated my skin and burrowed itself into my very soul to the extent that when I eventually returned home I could still feel it, my body yearned for it."

Places

CONTACT WITH THE ARCHITECTURE OF CHURCHES is an essential part of the pilgrimage experience for some pilgrims. Dennett and Myers both write enthusiastically of admiring the beauty of individual Romanesque arches. Kenney is "stunned by the beauty" of the illuminated glass in the León cathedral and "devours the divine sight" of the Pórtico de la Gloria in the Santiago cathedral. Wallis likens the varied churches along the Way to jewels in the Camino necklace. And for her, the true gems are those churches which date from the peak years of the pilgrimage. She loves the restraint, intimacy, and rounded feminism of the Romanesque as a place where God comes down from a-high compared to the authoritarian, angular masculinity of the Gothic where humans soar up to Heaven. Romanesque churches, Wallis appreciates, have a palatable feeling of cosmic dread by putting one right in the heat of the battle between good and evil whereas Gothic churches give one a view of distant paradise to be sought for. Stripped down to its Romanesque essentials, the exquisite church of San Martín in Frómista glows, according to Wallis, like a golden Adonis: "A soft evening light suffused the stone vaults, something like a consciousness floated among the walls. The church had a poise and order that contained but never denied the free play of the mind. It was impossible not to be contemplative." And in some of the finest language ever written about experiencing Camino architecture, Wallis beautifully describes emotions evoked by the Church of Santa María at Eunate:

> For a few moments, I could almost grasp the oneness of the medieval cosmos, feel what it was like to know, without any doubt, that the universe was a living union of the material in the supernatural. I could almost believe that God was still at play here, hidden in the shadows, then revealing himself on an issue of light. The Virgin and Child stared from the altar, absorbing all the space, then bestowing it once again in an gesture of austerity and tenderness on two souls from a far off, data-mad world who sat near the centre aisle, straining across the chasm of time for something forgotten.

At other times, northern sensibilities can be unresponsive to Spanish churches. Dennett is repelled by the push-button, coin-operated candles. Hoinacki is shocked by the "insane extravagance" of the excessive decorations that he considers so antithetical to the true Camino that he avoids all monuments. Dismissing the Disney-like legends and characters in the Santo Domingo Cathedral, Christmas jokes that she is drawn more to shoe shops than to Romanesque churches. Myers is made uneasy by his belief in the corruption represented by the churches.

It is not uncommon for pilgrims to be left wanting by the anticlimax of arriving in Santiago de Compostela. Myers regards Compostela as being less a New Jerusalem than a Disneyland due to the surrounding tourism and commercialism. Feeling revulsion at what he imagines to be a trivialisation of his pilgrimage efforts, joy is replaced by disdain and a palatable need to leave. "Finisterre beckons," he announces. Christmas feels indifferent to the cathedral and the crassness of the swinging *botafumeiro* and its elicited response of clicking cameras and clapping hands, something which is likened to a "circus act" by Wallis. "I passed the column where St. James was seated," Christmas continues, "his back to the tawdry spectacle we had just witnessed, and I shot him a look of disappointment. The simple and, by all accounts, moody fisherman from faraway Yaffa, son of Zebedee and Salome, Apostle of Christ, evangelist, martyr, and saint, had become Spain's Mickey Mouse." For Ward, Compostela is a place of sadness: "It is the great orphanage at the end of the road where the children of the Camino gather one last time before they scatter like dandelion seeds to their own countries, their old lives."

Sprawling and ugly urban development rankles both Dennett and Hoinacki on several occasions. Christmas is offended by the first view from the Mount of Joy of Compostela over an horizon of unregulated modernity. With the hilltop *refugio* behind exhibiting "all the warmth of a concentration camp", and the tarnished skyline in front, she realises that reality bore no resemblance to the naïve expectations she had imagined of her arrival: "In my mind's eyes I had pictured myself with the women in my group rushing down the grassy hillside of Monte del Gozo, holding hands as we sang, laughed and skipped our way into Santiago! Think of the poster for *The Sound of Music*, and you get the idea."

Connectivity to the past inspires many pilgrims. Dennett, for example, often feels "caught in a time warp" on the Camino, and takes comfort in knowing that thousands of pilgrims before her must have been similarly uplifted by viewing the wonderful sculptures. Kenney gently runs her fingers across an ancient castle wall to absorb its history and wonders if earlier pilgrims had ever done the same. Later, at the cathedral in Compostela, she too, like millions before her, inserts her hand into the well-worn depression on the Jesse Tree and feels "a sense of belonging with the many pilgrims who have been here before."

Often the most memorable parts of any pilgrimage account are the sensitive descriptions of the unexpected. Harmon is moved to tears sitting in a café, listening to Ave María on the radio, when a big dog ambles over and quietly lays its head in her lap. For Atman, a chance encounter with a very old and worn-out gate moves her to tears with the realisation that no one, when viewing her photographs, will ever be able to understand or appreciate "the moment of rapture" she feels at that moment. And while sitting on the rocks perched over the ocean at Finisterre, Ward watches as another pilgrim casts out her staff into the ocean with a shout of 'Gracias,' causing him to echo his own heartfelt thanks to the universe.

People

MANY PILGRIMS ARE OF THE OPINION that it is the interactions with people along the Way – the locals, those working in the *refugios*, and especially one's fellow pilgrims – that form the most lasting impact of the Santiago pilgrimage on their lives. At a time when there is a glut of pilgrimage narratives on shop bookshelves, almost all of which regurgitate the daily itinerary of walking intermixed with second-, or third-sourced historical didacticism, more than anything, it is the diversity and expression of these inter-personal contacts that is most interesting to readers.

Atman's pilgrimage account contains alternating judgmental comments about fellow pilgrims and statements about her own imagined capabilities in psychically healing the afflicted about her by "working with their energy." She falls in love with one emotionally fragile female pilgrim whom is made to feel uncomfortable upon receipt of the information. But at other times, Atman displays sensitivity in her interactions, as witness to the following encounter with a very old woman who offers her an apple: "She is so very poor – I can see from the clothes she wears – yet she wants to give. I can't deny her. I accept with a bow and putting my hand on my heart I say '*Muchas Graciás.*' She smiles and makes a sign of a cross in the air, blessing me. I bow low again. I turn and am on my way, while tears flow down my face."

At the end of a long day spent walking in bad weather, Dennett has an encounter with a horrible hotel keeper who demands payment in advance but when questioned grabs her pack and hurls it out into the street. When she begins to cry, he pushes her outside before slamming the door in her face. This is stark contrast to an encounter with a group of gypsies who call her out of the rain and bestow much kindness. At another time, Dennett is emotional as she departs from a home where she had stayed for several days: "Until I found myself surrounded by the affection and warmth of [the] family, I had no idea how frozen and self-protective my own emotions had become. I struggled along the shoulder of the road, weeping like one turned out of paradise."

Harman offers an interesting alliterative, typological classification of the pilgrims she encounters: those who are proper, pious, part-time, packaged, party, or pushy. Although like most pilgrims she too is touched by the many random acts of kindness, sharing, concern, and help experienced along the Way, it is often the locals of whom she is critical. This comes in the form of the anti-pilgrim sentiment she often feels in restaurants, and the obnoxiously rude and insensitive behaviour of loud-talking Spaniards on the Camino itself.

Hoinacki is grateful of the few words exchanged en route with fellow pilgrims who are respectful enough not to pry, but is disdainful of the loud, brazen, and uncivil cyclists who take over *refugios*. Of the natives, he is critical of those from the upper class whom he finds to be haughty, impolite, and selfish, in contrast to those from the lower middle class whom he believes to be open, friendly, generous, and considerate. Above all, it is the Spanish farmers – their honest work effort, sense of community, and staunch individualism – whom most interest Hoinacki: "But how I wish I could somehow have found the words to say: How much I respect you! How much I would like to honour you! How much your country should seek not to lose you!"

Kenney considers her inability to speak Spanish not to be a deterrent at all since it will enable her to be able to focus on herself with limited distractions. And she soon discovers that sometimes the most meaningful encounters are those free of words, as for example, glimpsing a local woman in a doorway who meets her gaze and clasps her hands together in prayer, silently blessing Kenney before turning back inside. As another New Age self-help aficionado, Kenney believes that she too is blessed with an ability to communicate with the troubled souls around her. Struggling with a resolution to remain independent, she, like many have before and since while on the Camino, succumbs to longing and falls in love with a fellow pilgrim.

For Meyers, solidarity grows with each leapfrogged meeting and re-meeting of pilgrims along the Way. He recognises too that many of these individuals are pushed and pulled by the contrasting attractions of solitude and companionship. Some pilgrims, however, are simply unapproachable; they are too different, too emotionally broken down, too demanding, too often drunk, too big assholes, etc. "As an archetype of life itself," Myers reflects, "the social fabric of the Camino would not be complete without its share of rogues, sociopaths and braggarts. Unappealing and unavoidable, they must be reckoned with." Toward which end, he seriously considers pillow-smothering one selfish individual in the bunk above him who persists in talking on his cell-phone late into the night.

Wallis' narrative is unusual in describing post-pilgrimage experiences. An exchange of letters with an elderly Spanish gentleman soon after she returns home leaves her tearful. Reflecting years later upon the various people she had met while on pilgrimage provides her with the opportunity to assess the importance of the Camino from a perspective of time: "In the deepest text of one's pilgrimage, I wondered, what meaning do such encounters have? Are they the heart of the story, or are they its sweet ephemeral gifts?"

The reduction of needs to only the barest of essentials while on pilgrimage allow, Thatcher supposes, even the smallest of goodwill gestures given or received to assume a weighty and memorable importance. In the word and act 'good' resides the word and concept of 'god,' he concludes. Thatcher lingers for several days in front of the cathedral in Compostela, once watching the arrival of an utterly exhausted and obviously bewildered pilgrim in her sixties who hobbles across the plaza filled as it usually is with a multitude of residents and tourists completely oblivious to the personal significance of what the moment means for an arriving pilgrim. Impulsively, Thatcher goes over the complete stranger and embraces her in a congratulatory hug. "The transformation from her look of anxiety, pain, and fatigue into genuine joy is worth the entire trip," he concludes. The next day Thatcher meets another pilgrim who recounts an incredibly sad story. Fifty kilometres from Compostela, this pilgrim came across a middle-aged couple struggling with exceptionally heavy backpacks. When he asked them why, he was told that their packs also contained all the belongings from the pack of their only son, who, just before undertaking his own Santiago pilgrimage, was diagnosed and soon thereafter died of cancer. The parents then decided to carry all his gear between them, in addition to their own. And after visiting Compostela, they were planning to go to Finisterre to offer their son's gear to the ocean.

Ward portrays the Camino community as an assortment of opinionated, generous, self-indulgent, thoughtful, obnoxious, and otherwise odd Chaucerian characters. In his pages, we meet a pilgrim who claims to have walked fifty thousand kilometres after being saved from a sinking ship but who is later found out to be a fraud, Spanish pilgrims who complain of the "French mafia" who run the Camino by manipulation, a pilgrim happy to meet someone from Saskatchewan because he loves that the name represents somewhere "so wide, so young" which unlike Europe is characterised by open spaces and minds, some pilgrims who regard staying in hotels like visits to brothels, dishonest students who rent out their apartments during the summer to live cheaply by masquerading as pilgrims, one mistrustful *hospitaliero* who insists on carrying bags upstairs to determine which pilgrims are cheating by gauging the weight of their loads, two artists who walk in medieval-styled white clothes designed to accumulate dust from the Camino as their project, a group of pilgrims who shockingly threw out a homeless man from a *refugio* where he had snuck in to get some sleep because he stank too much, a selfish pilgrim who zips off alone in a taxi to find accommodation in the next village leaving Ward stranded outside a completely full *refugio*, and a pilgrim with whom a beer is shared in a cool bar that seems to have been waiting for them for a thousand years. As he nears Compostela, Ward relaxes and becomes more accepting of the foibles of his fellow pilgrims where once he would have been judgmental. "I forgot about being a virtuous pilgrim," he states, "and settled for being a happy one."

Christmas' wonderfully iconoclastic recounting of her pilgrimage experience is one of few and best attempts to cut through the overly earnest and sanctimonious religiosity and platitudinous and self-indulgent New Age claptrap that has plagued much of the literature on the Camino in recent years. She accomplishes this with an absurdist sense of black humour and a sometimes cruel but always astute flair of penmanship.

Despite an aversion to large groups of women, Christmas organises a group of middle-aged females, most of whom she does not personally know beforehand, who turn out to be woefully ill prepared and ultimately unsuited, both physically and socially, for undertaking the Santiago pilgrimage. She jokes that many of today's pilgrims are those who backpacked across Europe thirty years ago and can now return in middle-age to "test out their knee replacements." Later, at one of their many meetings, this one in which they share their back-stories, Christmas realises the sort of people she is saddled with: "Some of the most overbearing, bitchy, and bullying women are found in faith-based milieus where everyone tries to out-God one another." Power often trumps piety, she concludes. She begins to rebel from the "psychobabble" and "New Age crap" being casually bandied about "'needing the group'!, 'bonding with our sisters'!, 'connecting with each other's souls,' and the 'incredible magic of the Camino.'" She continues: "It began to piss me off. If I heard the word 'awesome' one more time, I was going to scream." When it becomes her turn to share her reason for being there, Christmas matter-of-factly states her goal is Santiago de Compostela which they can all achieve if they treat the undertaking like a serious pilgrimage and not a casual shopping trip to the Outlet Mall. After getting over their shock, one member of the group says that she thinks they all need to give Christmas permission to walk her own Camino. "That was it. I was ready to slug someone," Christmas writes.

For a while, Christmas remains with the group, tempers among all becoming shortened as the walking distance is increased, until she breaks with them to head out on her own, the reason given being that "the idea of re-entering the estrogen-pit turned my stomach. The Camino was no longer about fulfilling my heart's desire but about placating a pack of women who did not know what they wanted and who based every decision on what others thought." Once on her own, Christmas turns her critical attention to other pilgrims she encounters. When meeting someone on his seventh pilgrimage who insists that each journey is wonderfully different, she thinks: "Right buddy. There's a big world out there, more lovely and stirring than the Camino de Santiago de Compostela", before offering the following astute comment: "The Camino has its share of groupies and junkies, and sometimes it grips those who gravitate into its sphere a little too tightly."

PART II

Walking the Way

"No one wanted to hear the diary version of the walk – the day-to-day home movie tedium of where and when and what…Where were the good bits?"

– Jack Hitt, *Off the Road: A Modern-day Walk Down the Pilgrim's Route Into Spain*

PRE-AMBLE

"People at turning points in their lives — looking for peace, or enlightenment, or just an escape from the daily rat race."

– David Lodge, *Therapy*

"My life was a shambles, I felt exhausted by work, my marriage was foundering. When finally I had the time to make the journey [to Compostela], I prepared my backpack, found a walking staff, flew to Spain and took to the road. I knew what I was fleeing from, not what I was seeking."

Those are not my words. They belong to another university professor, Edward Stanton, and are the fifth through seventh sentences at the beginning of his 1994 book *Road of Stars to Santiago*. These also happen to be the fifth through seventh sentences that I ever read about the Camino from any pilgrim's narrative. If I could be as brave and honest as Stanton, how, in a similar vein, might I begin my own narrative? Let's give it a try.

On the cusp of my fiftieth birthday, my life was, even by the most optimistic of measures, at its midway point. A string of failed relationships had left me remote and emotionally jaded. Most friends lived elsewhere and I was homesick for my country of birth. After a decade working at one of the world's most prestigious academic institutions my position had been terminated and I would soon be unemployed. I was exhausted by the toll that work had taken upon my spirit. Finding it difficult to be happy about much of what was around me, I needed to escape from the familiar, the comfortable, to lose myself in an undertaking that was bigger than the solipsistic melancholy into which I had settled. I needed an opportunity to remember, to review, and to celebrate those events in my life that had defined me. I owed it to my life that had been and to the life that would be, to pause and to give witness to the past. At the same time, I needed to accumulate new experiences, shared by others, that could be used as positive memories – talismans – to be carried ahead to buttress myself against the dark days that might lie await in the future.

The Camino Francés is sometimes also referred to as *la ruta de la terapia*, the therapy route. Because of this, it is not uncommon to meet the walking wounded along the Way; those who have lost a friend, a family member, like me – a job, or those who are hoping to lose something, such as an unhealthy relationship with a substance or perhaps an individual. Much of my own unhappiness before setting out was related to turning fifty; to the knowledge that more sunrises and sunsets have been than will be seen; that perhaps I should begin to take steps to turn the ship back towards the harbour. More than anything – the lack of a life-partner, the imminent lack of a job – it was this realisation of the lack of a personal future of a duration as long as that of the past, that I was having difficulty coming to terms with.

My reading at the time certainly didn't help assuage my self-indulgent, mid-life crisis. By chance (?) the last book I read before heading out the door to Spain was one from my collection of Nobel Laureate Anatole France's works. Knowing that I would soon be walking along our mutually eponymous Way of those from France (i.e. the Camino Francés), I used this as the inspiration to select France's *My Friend's Book* which had been sitting on the shelf unread for several years. Writing in December 1885, France began his loosely autobiographical book with the following Dedicatory:

> 'Nel mezzo del cammin di nostra vita'
> 'In the midway of this our mortal life.'

> This line, wherewith Dante begins the first canto of his *Divina Commedia*, steals into my thoughts to-night, possibly for the hundredth time. But never until to-night has it really touched my heart.
>
> Yet now how intently I ponder it in my mind; how gravely beautiful it seems; how full of meaning. The reason is that now for the first time I can apply its meaning to myself. I, too, have reached the point where Dante stood when the old sun set upon the first year of the fourteenth century. I, too, am in the middle of life's journey – if, indeed, that journey were the same for all, and if for all old age were its goal.
>
> Ah me! I knew twenty years since that it would come to this. I knew it, yes, but I did not realize it. In those days I recked as little about the way of life as about the way to Chicago. But now that I have mounted the hill and, gazing backward, survey at a glance all the distance that I have traversed so swiftly, the verse of the Florentine poet fills me so deeply with the spirit of reveries that I would fain sit through the night here at my fireside calling up the spirits of the past...
>
> Sleep, my beloved ones; for to-morrow we set forth upon the road once more...

And so, I too wished…And so, I too did…And so, once more I headed my life-ship back out into the beckoning waves – this time toward the sea of grain of the Spanish *meseta* – it not yet being time to turn the wheel shoreward. I replace France on the shelf and seek out my copy of Anne Bronte's *The Tenant of Wildfell Hall.* Thumbing through I find the page, dog-eared from first being encountered many years before, that seems to encapsulate what France had written about and what this France will undertake in the weeks ahead: "Through life's pilgrimage…"

On Landscape…

CHAPTER 5

OVER THE HILLS AND FAR AWAY

"For the majority of the eleventh- and twelfth-century pilgrims to Santiago…[this was their] only occasion to cast a glimpse upon broader existence, to measure for once the world and its wonders, to see, once in their lives, the mountains and the sea…[to feel] the invigorating air of the new world gradually unfolding before their incredulous and astonished eyes."

– Walter Melczer, *The Pilgrim's Guide to Santiago de Compostela*

Fields

The pilgrim Way between Obanos and Puenta la Reina is a gravel track contouring along a hillside parallel to and slightly above a small road. Although quite tired from the lack of sleep on the trans-Atlantic flight and an inability to catch a nap during the purgatory hours spent in Madrid airport waiting for the flight to Pamplona, the scenery lifts my spirits, and with that, my dragging feet and the still unfamiliar weight of the pack. Fields of russet and golden crops in their winter senescence, intermixed with copses of trees and small patchwork farmsteads, all bordered by telephone lines and quiet country lanes feed my hungry eyes. This, more than anything, is what I've been so desirous of experiencing during my walk across northern Spain; what I've come all this way to purposely seek out: a view of well-tended and well-

loved domestic fields, a place where nature blends seamlessly with culture, a location of historical thickness which occasionally, so I hoped, might offer glimpses of earlier human tracings on the palimpsest landscape. Infused with happiness after what has only been a few kilometres of walking at the very start of the long pilgrimage route, I stride forward with renewed vigour to find my lodgings for the night.

❖ ❖ ❖

After a detour to visit the monastery at Cañas, the alternate route crosses large fields empty of any human structures before rejoining the pilgrim Way in Santo Domingo de la Calzada. Decked out in my rain gear for both warmth and protection against the on-and-off drizzles, I am forced to use my walking stick to keep balance while moving along in the muddy track bisecting the lonely fields. Mindful that one early definition of a pilgrim was that of a stranger moving through the fields of a foreign land, I begin to feel like a true pilgrim, striding ahead in the wet mud, walking stick as my pilgrim staff. "Squish, squish, plunk" are the only sounds as my feet and staff hit the wet earth. I am conscious too that these three points of anchoring symbolised the Trinity upon which medieval pilgrims would meditate as they strode ahead. Paradoxically, I also begin to feel at home, experiencing with a rush, 'topophilia' memories of the landscapes of my youth. And as in many such planar places like those of the Canadian prairies where I grew up, it is the sky here that commands attention.

The rain lets up, the cumulus clouds start to lift, and the ground-hugging mists dissipate. Then, as if by special effects in some Hollywood film, the sun partially emerges, sending its rays shining down to the earth in the shape of a giant pyramid. For five minutes, Christian pilgrimage completely forgotten, I stand transfixed by the splendour as I am wrenched backward to time spent in Egypt on another pilgrimage. No accident that the pyramids, humankind's largest religious structures, are shaped just so, and that monotheism began with Akhenaton's *Hymn to Aton*, his solar deity. Awash in transcendental bliss, it is an effort to turn my eyes forward again and set off once more in the clinging mud. Within moments the skies clear and the solar pyramid disappears, being replaced immediately by a view of the steeple of the cathedral at Santo Domingo rising proudly up out of the earth, many kilometres ahead, drawing

me toward it like a lightning rod as if as to counter the pull of the pagan pyramid. Smiling at my imaginative hyperbole, and quickly dispelling the rather profound theological implications of what might have just occurred, I recommence my walk, soon giving in to the urge to start singing at the top of my lungs… purposely secular songs. Only a solitary hawk flies by in witness to the scene.

❖❖❖

AS I PAUSE TO TAKE A PHOTO OF THE enormous Camino map and sign notifying of the regional border between La Rioja and Castilla y León (Old Castile), Jean-Olivier and Emmanuelle zip by without so much as a pause in either step or their ongoing conversation. Although the latter looks Canadian bundled up as she is in her pile and toque, the former looks positively Gallic with his ever-present black beret perched, as always, at a haughty angle atop his head. Thinking of that other hyphenated and similarly bereted Frenchman,

Jean-Paul Sartre, and remembering that this is after all the Camino *Francés*, the Way of those from France, I cannot resist taking a photo of the two as they move along the gravel road ahead, dwarfed in the existential magnitude of the surrounding landscape. Soon I follow behind, comfortable in my solitude and happy to be enjoying the 'entertainment' offered by reviewing with each step the unfolding panorama of my own memories.

❖ ❖ ❖

"F~~K…F~~K…F~~K!", I SHOUT IN PANIC as I look at the taxi speeding away after dropping me off early on a Sunday morning in the tiny village of Tardajos at the western edge of the Burgos suburbs. The cab soon disappears into the dark and I once again look down with shock at the broken backpack at my feet, reviewing the entire pilgrimage flashing by in a second, culminating right here and now with my failure. For the entire back assembly of the carrying system has split, one of the thick shoulder straps completely ripping through its plastic anchor to the pack frame and now hanging free, attached to the pack only by its narrow bottom strap to the hip-belt. I look around at the few unlit houses and the forbidding plains of the dreaded *meseta*, the remotest section of the Camino. I shake my head in disbelief. "Just f~~king great. Now what am I to do?" After the initial rush of panic, a tempered and analytical calmness automatically clicks in, honed from decades of engaging in danger-filled, outdoor pursuits, where a cool assessment of alternatives was what saved lives. I breathe deeply to calm down and run through a series of corrective possibilities of adaptive management. Okay, perhaps this is actually a *good* place for this to happen after all, for (1) I can walk the nine kilometres back to Burgos using only a single strap or carrying the whole damn thing in my arms and wait there for shops to open on Monday… (*Are* shops in Spain open on Monday?) …or on Tuesday then, to see if I can find an outdoor equipment store from which to purchase a replacement pack (*Certainly* given a city with a population of one hundred and seventy thousand they must have some good shops, right? *Right?*); or (2) looking down at the pack once more, perhaps I can try to repair it here (*Can* it be fixed and if so is it wise to proceed into the remote plains when the next place of any significant size, León, is located a week of walking away?).

After a few moments of weighing the options I decide on the latter and withdrawing one of my two water bottles from the pack begin to peel off the duct-tape (where would the world of emergency repair and relief be without that most marvellous of all inventions?) which I had carefully wrapped around the bottle…*just… in… case*). My triage complete, I spend a few minutes hoisting up and taking off the pack, much more gently and through use of the other, undamaged, shoulder strap of course. As it seems to be working, I put away the water bottle lined with miracle tape and with a very restrained mouthing of "*Ultreia*", gingerly move forward into the dawn of a new day. For the next hour, however, I remain extremely nervous about the band-aid repair job. But as everything keeps holding together I eventually stop fretting and start enjoying the incredible beauty of the scenery unfolding around me, the fields bathed in an almost unbelievable orange glow from the rising sun. From the edge of disaster to the verge of ecstasy in the space of a single hour. The experiences of the Camino come fast, indeed.

The day, despite its in-auspicious start, turns out to offer the best walking yet. The Way follows a narrow gravel track running through rolling, grey-brown fields enveloped in winter silence and linking a series of atmospheric hamlets like beautiful pearls on a necklace. These quaint dwelling places are inevitably tucked down in the arroyo valleys in attempt to seek out what little shelter might be had from the fierce winds that blow across the vast, treeless tablelands of the *meseta*. What a joy it is to suddenly come across such a hidden hamlet and be able to see the Camino snaking its windy way down into, through, and up the other side of the valley in the distance. No images spied in the dozens and dozens of books read over the years long before undertaking this pilgrimage had captured my imagination more than such scenes wherein the loneliness of the road is contrasted with the hospitableness of the village, the lure of wayfaring versus

the pull of domesticity. Not far beyond the hamlet of Hontanas I pause for lunch beside the romantic ruins of a medieval hospice and leaning up against my repaired and henceforth always-to-be-babied backpack, commence to wiggle my exposed toes in the crisp air, content beyond words.

❖❖❖

IT IS COLD AND STILL DARK WHEN I HEAD OFF in the early morning from the *albergue* in Sahagún toward Mansilla, about half way along the Camino. This is also the middle of the *meseta*, that one-time dreaded tableland covered by grain and, if one is to believe the legends, haunted by the cries of pilgrims driven to madness by the monotony of the landscape. No wonder then that this is the section most often skipped over by modern pilgrims as they race by between Burgos and León, sequestered within the safety of their buses, free from having to face either the harshness of outside nature or that of their own reflective inner natures. Cowards! For it is the *meseta*, more than anywhere else on the Camino, where, in the absence of external stimuli, one travels the 'road within', that personal pilgrimage to the heart of one's true identity. In such a spirit and inspired perhaps by being swaddled in numerous layers against the frigid temperatures, I would later use the long day to systematically review every Christmas celebration of the past decade. At the present time, however, in the early hours of the November morning, I find the beauty of the landscape to be so sublime to make it impossible to concentrate on that inner journey.

I have opted for the longer, nearly forty-kilometre, alternative route that traverses the remote countryside. The fields and few solitary trees here are covered with a dusting of hoarfrost, the ploughed ridges of icy soil resembling *sastruggi,* that wind-blown hard snow I remember from my time spent pulling a sledge on an expedition in the High Arctic. I am enveloped by a profound silence broken only occasionally at the start of the day by the crunching of the frozen ground beneath my boots. Once or twice, increasingly conscious of my solitude, I try to catch a glimpse of a fellow pilgrim, the only other to be walking this section today it turns out, who had left the *albergue* about a half an hour before me. Unsuccessful, I reconcile myself to being totally alone. Only I seem to be moving. Even the non-existent wind appears to have been frozen in place.

Copses of trees, their skeletal black forms isolated against the whitened fields and pale blue sky, stand as mute sentinels to mark my progress. The complete absence of trees in other locations, however, where the horizon crests and then disappears out of sight, produces the unsettling feeling of somehow being precariously perched on the lip of a small planet, ready at any moment to slide off into the swirling void of space. Once I pause while crossing over a rail-bridge and spend several moments swivelling around, soaking in what is the most beautiful landscape I have yet encountered and again wonder about the impatience of modern pilgrims who pass this all by. And it is while on the bridge that I see the white cross in the sky. After several moments of awe and shaking with emotion, I put away the camera and, tears frozen on my cheeks, descend back down to the vastness of the *meseta* and the solace of its open spaces.

Hills

Soon after leaving the suburbs of Estella and the Monasterio de Irache with its famous wine fountain the pilgrim way splits. I take the route heading toward Villamayor de Monjardin whose hilltop castle beckons on the horizon. The next several hours of walking will be through some of the most wonderful, bucolic scenery of the entire Camino. The gravel lane, empty of all activity at this early hour in the morning, peacefully traverses grain fields and orchards that skirt the lower slopes of the gently rolling hills. Again and again I pause and stare, fascinated by the complexity of the landscape mosaic about me, in particular the manner in which the green forested hills of wildness seem to send down giant amoeba-like arms to tentatively probe the cultivated fields below. Come spring, I wonder, as the fields shake off their torpor, do the farmers, those servants of the soil, have to cut back these exploratory forays of wild nature? In the absence of such manicures, how long would it take for the landscape to revert back to its forested state as it was before the Romans and Visigoths arrived?

◆ ◆ ◆

WHILE ON THE WAY TO VIANA my nervousness increases as the trail switchbacks down the side of the ominously named Barranco Mataburros canyon. I feel as if I am entering a Sergio Leone spaghetti western. The region is very arid and in consequence, the vegetation sparse. Only a few trees offer anything in the way of shade. Come mid-summer the temperature must be brutal. As I proceed down the dry gulch the otherwise still Sunday morning air is repeatedly shattered by the menacingly loud sound of rifle shots. With echoes ricocheting about it is impossible to tell exactly where the hunters are, and more importantly, where they are pointing their guns. The predominant plants are knee-high shrubs barely able to conceal the parched soil and unable to offer any protective cover should the bullets begin to be directed my way. There is nothing to do but embrace the situation with black humour and mordant enthusiasm. So turning up and buttoning the sides of my Tilley hat cowboy style and whistling Ennio Morricone's theme music from *The Good, the Bad, and the Ugly* I assume the best squint-eyed Clint Eastwood stare I can muster and quicken my pace while the rifle shots continue. Later, upon gaining the lip on the other side of the ravine I count seventeen cars yet at no time do I ever spot a single hunter.

❖❖❖

THE CLIMB UP THE SIERRA DE ATAPUERCA is brutal, forcing me to frequently pause to catch my breath. This is the longest and steepest ascent so far, making me question, in what will by no means be the last time doing so during the pilgrimage, what weight (particularly books) I could jettison that would lighten my load. Knowing the area to be riddled with caves in which the eight-hundred-thousand-year-old remains of 'Atapuerca man,' Europe's oldest human ancestor, were discovered, keeps my mind off the gruelling task. It is extremely exciting to be walking – okay, at this point in the ascent, more accurately stated 'crawling' – through the ground floor of the continent's hominid creation, its original Eden. Body hunched over, eyes just a metre from the steeply sloping trail, I try to resist resorting to the use of my knuckles to propel myself upward, thus setting evolution back on its head.

From the top of the sierra, medieval pilgrims would have revelled in their first glimpse of the distant Burgos cathedral, its twin spires soaring triumphantly from the flat plain like the masts of a tall ship amidst the sea of grain waving in the wind. The view that greets the modern pilgrim is much less inspiring. Today Burgos' skyline is characterised by the secular, not the sacred. Its sprawling suburbs and smoke-discharging factories register the strongest impression.

Turning my eyes earthward in disappointment I notice with surprise the large labyrinth that has been laid out with stones on the crest of the ridge. At other locations along the Way, perhaps while they paused for lunch or a water break, modern pilgrims had constructed small cairns of precariously piled stones. These impromptu little *innukshucks* had always caused me to smile. Here, however, the labyrinth is a different thing altogether, its construction no doubt having required hours of deliberate labour by a dozen pilgrims. Still breathing heavily from the recent ascent, my immediate impression I'm forced to admit is not one of admiration for the imaginative creation but rather one of astonishment that anyone could have had the energy to divest in such an enterprise after such a steep climb. Astonishment is soon, however, supplanted by temptation. Negotiating one's circular way around such

PART II | 67

labyrinths I knew to be symbolic acts in medieval times to the undertaking of actual long-distance pilgrimages. How easy it would be to simply spin around a couple of quick laps and then call it quits in nearby Burgos. Shocked that I could even be capable of such heretical thoughts, I guiltily look about to see if anyone or *anything* might have noticed my hesitation or been able to read my mind. Quickly descending from my own Mount Tabor, I continue on toward Compostela.

❖❖❖

YESTERDAY WHILE APPROACHING RABANAL, the contrast between the blue skies over the *meseta* plains behind and the dark, ominous storm clouds encircling the wall of mountains ahead had made me think that I was on a perilous journey to Mordor. Not surprisingly, this made for some fitful nightmares last night. Today, however, the weather is grand with barely a cloud in sight as I make my slow way to Monte Irago, all trepidation from the day before forgotten. Greeting the monks from Rabanal out for their morning walk, my spirits lift and I move upward savouring the views of the rising hills. With their flanks covered in tall grasses over which the wind moves, producing long, sinuous waves, the hills seem alive, an impression reinforced by the slowly whirling blades of the giant windmills on the horizon. Nothing prepares me, however, for the spectacular view that greets me as I crest over the summit and walk toward the village of El Acebo perched on the rim of the large valley spreading out below.

The area between the two ranges of bordering mountains on either side of the valley is filled with an impossibly flat white surface. My first impression is

of viewing an enormous icecap and I am suddenly wrenched back to memories of traversing several such while on arctic mountaineering expeditions. I stand transfixed, trying to adjust to the incongruity of my eyes perceiving polar ice sheets and my body registering pleasantly warm temperatures. It therefore takes a moment to realise that the sheet of white is actually the top of a cloud bank that has completely sealed in the valley, only a few plumes of distant factories from what might be Ponferrada poking out above the atmospheric inversion. Lovely though the view is, I cannot but help to wonder about the quality of air I will be exposed to during the two days it will take to cross the valley floor before ascending the mountains that I can see shining in the warm sun more than fifty kilometres away on the other side.

♦ ♦ ♦

FROM SOMEWHERE NEARBY but thankfully hidden from view comes the panicked squeals of another pig being butchered, adding to my anxiety about the imminent climb up to O'Cebreiro, generally acknowledged to be the most difficult section of the Spanish Camino. Swirling mists clog the small valleys leading out of Villafranca del Bierzo making untenable the high-level route option. In consequence, I am walking through a series of small villages in which everyone seems to be out on the side of the road in the cool morning mountain air huddled into small groups around recently killed pigs which have been hoisted on spits to which blowtorches are being applied to burn off the hair. Again and again this scene is repeated and I wonder how Sandra, a vegetarian pilgrim I met last night, will fare as she walks through this Dantesque landscape; the gateway to Mordor indeed.

At the village of Herrerías I make a bad decision, committing what will be my worst route-finding mistake on the entire pilgrimage. Instead of turning into the village and thereby losing some hard-gained elevation before the climb recommences, I opt for continuing on the road which my maps suggest might link up with O'Cebreiro. The problem I am soon to discover is that these maps from various pilgrim guides are woefully inaccurate when it comes to anything but the established, traditional Camino route. A villager shouts at me to descend into the village and follow the waymarked signs. Waving a thank you but indicating with my swirling arms that, as suggested from my maps, that the road that I'm presently on will eventually meet up with the pilgrim way, I ignore the helpful advice.

After an hour and five kilometres of walking I begin to realise that something is not right as my road weaves increasingly farther away from where the pilgrimage route runs. And like a poker player with a bad hand yet forced to up the ante in the hope that a good card might be drawn the next round rather than folding, I keep slogging forward into the great unknown rather than biting the bullet by turning around to make my way back down the road to the junction where I had parted from the Camino. After another hour I come across a group of individuals on the side of the road near their cars and ask them in my next-to-useless Spanish where I was on one of my maps and if I kept on this road whether I would eventually reach O'Cebreiro. Like most locals anywhere, they refuse to look at the map, instead speaking rapidly and gesturing widely, telling me confusingly to my rudimentary understanding, that my destination was either twelve or twenty-one kilometres ahead. Reconciling myself to what therefore could be another four or five hours of walking, I pick up the pace, conscious that this is turning out to be my first real adventure on the Camino and that a roadside bivouac somewhere that evening might be a distinct possibility.

The lack of any roadside directional signage is alarming as are the thickening mists that obscure any views to aid navigation. The only real hint that I might still be on the road shown on my inadequate maps is that every once in a while I am surprised to hear the bizarre sound of automobiles racing by through the cloud-filled skies high above me! Occasionally as the clouds lighten I can discern the improbably tall bridges supporting the regional highway viaduct marked on my maps. Finally, hours later and after several nervous unsignposted road-splits, I see my first sign for O'Cebreiro and eventually reach the town of Pedrafita which I'm happy to see is clearly marked on my maps and which hosts a modern pilgrim statue suggesting that cycling pilgrims might come this way. As I traverse toward O'Cebreiro, finally visible perched on the valley rim in the distance, I realise that never once during the last three hours had I thought about the elevation I was gaining. Nothing like being spooked about becoming lost to take one's mind off the struggles of a steep climb, I muse.

Entering O'Cebreiro, the views back eastward to the beautiful cloud-filled valley out of which I had just climbed makes me imagine that I've emerged from some primordial white slime ready to start a new life. Strolling through the village, I then look out toward the westward rolling hills of green Galicia beyond and wonder about what other adventures might be in store for me in the new life to be faced ahead.

COMMUNITIES

IT IS A RELIEF TO BE ABLE TO LEAVE THE DANGEROUS highway behind and to once again walk a traffic-free country lane winding its peaceful way across the hibernating winter fields. Relief soon turns to joy when just a few kilometres later, as a light drizzle begins to fall, I enter the small, incredibly picturesque village of Pieros. Here, the ramshackle buildings offer those romantic feelings of an embodied, living history that I've been vainly hoping to encounter ever since the first day of this pilgrimage. I have missed the decrepit charms of many of the rustic villages along the pilgrimage routes of southern France. And now

here, three-quarters of the way to Compostela, my appetite is finally satiated. The crudely constructed fieldstone and brick houses register both the squalour and tenacity of the hard lives of their past and occasionally present inhabitants. More than anything it is the porches, attached higgledy-piggledy to the outside of the buildings by rough-hewed timber beams, that most easily draws the eyes and imprints upon the memory.

❖❖❖

VILLAFRANCA DEL BIERZO STANDS WATCH at the entrance to the mountain pass leading up to O'Cebreiro and Galicia. Arriving by mid-afternoon leaves opportunity to explore the atmospheric charms of the old town. The most notable feature, visible from almost anywhere, is the towering bulk of the Iglesia de San Francisco which repeatedly appears and disappears in an out of the swirling mists like an eerie apparition. The contrast between the rustic dilapidation of my accommodation in the *albergue* and its nearby neighbour, the Castle of the Marquesses, is striking. Unlike the Disneyfied Templar castle seen earlier in Ponferrada, this private home, still occupied by a wealthy family five hundred years after its construction, looks real. Ignoring my Canadian prairie socialist discomfort at the demonstration of such opulence, I ponder knocking on the front door and brazenly inviting myself over for dinner, guaranteeing the almost-certain-to-be-alarmed host that my captivating raconteur of personal stories would more than pay for any hospitality I might be offered. The daydream lasts only a moment. Instead I venture into the heart of the town where the pilgrim Way runs along the narrow Calle del Agua, lined with an impressive array of old buildings.

Saving the best for last, I circle around the Iglesia de Santiago to arrive at the Romanesque north portal which contains a capital with a lovely carving of the Three Wise Men. More significantly, this Puerta del Perdón was where sick pilgrims too incapacitated to undertake the arduous climb up to Galicia the following day could enter and be granted a pardon for their sins as well as receive the plenary indulgence equivalent to having reached the tomb of Saint James in Compostela. What a lovely escape from the bedbugs, the cold temperatures, the sore shoulders and feet, and, glancing over my shoulder at the cloud-cloaked mountains, mostly the ascent of tomorrow. My gaze wanders from the far to the mid horizon and spotting Saint Francis' church I feel

ashamed about even just hypothetically contemplating giving up when my favourite saint had persevered, if the stories are true, all the way to Compostela. Thus, in the waning light of a December afternoon, and suddenly feeling bone-weary from the near five-hundred-kilometre-long travail, I lay my forehead against the cold stone of the portal and pray to the saintly beggar fool from Assisi for strength for the rest of the journey.

❖❖❖

LONG HAD I BEEN HAUNTED by photographs of the strange, hobbit-like dwellings of O'Cebreiro. The oval-shaped, fieldstone-walled, and straw-thatch-roofed dwellings, called *pallozas*, represent an architectural style dating back to the early colonising Celts. Today, prissily tarted up, they occupy centre stage in the modern tourist-filled village. As a pilgrim who has laboured to get to this village eyrie perched atop the saddle between León and Galicia, it is hard not to feel a tad superior to the groups of gawking tourists who wander about the village ducking in and out of various shops doing their Christmas shopping before hopping back in their cars for the drive home. Until recently a fairly remote and authentic village, O'Cebreiro has become a Galician Celtic theme park that suffers from trying too hard. Case in point: I am forced to retreat to the peace of the pilgrim *refugio* when I hear the normally enjoyable Celtic music of fellow Manitoban Loreena McKennett blasting out of one Celtic shop. It all just seems so incongruous; so forced.

✦✦✦

AFTER A MARVELLOUS FORESTED WALK I meet up with fellow pilgrims Tony and Sandra on the outskirts of Sarria and follow them into town, enjoying the interesting hotchpotch of old and new buildings along the Way. After settling into the *albergue* and savouring a hot shower I go out for a walkabout, almost immediately stumbling across an attractive pilgrim mural. Reconnoitring the route out of the city – always a wise move if one intends on departing at daybreak the following day – I encounter the small Romanesque church of San Salvador. My spirits soar when I see the Mozarabic archivolt portal surrounding one of my favourite pieces of sculpture of the entire pilgrimage route: an image of a happy Christ, hands held upright. I wave warmly at him and continue my wandering about the town.

Being an early Saturday evening two weeks before Christmas, people are milling about gift shopping. I marvel at the limited selection presented in the storefront windows, amazed at how far removed this all seems from the mass consumerism so characteristic of this time of the year back home in America. As I stroll amongst the happy families and under the Christmas lights and brightly coloured street decorations I suddenly experience a growing sense of aching loneliness and intense homesickness, almost to the point of tears. Not wishing to upset any of the children I return to the *refugio* and wrap myself in the solitude of my sleeping sack, attempting to circumvent depression by drugging myself to sleep.

❖ ❖ ❖

AFTER THE HAUNTING, MEDITATIVE SILENCE of the vast plains and the picturesque, rustic beauty of the tiny wayside villages, one cannot help but feel sorry for the city of Santiago de Compostela and its inability to match these marvels. Things here are simply too new, too frenetic, too crass, too…in short, much of the contemporary world. Most modern pilgrims share in common a desire for and appreciation of the Camino Francés as a vehicle of escape from the patterns of the modern world. In some respects it can be regarded as an opened and elongated cloistered walk. Sitting in the central Plaza de Obradorio, watching the hustle and bustle of students and shoppers, tourists and tramps, pilgrims and police, is exhausting to senses accustomed as they have been to the more temperate, more deliberate, more mindful life of the last month spent along the Way. I am so grateful that this is not my final destination, that tomorrow I will be leaving here and off walking again through the forests of Galicia toward the end of the world. In the meantime, I try to banish anticlimactic thoughts and attempt to enjoy the city.

Crossing the plaza, I pause in front of the portal at the Colegio Mayor de Fonseca and admire the retro-Renaissance statue of Santiago *Peregrino* which I've been disappointed to have found is not as well represented here in Spain as he is along the pilgrim paths in France. I then move into the centre of the plaza in front of the cathedral and take a photo of my foot beside the very last scallop shell insignia of the Camino

Francés. All about swirls a boisterous crowd oblivious to my little accomplishment. With humility I smile in recognition of the true significance of that accomplishment, being of course of only personal importance and of absolutely no consequence whatsoever to the complicated contemporary lives of all these people. And so with a content acceptance of the zero impact of this past eventful month of my life upon the greater world, I stride off to an Irish pub I had earlier spotted, therein to reward myself with a celebratory pint (or three) of Guinness. I justify the indulgence (funny to use that word here in front of the cathedral where so many came at one time to receive such from the ecclesiastical authorities) based on a rationalisation that I will need to draw upon the purported claim of that black nectar from the Liffey "for strength" in the coming days of walking to Finisterre.

Woods

THE RAIN BEGINS IN EARNEST AS I CONTINUE along the track through the dense pine forest. The logging road is straight as an arrow, requiring no attention for route finding. Even had the rain and leaden skies not obscured distant views there would be little here to excite interest. The monotony of the dark trees and the constancy of both rain and terrain allows the mind to wander, the melancholy of the moment pushing thoughts toward uncomfortable places. The solitude of the day conjures reflections on the larger issue of the solitude of my life. Morbid reflections about dying alone produce silent tears that soon, with no one around in front of whom to be embarrassed, I let progress into outright sobs. Awash thus in sombre, self-indulgent ruminations, I trudge forward in the rain. I am a sorry sight when I finally arrive at the monastery of San Juan de Ortega in its little clearing in the woods. I approach fellow pilgrims Jean-Olivier and Emmanuelle who are huddled underneath the front portal of the church, resembling two Quasimodos with their grey ponchos hiked up over their backpacks. I am grateful for the rain that masks my tears. We enjoy a few moments of company, mostly complaining about the abysmal weather. Having already had their brief lunch break, they soon head off leaving me once more on my own, munching a cold, bruised apple and soggy bread, outside the locked church, surrounded by the lonely woods, feeling ever so sorry for my oh so pitiful self.

❖❖❖

THE APPROACH TO SARRIA OFFERS some of the most pleasant walking of the entire Camino. Disappointed at finding the famous monastery of Samos closed, my mood lifts when, a few kilometres later, the Way leaves the side of the road and begins to wander through a dense forest of ivy-covered trees as it follows the course of a small stream. The sylvan splendour feels so comforting coming after the many weeks spent out on the exposed plains of Castille and León. Unlike the sublime grandeur of the *meseta*, here I lose myself in admiration of the intimacy of the picturesque. There is also a need to focus on the immediate environs due to the carpet of fallen leaves that covers the ankle-twisting, irregular terrain of the trail as well as the paucity of waymarking signs. Engaged in such concentration and beginning to become slightly concerned about the uncertainly of the route, I am startled when Tony suddenly pops up behind me with a cheerful *buenos dias* and

expresses his gratitude in having found me as he had feared that he had become lost. Looking at his smiling, friendly face and thus leaving unsaid the disquieting possibility that it is entirely possible of course for *two* pilgrims to be just as easily lost in a forest as it is for one, we walk together through the remainder of the woods and eventually gain another road where he takes a break while I continue onward.

❖❖❖

IT IS A PLEASURE TO SEE another burst of light in the distance ahead, signifying that the lovely trail winding through the countryside upon which I am walking is about to exit from the gloomy woods. And just as anticipated, the trail soon emerges into the bright sunshine as it runs alongside a small, flat field bordered by stone rows and wood and wire fencing. This is a wonderful reprieve from the steep descents and ascents that have occupied most of the late afternoon spent crossing the many river valleys on this section of the Way approaching Arzua. I feel exhausted due to having already covered almost forty kilometres since leaving Gonzar more than eight hours ago. The pretty field, completely surrounded by a glade of large oak trees, is simply too tempting to resist. I drop my pack right in the middle of the trail and taking out a water bottle and a fresh pair of socks, gingerly step over the fencing, and liberate my feet from their hiking-boot prisons while I lie down and relax by watching the swaying dance of branches in the wind.

❖ ❖ ❖

COULD ONE REALLY EVER IMAGINE an icing that was more perfect? I was on my first day of walking to the sea after having successfully completed the Camino Francés at Compostela several days before. My body was fine, free of blisters, shoulder strains, and pulled leg muscles. And my soul was buoyant, filled to the brim with pride of accomplishment and a revitalised spirit of purpose. So here I was on my way to the end of medieval European world and everything about me, everything I was experiencing, was simply extra…an icing on what has been one of the sentinel events of my life. And what a sweet icing on that life-cake it was turning out to be! Again and again over the last month I had found myself writing in my journal that the landscape passed through on that particular day was the most beautiful one yet encountered, etc. And this evening I would find myself doing the same once again. For the country lane I was traversing was bucolic perfection, its route ducking in and out of or skirting along the edge of copses of oaks, pines, and poplars, all pushing against, as in a loving embrace, meadowlands of cornstalks and hay. Had this not been at the end of the continent I

feel that I could continue to walk the trans-Atlantic distance home should the landscape remain as beautiful as that which spread out before me.

◆◆◆

ALREADY PREDISPOSED TO DISLIKE the mono-specific eucalyptus forests that have, cancer like, taken over Galicia and contributed to its serious decline in biodiversity, I begin to curse the trees as if it was somehow their fault for the lack of waymarking that had resulted in my becoming completely lost. Unmarked logging roads branch off every which way and the nondescript sameness of the woods confounds being able to determine one's location on the map. Not that that would help anyway, given its degree of cartographic imprecision. There is nothing to do but muddle through relying on my built-in compass to direct me toward Muxia. But even with this compass I become totally confused after reaching a highway and heading off in what, after a kilometre and finally coming across a sign identifying the village, I realise to be the opposite direction to that which I need to take. Backtracking to and then passing the original forest road I had been traversing I continue along the highway strangely empty of any vehicles for several more kilometres until another sign sends me back into the glades of eucalyptus on my way toward the nearby ocean. The *ocean* for Saint James' sake! How can one lose an ocean?

How embarrassing is *that*? Later, meeting up with Pasquale in the pilgrim *refugio*, I am mollified to learn that he too had become lost in the exact same location. For too long we had had such an easy time of it while on the Camino, its way-marking nearly idiot-proof. Now, post-Compostela, it has been a different story altogether. No underestimating the waywardless idiots here!

COASTS

WHERE IS IT? WHERE IS THE OCEAN? For the last hour I've been rubbernecking every few minutes, peering again and again toward the west with a near uncontrollable hunger, yearning to catch that first, that precious, that soul-imprinting glimpse of the sea toward which I have been struggling for all these long, long days; that memory that should the circumstances develop so, I know will be replayed again and again on that life-review rolodex while on my deathbed. I know that the sea is somewhere up ahead only a kilometre or so away. Frustration builds and builds and I start to verbally curse all the eucalyptus trees that have continued to block the view. Not until I enter the coastal town of Munios do I finally get to see the peninsula of Muxia extending bravely out into the north Atlantic. For more than five minutes I stand transfixed. And because this has always been my final destination, not an

afterthought as seems to be the case for many of those deciding to come here from Compostela, I am completely and totally floored by the emotion of the moment. A short time later, I jog the few remaining metres across the beach, and throwing my pack off into the sand while both simultaneously laughing and crying, I walk over the rocks and stick my still-booted feet into the crashing waves. I'm there... *finally* I'm there!

❖❖❖

THE FIRST RUSH OF EXCITEMENT has passed; now is the time to reflect back on the long walk as I watch the sunset from the base of the lighthouse at the end of the Muxia peninsula. In a place famous for its incessant rain, I have been blessed with a perfect evening. Only a thin band of clouds hovers near the western horizon. Nestling into a comfortable depression scalloped (how appropriate!) into an enormous, wave-smoothened boulder as if it had been designed for just such a purpose, I settle back to enjoy the view. As the setting sun makes its way from sky to sea I review my journey along the Way from the shadow of the Pyrenees to this rocky outcrop on the edge of the north Atlantic. For several hours I sit thus, rooted to the solidity of the bedrock beneath my body while my mind wanders afar, tracing the nuances of every marvellous day of the past month spent on the Camino. Later, despite the December chill, I open my shirt and roil up my pant legs, and like a parched amphibian present

my skin to the sea in an attempt to absorb its offering of salty mist sprayed up from the nearby splashing waves. And then, in a parting gift from Spain – as if it had not been given me so much already – the disc of the sun, upon reaching the clouds just above the horizon, spreads out laterally in a final glory of yellow and orange before it disappears into the western sea, merely another day, and another pilgrimage, over.

❖ ❖ ❖

IN MY PLANNING I HAD VERY much looked forward to the walk from Muxia south to Finisterre, imagining it to be perhaps similar to the Cleveland Way or any of a number of such spectacular costal walks in the United Kingdom. Due, however, to the infestation of view-inhibiting eucalyptus trees, I decide to follow Pasquale's lead and travel there instead by bus. The plus to this is that it will allow another relaxing day to be spent in Finisterre before I needed to return to Santiago and my plane flight home. The happy wisdom of this decision becomes manifest as I take another sip of Spanish wine and savour my end-of-the-pilgrimage lunch of *pulpo*, local octopus, and of course, *coquille St. Jacques*, or scallops as the French so wonderfully call them in homage to the saint. It is a sunny Saturday afternoon and the harbour is a whirl of activity with fishermen rowing back and forth from the shore to their moored boats. The peaceful moment expands and for the first time in a month I abandon myself uninhibitedly to the hedonistic pleasures of lassitude, enjoying watching the bustle of others while I remain sedentary.

Ordering another carafe of white wine I reflect on the definition of the Spanish word 'camino,' often translated as 'road' but really meaning 'way' in

English (as in 'pathway') or 'chemin' in French. A 'way' of course is not the same thing as a 'road.' Fuelled by more wine, I finally decide that the Taoists are probably the closest to understanding the special nature of a pilgrimage journey, with the 'Tao' (or 'Dao' as it now seems to be spelt) literally meaning the 'Way' or spiritual path. Nodding in appreciation of my wine-induced enlightenment, I return to the immediate subject in hand. Leaning my head back with closed eyes, I enjoy the warmth of the sun, unexpected at this time of year in Galicia, and ponder another Asian insight that seems to fit my present mood perfectly: *wo wei* or purposeful inactivity.

Later I return to my hotel room and totally exhausted in body and mind, collapse fully clothed on top of the inviting bed and sleep for thirteen hours, something I cannot remember ever having done before.

✦✦✦

I CREST OVER A RIDGE OF ROCKS near the ancient place of early Celtic mystical worship, and there it is: the beach! Rather than approach it by crossing the peninsula from the town of Finisterre on the other side, I'm high up on the ridge returning from the lighthouse at Cabo Fisterra. From here, the view down to the beach and its crashing waves is truly spectacular. A half hour later I am on the sand traversing the length of the beach waiting for the sunset to begin and the winter sunbathers to depart.

In several locations I walk tentatively to the edge of the breaking waves and step into the receding water to allow my trail-beaten boots to touch the ocean so that I can take photos of my footprints leading into the sea, symbolic of the end of the pilgrimage. Once, however, I misjudge the distance and a rogue wave leaps up at me. In a panic, I hop, skip, and jump backwards to avoid a soaking. Feeling lucky at my escape from the capricious ocean it is not until half an hour later when I take off my pack to place the camera back inside that I am devastated to notice that I have somehow lost my walking stick, my trusty companion of all these many weeks. [It is hard for the uninitiated to underestimate the strength of attachment that develops between a pilgrim and her or his pack, boots, and especially walking staff or stick. Case in point: the following day as Pasquale and I are waiting for the bus to Compostela, we are surprised to see Sandra whom we had understood was to be walking the final few kilometres to the lighthouse at that very moment. Almost embarrassed, she says that after her morning coffee in a nearby bar she was shocked to realise that she had forgotten her walking staff, carried all the way from her native Cologne, in the pilgrim *refugio*. And then upon rushing back there she had found that like most hostels the building was locked until the end of the day. Unwilling to finish her pilgrimage without her trusted wooden companion, she had opted instead to spend the day in town, postponing her finale until the next day. Although incredibly homesick at this point, she was nevertheless willing to delay her departure even if it meant the possibility of missing Christmas at home with her family all so she could finish as she had begun, with her staff at her side!] Retracing my steps (luckily an easy thing to do in the sand), I eventually find my stick lying forlorn in the sand at the very place where I had gyrated away from the attacking wave and where it had slipped out of its bindings on the pack. Restored with my trusty Camino companion, I find a secluded place to sit down on the rocks at one end of the beach and wait for the last visitors to depart.

    As the sun sets I strip off all my clothes and with a good deal of trepidation begin to gingerly scramble over the rocks and approach the water. Many are the rituals that modern-day pilgrims have established upon reaching Finisterre. One of these is the obvious one of plunging into the ocean in celebration of completing the Camino. I had always intended to do this at the fiftieth anniversary of the precise moment of my birth, and indeed had planned out my entire pilgrimage around this particular event. Recently, however, being a few days ahead of schedule and bone weary from the travails of the Camino, I had rebooked a new flight home, the only time available necessitating my departure from Spain the day *before* my fiftieth birthday. Still, I wanted to do this immersion, which until yesterday I had always envisioned to be a quick in and, given the expected frigid end-of-December temperatures of the north Atlantic, an even quicker out. Yesterday, however, Maria, with whom I had walked portions of the Camino and who had arrived here several days before to do her ritual plunge, instructed me about the proper way to undertake this immersion (which I was later to learn has as its inspiration a medieval Galician fertility ceremony referred to as "*El baño de las nueve olas*"). Following her lead, I kneel in the water of a receding wave (which doesn't feel too bad so far). With nervousness, I then wait for the next wave to break over me. And when it does, it is of course bone-chilling.cold! Rather than flee as every cell in my body tells me to, I wait and again another wave hits me in the chest. Despite losing all sense of feeling in my legs and feet I remain in this position for the total of the nine waves that are supposed to symbolise time spent in the womb. And thus at the very edge of death (or at least hypothermia) I am symbolically reborn. Although I hear some approaching voices, it takes a few minutes for my recalcitrant fingers to warm up enough so I can dress myself, a task made all the more difficult by my body shivering as if experiencing an epileptic seizure. Jogging in the dark over the peninsula back into town, I hurriedly return to my hotel room and immediately submit myself to a final, post-partum, tenth wave, this time a prolonged jet of near-scalding water from the shower-head.

❖❖❖

It is nearly 3a.m. on the twentieth day of December and as I walk along the leeward side of the high ridge of sand dunes on Plum Island, Massachusetts, I hear the Atlantic Ocean before it is seen. The wind is blowing fiercely as I navigate the slippery iced walkway in the bright moonlight to finally catch a glimpse of the crashing waves. Despite feeling weary from my Compostela to Madrid to Boston flight having arrived only six hours before, I am also very happy, excited, and of course nervous. I time the cycle of waves and do some hurried calculations. Then, after waiting for a few minutes and shaking my head in disbelief, I peel off my clothes, understandably wondering (worrying) about the craziness of the forthcoming act, a repeat of that accomplished less than two days before on the other side of the ocean. Naked, I stand shivering on the beach and giving one last check of the watch to make sure it is the correct time, proceed to walk into the ocean and kneel down to await the first of the nine waves to wash over me. By the time it is over I can barely raise my arm up to check the watch and confirm the time. Then at the precise fiftieth anniversary of when I first entered the world, I re-enter it a second time, wailing in pain and terror…just as I've been told I did before.

On Architecture…

CHAPTER 6

THE PRESUMED ETERNITY OF STONE

"How amazing and ironical it is that this legend, so improbable, so flawed, so disreputable, should have trodden a path through the history of western Europe that is flagged by some of the brightest achievements of our civilization."

– Edwin Mullins, *The Pilgrimage to Santiago*

STRUCTURES

THE TAXI FROM THE AIRPORT QUICKLY races away leaving me standing alone at the side of the central square in the sleepy village of Obanos, backpack at my feet and heart on my sleeve. I assume a frown of disappointment wondering why there is not a soul in sight to witness such an historically auspicious event. Where is the mayor to see me off? Where are the press to inquire about my *feelings*? Where is the crippled leper asking me to give the Apostle a hug for him upon reaching Compostela? Where are the prayerful monks to give me a Godspeed blessing? Better yet, where is the bodacious señorita to give me a kiss goodbye and whisper in my ear that she will wait for me? I smile at the affected hubris. This is it: the location where the two pilgrimage routes from France converge to become one. The Camino Francés. My very own namesake road!

Confused about my bearings, I look around and notice the portal in the old city wall. And there – my heart almost bursts with excitement at the recognition – is the yellow and blue waymarking scallop shell insignia that after fourteen-hundred kilometres of walking pilgrimage routes in France, I have grown to so love. The gate is open…beckoning…luring me forward with dreamed of experiences of adventure, joy, contact, and contemplation of the outer Camino to be, as well as daring me to face the challenges of confronting memories of the inner Camino that has been. Smiling with anticipation at the same time as acknowledging a feeling of trepidation, I bend down and in an oft-repeated move from my months of pilgrimage in France, hoist the pack first up on one shoulder crying "*Ultreia!*" the medieval pilgrims' rallying cry of 'onward,' and then on the other shoulder with a shout of "*Suseia!*" or 'upward,' before heaving the pack high on my back and cinching it tight around my waste with a concluding "*Deus aia nos!*", 'God help us.' I am ready to begin.

Slowly I walk toward the opening and passing through reach up to touch the scallop shell waymarker sign for good luck. I pause for a moment in contemplation. Before me, stretching across northern Spain like a necklace of pearls that for so many years has beguiled my imagination, are the towns of the Camino: Puente la Reina, Estella,

Lograno, Nájera, Santa Domingo, Belorado, Burgos, Castrojeriz, Sahagún, León, Astorga, O'Cebreiro, Sarria, Arzua, and finally Santiago de Compostela. Hundreds of times, a finger tracing the route on a map, I have visited these towns in my mind. Now, moving forward once again, I will visit them with my feet…my eyes…my heart. Onward! *Ultreia*!

❖❖❖

ESTELLA IS BRIMMING WITH WONDERFUL BUILDINGS. In front of me is the twelfth-century Palacio de los Reyes de Navarra, one of the most beautiful medieval secular buildings in all of Spain. The sturdiness of construction, the gently rounded arches, the non-flamboyant harmony of its design are all signatures of the Romanesque, a word that though it seems to somehow imply a diminishing of something better through use of the "esque", is really one of the most highly accomplished, approachable, and therefore loved of all forms of early architecture. The decreasing size of the windows on successively higher floors is a particularly attractive feature. I walk down the steps to examine what are thought to be the building's highlights: its carved capitals. One in particular draws most of my attention. Here the hero Roland, mounted on a horse and recognised by his elongated crusader shield emblazoned with a tiny cross, jousts with the Muslim giant Ferragut noted by his round shield and oriental style of chainmail. Though both are approximately equal sized in this scene on the front of the capital, glancing around the corner at the continuation of the fierce battle I see that here clearly the much larger Ferragut appears to be the more formidable of the pair. But as the Biblical story of David and Goliath has taught us: "the bigger they are….". Roland of course, as the famous Chanson tells us, would unfortunately have little time to savour this particular victory.

❖❖❖

Whereas the cathedral in Burgos left me cold, the Monasterio de las Huelgas on the outskirts of the city is redolent with great character and kindles imaginative flurries about what life might have been like for its inhabitants during the Middle Ages. Staring at the architectural splendour in front of me I am tickled by the inherent irony of the very place itself, designed as it was to be the most lavish Cistercian convent (huh?) for housing widows and unmarried women from Europe's nobility (Eleanor Plantagenet, daughter of King Henry and sister to Kings Richard and John was the first abbess). My eyes dance over and eventually become tired from looking at the complicated north side and trying to take it all in. For what is displayed is a fascinating mishmash of architectural forms: church, towers, gable, pediment, rose window, doorways, buttresses, chimneys, and arcades. The dark, mysterious and, it must be admitted, slightly ominous, arched openings of the long colonnade raise questions about what might have transpired therein. How devote and well behaved were the young women? Or were they like those famously rambunctious and lascivious members of Venice's aristocracy interred against their will within in that city's many convents? How many came here on their own accord, possibly grateful to be finally rid of violent spouses to whom they had been given as chattel through arranged marriages?

Pondering such questions, I enter the courtyard to begin my guided tour which, given the early hour in the morning, turns out to be for me alone. Regarding my private and strikingly fetching tour guide I wonder about how many of the young female noblility resident here during the Middle Ages, referred to by decree as *Señora* rather than *Sor*, displayed the same classic raven-haired beauty?

❖❖❖

For more than an hour the castle high atop the prominent hill overlooking Castrojeriz has drawn my eyes. Not till I get closer to the village do I see the fourteenth-century, skeletal ruins of the monastery and hospice of San Anton. Incredibly, more than half a millennium after their construction, two gothic arches still boldly span the pilgrim route upon which I am walking. I linger underneath, marvelling at the incongruous combination of their seeming delicacy and obvious rigour beautifully silhouetted against the sky. The back of the church likewise emphasises bulk strength in its solid brickwork which is contrasted with an incredible lightness of the tracery of the small rose window.

I pause and try to imagine this place at the height of the great pilgrimage age when late arrivers would have been allowed to sleep under the then-covered archway, eating the meagre food left out for them by the monks, and perhaps if it was winter as now, huddling together over a brazier for warmth, sharing their varied yet possibly familiar stories. Sadder would have been those tended by the monks inside the hospice, suffering from any of a number of ailments rampant in medieval times. Setting down my pack I spend a few minutes searching for intimate carvings of good luck of the type left by pilgrims that I had seen on the stone walls of a similar hospice arched over the pilgrim route in the French town of Pons. Unsuccessful, I shoulder my pack once more and continue forward to find more habitable accommodation for the night.

❖❖❖

AT MY FIRST SIGHT OF THE MAGNIFICENT, thirteenth-century Templar castle in Ponferrada I erupt with a throaty laugh. I know it is supposed to be a crowning jewel of Spanish military architecture and of course I'm well aware of the sad plight of the controversial Templars (unlucky Friday the thirteenth and such). But it is for all that simply just too silly-looking not to invoke a chuckle. The long ramp leads up to the entrance flanked by over-restored walls and towers crowned by turrets and machicolations over which a colourful flag flaps in the cool breeze. The whole scene, framed by a brilliant blue sky, looks undeniably like a Disney postcard. As I enter through the tarted-up double gateway I half expect and am slightly disappointed *not* to see the ticket agent dressed up as Mickey. The feeling of unreality is inescapable as I tour the enormous sixteen-thousand-square-metre fortification. I feel like a young boy wandering about a clichéd castle of my childhood imagination. I walk around the walls and in a playful mood startle my fellow pilgrims Jean-Olivier and Emmanuelle walking below by hollering insults at them in my most over-the-top, Python-esque, bad French-accented English. I'm gratified when my "you dirty English pig-dogs" etc. elicits a big laugh from them, demonstrating the cross-cultural familiarity of British comedy.

BRIDGES

I AM ABSOLUTELY STAGGERED WHEN, after only a few minutes of walking along the Calle Mayor through the pilgrim town of Puente la Reina, I catch my first glimpse of the magnificent Puente de los Peregrinos. Built in the early eleventh century at a time when engineering and aesthetics were one, the bridge is a masterpiece of Romanesque architecture. I spend more than an hour walking back and forth across its length as well as upstream and downstream along both sides of the Rio Arga admiring the structure from every possible angle. Never have I been so struck by the incredible lightness and delicate beauty of any bridge: the five graceful arches balanced atop their fusiform abutments, punctuated by spandrels cut by the remarkable windows designed to lighten the weight of the structure while providing beauty in an almost unequalled display of form serving function. Also remarkable is the surface pavement which, though composed of rough-hewn stones, has the impression of being laid down as a thin gossamer layer.

I sit down on a quiet bank-side bench and imagine the scene a millennium ago when the place was a-bustle during the bridge's creation, and try to guess at the mind-set of its designers. I remember Dickens' reflections from *Pickwick Papers* that the difference between something created and something constructed is that whereas the latter can only be loved after it was built, the former can be loved even before it exists. I am certain that the designer of this particular bridge, whose identity has long since been lost in the medieval shadows, when looking at his plans scratched upon a sheet of vellum, must have loved his creation from its very conception.

Standing up, I walk back to the town-side guard tower and look through the portal across the hump-backed span that I will cross early the next morning. Can there really be any better location to begin a pilgrimage? The feeling of the beckoning road ahead is palatable, the forward draw toward unknown experiences and promising adventures, almost irresistible. Standing within the tower, I feel like a racehorse chomping at the bit eager to bolt out of the starting gate to begin my journey. "*Mañana… mañana*", I intone as with effort I force myself to turn back to the pilgrim hostel for the night.

♦ ♦ ♦

IMMEDIATELY AFTER LEAVING THE TINY hilltop village of Cirauqui the pilgrimage route descends to a Roman bridge on the best-preserved section of the two-thousand-year-old Via Traiana. Knowing that much of this ancient roadway ahead upon which medieval pilgrims would have strode has long ago disappeared beneath the modern highway, I savour the opportunity to be walking along one of the few, truly authentic sections of the Camino Francés. While another pilgrim rushes by oblivious of the history upon which he is treading, I purposely slow my pace, allowing my feet and legs to twist and turn this way and that as they register the uneven surface of closely fitted stones and, straw like, attempt to draw up the ancient Roman history into my body and being.

✦ ✦ ✦

THE BROAD FLOOD-PLAIN OF THE Rio Odrilla located outside of Castrojeriz must have always presented a difficult challenge to cross in remote antiquity. Until such time that is, however, as the coming of Roman engineering. Raised a metre above the expansive riparian marshes is a serpentine causeway still flanked by its original Roman stonework. Demonstrating an intelligence about

the natural world more astute than that held by of many of today's engineers, including those who designed the modern road running parallel, the Romans had permeated their long causeway by numerous arches in order to enable the passage of water. Being a co-author of the only published book about road ecology, I professorially admire the lesson shown by the contrasting juxtaposition of the ancients building *with*, compared to the moderns building *over*, the landscape. In homage to the early, more environmentally sensitive form of engineering, I abandon the modern road and opt to cross the marshes on the Roman causeway. When several hours later my day of wonderful water crossings continues with a much restored but still atmospheric, multi-arched bridge dating from the twelfth century, I realise that such structures have become for me the defining architectural feature of the pilgrimage route in Spain.

❖❖❖

I'M HALFWAY ACROSS THE SINUOUS BRIDGE leading into Hospital de Órbigo, which at over two-hundred metres is the longest medieval water crossing in Spain, when I see the individual walking toward me. In a sudden mood of boyish playfulness, I identify him as being my opponent. As the backpacked and bushy-bearded pilgrim approaches, obviously on his homeward return from Compostela, I shift my position slightly to the left of the medial line of stones and raise up and tuck my walking stick under my arm, business end pointed toward him. With only the slightest hesitation, the pilgrim, who I'm elated to see is likewise aware of the history of this particular bridge, enters into the spirit of the moment and raises up his own, much more robust and menacing looking, wooden walking staff. We thus purposely stride toward one another and slowing, complete strangers sharing a loud laugh, each lightly taps the other on the shoulder edge of the pack in passing without so much as a break in our steps or a word spoken. For this is the famous La Puente del Passo Honoroso, where in 1434 a Leónesse knight attempting to free himself from the melancholy of unrequited love, challenged the nobility of Europe to participate in what would be the last major jousting tournament of the Middle Ages. At the end of the bridge I turn around and see that the now distant pilgrim has done likewise. Simultaneously, we both raise our staffs-cum-lances in salute before returning to our respective pilgrimages.

♦♦♦

IT IS STILL DARK AND COLD WHEN, on the way to Finisterre, I arrive at Ponte Maceira, the wonderful, late-medieval bridge stretching a hundred metres across the Rio Tambre. Knowing this to be the last structure of such magnitude that I will see on my pilgrimage to the end of the world, I linger in the early morning quiet, savouring all those elements that I've so grown to admire: the hump-backed shape, the rounded arches, the rough-hewn field stones, and the mid-channel twist that produces a quaint organic nonlinearity to the whole. Not a soul is moving along the attractive, mansion-lined streets leading to the bridge. With the cooling river releasing great amounts of steam into the December air, the entire valley is clouded in atmospheric mist. Crossing to the middle of the bridge, I look downstream to where the remains of the older Roman bridge lie underwater. According to a local legend, this earlier bridge was destroyed by God in order to prevent solders from pursuing the fleeing followers of Saint James. Staring into the swirling mists it takes little imagination to hear the sounds of surprised legionaries and relieved early Christians.

SCULPTURE

THE LATE-TWELFTH-CENTURY CAPITALS in the partially ruined cloister of the church of San Pedro de la Rúa in Estella are much admired masterworks of Romanesque sculpture. No church structures appeal to me more, inveterate meditative walker that I am, than do cloisters. As such, all day I've been looking forward to visiting the many notable carvings and the famous, single twisted column symbolising the imperfections of our corporeal world. Again and again I slowly circle around the cloister pausing frequently to examine the capitals. Represented didactic scenes include those from the Bible and the life of Saint Andrew, including one I especially enjoy of a king blessing solders that remarkably

still displays vestiges of blue paint. Additional capitals contain wonderfully rendered and singularly expressive images of foliage as well as of harpies, griffins, sirens, and many other fantastical creatures of a type that would later so bother that self-righteous stick-in-the-mud art critic, Saint Bernard. Finding it remarkably easy, however, to ignore Cistercian criticisms, I continue walking about, returning to my favourite carvings to study them again and again as the sun sets on this, my first full day of pilgrimage.

❖ ❖ ❖

DOÑA URRACA LÓPEZ DE HARO, Abbess of the Cistercian Monastery of Santa Maria de Cañas, must have been extremely well loved. The evidence is displayed on her thirteenth-century tomb, recognised to be one of the most spectacular sepulchral monuments in all of Spain. It is not, however, her effigy that draws my attention as much as do the accompanying carvings of the mourners displaying emotion to such a degree that one can almost feel the painful loss of their revered leader. Squatting at the feet of the surface effigy of the Abbess are several novices who hold hands up to the sides of their tearful faces. Most spectacular is the frieze showing the funeral procession that wraps around the sides of the sarcophagus. Here monks, bishops, and nuns, prayer books, sceptres, or handkerchiefs in hand, sombrely file past preceded by women wearing elaborate headgear whose hands are clenched to the sides of their cheeks in palatable grief. In front of them, at the edge of the depicted coffin, a group of monks are pictured pulling at their hair, pain etched upon their simply rendered faces. And most remarkably, in one case, a monk, his face unseen, has dropped his tonsured head onto the surface of

the Abbess' coffin as he clutches its sides. On my knees studying the carving, I am absolutely transfixed, almost believing for a moment that I can actually see the figure move up and down as he sobs in grief. Shaking my head and regaining my feet, I blame the temporary illusion on the atmospheric music of Gregorian chants that has been playing softly in the background throughout the visit. Finally, at the base of the sarcophagus is a pleasant carving of the smiling, heaven-bound Abbess suspended aloft in a shroud held up by angels. It takes an effort to finally drag myself away from the monastery, and as I do so it is impossible not to feel sorry for the bulk of pilgrims who, either in ignorance or unwillingness, do not walk the meagre five kilometres off the Camino to visit this memorable site.

❖❖❖

SPOTTED FROM A DISTANCE ALONG the narrow street, the west façade of the twelfth-century Iglesia de Santiago in Carrión de los Condes at first glance does not illicit much attention relative to other such structures recently observed in several nearby churches. Closer inspection, however, reveals these carvings to represent masterpieces of Romanesque sculpture. My eyes are first drawn to the image of Christ in Majesty in the centre of the upper frieze over the portal, and in particular, the delicate folds of his robe. Single columns straddle either side of the door, remarkable for being carved along their complete lengths, one sporting an elegant, beautifully winged angel holding a harp. It is the archivolt, however, that is most interesting in its detailed depiction of medieval tradesmen with their appropriate tools in hand. I am always warmed by such scenes of the mundane. This is the great gift of Romanesque sculpture: its uncompromising focus on the human scale, its ability to capture the zeitgeist of the Middle Ages with an incredible intimacy that would later disappear with Gothic's emphasis on vertiginous grandeur.

❖❖❖

I AT FIRST SMILE AND THEN LAUGH OUTRIGHT at the façade of the Renaissance church of San Marcos on the edge of León. Normally when present, the scallop shell of Santiago, the long-acknowledged symbol of reaching the Galician sea coast, is pictured subtly, often tucked into a corner or kept in the background so as not to distract from the portrayal of the Saint. Here, however, that piece of saintly bling has itself become the major decorative element of the church front. Hundreds of bas-relief shells are shown marching their way in gay exuberance in ordered rows across the entire façade. Spirits soaring from the image, I reach up and touch my own scallop pilgrim badge on my hat, nodding my head downward in acknowledgement and gratitude, before striding off toward Compostela with a renewed vigour. Was this, I wonder, notwithstanding their decorative intent, an ancillary purpose of these particular uplifting carvings?

❖❖❖

AS I STARE IN AMAZEMENT AT THE BEAUTIFUL sculptures bordering the portals of the church of San Nicholás in Portomarín I have to keep reminding myself that every single stone has been reassembled here several decades ago after having been transported, Abu Simbel-like, from its original location, now buried beneath the nearby reservoir. What would the Knights of Saint John have thought of this transference, I wonder, having built their church as a monumental fortress to withstand besiegement of all…except of course rising water?

On the tympanum above the west portal is a weathered image of Christ floating on his flying-saucer-like mandorla over a pair of monsters carved on the mènsula corbels straddling the door. As in previous churches I find my eyes drawn to the archivolt and its couplets of musicians playing a diversity of medieval instruments, some recognised as being prototypes of those still in use today; others, however, of unknown nomenclature and mysterious, only to be guessed at sound. Racing to beat the threatening rain clouds, I dash around to the north façade and am struck dumb by the portal there. Three columns bracket the door and are capped by finely carved capitals displaying, most notably, monsters such as harpies, sirens, griffins, and dragons. It is the tympanum, however, that is most striking with its oddly unsettling depiction of the Annunciation. Wings wonderfully outstretched for dramatic effect (or

possibly intimidation), a menacing looking angel thrusts his finger at Mary who, far from being in acquiescence, much less welcoming of her divine role, is holding up her hands in fruitless protest. This well-known Biblical scene, a favourite of so many, is here transformed from one of blind acceptance to a much more moving one of knowing reticence. Mary's triumph and then tragedy feel all the more significant as a result.

THE FORTRESS-LIKE BULK OF THE Iglesia de San Miguel in Estella sits, as one would expect for a church dedicated to the Archangel, high atop a hill overlooking the town and river. Anticipation builds as I ascend the steep medieval steps, for the famed north portal is said to contain some of the very finest Romanesque reliefs found in all of Spain. Arriving in the little courtyard I am first struck by the small size of the portal tucked away from the elements under a modern protective awning. Moving closer I soon realise that size is completely secondary to the spectacular beauty displayed by the carvings. Having visited many masterpieces of Romanesque sculpture and architecture along the four pilgrimage routes in France, I had simply not expected anything in Spain to be of comparable character. But here, on only my first full day of walking at the start of the Camino Francés, I find myself happily surprised and completely dazzled.

As was the intent, the eyes are drawn first to the central tympanum showing Christ in Majesty floating on his nimbus (mandorla) cloud and surrounded by the saintly Tetramorphos of which, given my personal close association with Venice, I'm most taken by that of Saint Mark's flying lion. Next, I slowly walk from left to right admiring the pedagogical lesson on the capitals of Christ's life: the Annunciation (great large-headed figure behind Mary), Visitation and Birth, Angels and shepherds, and the Adoration, and Presentation on the left-side; and the Flight to Egypt (my favourite), Herod and the ever-disturbing Slaughter of the Innocents, and wonderful carvings of hunters and prey amongst an extremely realistic-looking tangle of vegetation on the right side. To my mind, most impressive are the five archivolts displaying from the centre: angels (not too exciting), the Old Men of the Apocalypse with recognisable instruments in their laps (absolutely breathtaking), prophets with long scrolls draped over their shoulders (nice), scenes from Christ's life (boring), and episodes from the lives of the Saints (I particularly enjoy the iconic one of Martin dividing his cloak). And finally, apropos to the overall theme of the Last Judgment, is the outermost (and

therefore farthest from the central Christ) archivolt that portrays the doomed sinners suffering from various tortures. As always, the gruesome details displayed, closely examined with my monocular lens brought along for just such a purpose, are morbidly fun to behold. But how different and how terrifying must it have been when viewed through the medieval eyes and mindset of the truly ardent and the obsessively fearful?

❖❖❖

EVER SINCE I HAD FIRST GLIMPSED photographs of the tiny Romanesque church of San Martin in Frómista I had longed to visit. Here now, after spending a cold day battling the searching winter wind pouring off the *meseta*, I find the church, standing as it does in proud isolation in the centre of town, to offer little in the way of warmth. That said, I still admire the minimalist simplicity and architectural purity: the octagonal cupola, the perfect proportions of the gently rounded apses, and the stark lines casting shadows across the yellow limestone walls. Upon closer inspection I discover something indiscernible from the distance as well as also from those earlier photographs. For running around the entire church, just underneath the eaves, sometimes layered in two parallel rows, are the most incredible group of carved corbels. Again and again for over an hour I circle about the church and with either monocular or camera held in gloved hands I study the hundreds and hundreds of carvings; a complete menagerie of grotesques and fantastics, each unique from its neighbours. Favourites include lions ingesting the heads of sinners, a turbaned infidel doomed for Hell, and a large-headed demon sporting a bad case of Austin-Powers-like teeth. Enjoying the artistry of the imaginative sculptures finally does warm me but not nearly enough. I therefore abandon my ecclesiastical investigations and follow fellow pilgrim Amador into a little restaurant to experience my first mid-afternoon *comida* of the journey.

❖ ❖ ❖

FREE OF LATER OVERT ALTERATIONS that mar its sibling in Burgos, the cathedral in León reigns supreme along the Camino for its pure French Gothic artistry. Following my long-established ritual of studying the exterior before entering the sanctuary, I marvel at the unbridled exuberance of the soaring spires and vertiginous towers pulling, as was ever the intent of the Gothic, the eyes always upward to God's heavenly home; at the patterned feminine symmetry of the rose windows balanced above the masculinity of the pointed-arched triforia on both the west and south facades; at the complicated Celtic-like tracery of the high gable window on the south façade; and at the boldness of the phalanxes of flying buttresses, those apogees of Gothic form and function that brazenly hold all together. Then I stand rooted in front of the three portals on the west façade, savouring for the longest time the carved artistry of their tympana and archivolts, in particular the varied clothing on the commoners shown engaged in scenes of thirteenth-century life and the tortured expressions on the faces of the damned in the disturbing scenes of their grisly torments in Hell.

As wonderful as all that is, it becomes immediately apparent upon entering the cathedral why this is one of the greatest pieces of Gothic church architecture, not just in Spain, but anywhere. For more than two decades I have travelled throughout Europe visiting many of its cathedrals and it takes but seconds to realise that I am standing in one of the most marvellous buildings that I have seen. The "jewel of León" it is called with good reason, for the luminosity from the expansive stained glass windows – only Chartres has more – bathes the interior in a rainbow of dancing colours. Joining the other gawking visitors I wander about the nave, lingering longest at the crossing, neck craned upward, completely lost in admiration at the incredible, almost unbelievable, lightness of a building that is more glass than stone. What a shattering effect this splendour must have had on those simple peasant pilgrims of the Middle Ages, some of whom might never have seen anything like this in terms of scale and beauty. As a vehicle to inspire awe, this Gothic glass house might well have registered some of the strongest memories and most often retold stories for peasants returning to the squalor of their hardscrabble farmsteads. It takes an effort to wrest my eyes away to focus on the other star attractions of the cathedral, namely the handful of elaborate tombs with their lovely Mozarabic-lobed fringeing arches and haunting carvings of funeral processions and scenes of the Crucifixion.

Finally I enter the ornately decorated Renaissance cloister. I am here to see the fading murals, tickled by the idea of (Robert) France's viewing the artistic work of (Nicholás) Francés on the Camino Francés. Humour aside, I am once again awestruck. Will the wonders of this cathedral never cease? The image of the Crucifixion is one of the most powerful I have ever seen, the blind methodical nature of the medieval garbed solders in striking contrast to the knowing compliancy of Christ. And as an added bonus, just who exactly are those three pilgrim-staffed individuals in the corner supposed to be? If one imagines removing the halos they look not dissimilar, I realise with a laugh, to myself and my fellow pilgrims, Pasquale and Jean-Olivier.

❖❖❖

ARRIVING IN THE SQUARE IN FRONT of the Basilica de San Isidoro in León after just having visited the nearby cathedral provides a clear lesson in the differences between medieval architectural styles. For whereas the Gothic cathedral was all about display (light, glory, and awe) the Romanesque basilica is about intimacy (education, contemplation, and mystery). And it is for these reasons that I have opted to attend mass here in the older basilica rather than the cathedral. But first, to be a tourist and study the building.

The squat bulk in front of me is broken by two portals, each presenting an exquisitely carved tympanum. The right one is particularly marvellous with its depiction of the descent from the cross and the Ascension, all figures displaying unusual round-cheeked faces and pudgy limbs. The two angels giving Christ a boost up to heaven are especially amusing. Underneath, on either side of the door is a pair of impressive ménsula corbels representing the heads of growling beasts. The other portal's tympanum depicts one of the most unsavoury, and my least favourite, of Old Testament stories. Here carved in remarkable detail is annoyingly compliant Abraham's supreme test, the sacrifice of Isaac being halted at the very last moment by the appearance of God's outstretched hand.

Within the building, a forest of hefty columns, rounded arches, barrel vaulting, and above all, gloomy darkness radiate the spirit of the Romanesque (architecturally this basilica was to become one of the most influential buildings in northern Spain) and give the impression that one has entered

the most holy of holies. For this was indeed one of the major sites along the Way at which medieval pilgrims were instructed to pray; in this case, before the tomb of the sixth-century archbishop (later canonised) from Seville, Isidoro. Unlike the dubious San Iago (Saint James), purportedly now of Compostela, whose major historic distinction seems to have been being a loudmouth ("the voice of thunder" in the Bible) and having the bad luck to be the first martyred Apostle, Isidoro is an early Christian who is truly worthy of respect. For as well as being an important cleric he was also a scholar. Indeed Isidoro, as the most learned man of his age, assembled, more than a millennium before the French Academy or Dr. Johnson, the world's first encyclopaedia and dictionary. His *Etymologies* would become the major educational tool of the Middle Ages, containing entries on theology, botany, zoology, physics, geography, astronomy, medicine, law, architecture, agriculture, history, etc. And so it is here rather than later in Compostela, with head bowed in reverence, that I offer a prayer of acknowledgement for the accomplishments of the most worthy of the four saints whose remains/relicts lie on the Spanish Camino.

After the service I proceed to tour the adjacent Panteón de los Reves, the crypt filled with dozens of royal tombs. Never have I so wanted to sneak away from a mandatory guided tour and spend extra time at a location. For not more than a few metres above my head and covering every square centimetre of vault and spandrels are what many experts contend to be some of the finest frescos in existence. This has led the crypt to be referred to as the "Romanesque Sistine Chapel." And like that noted Renaissance masterpiece of Michelangelo, the art here is capable of bringing viewers to the edge of tears in appreciation. Splashed against a white background so close that one could reach up and touch them (hence I suppose the omnipresent guards) are thousands of brightly coloured images from the life of Christ, as well as of saints, signs from the zodiac, and the especially exquisite agricultural animals exhibiting a diversity of facial expressions. After seeing many thousands of pieces of art through walking thousands of kilometres along the pilgrimage pathways of France and Spain, possibly only the famous Last Judgment tympanum at Conques or the statue of Jeremiah at Moissac are the equal for their beauty as these frescos. I wrench my eyes from the ceiling and glance at the other visitors and see some, like me, shaking their heads in disbelief at the masterpiece above them. Too soon we are herded away to visit the museum which although containing many notable pieces of medieval art cannot but pale in comparison to the crypt. As photographs are prohibited I visit the shop and buy a souvenir booklet filled with images, knowing that my words alone will never be able to do justice to the marvels of the crypt when describing it to others.

❖ ❖ ❖

So THERE IT FINALLY IS, the ultimate destination for so many of the faithful over so many years: the cathedral of Santiago de Compostela. Despite my prejudice against Renaissance embellishments, I am surprised to find myself admiring the verticality of the Obradorio façade. My eyes are drawn upward and there he is: the famous, large statue of Santiago *Peregrino*, poster boy from the covers of a dozen contemporary pilgrim accounts and guidebooks.

Suffused with pride of accomplishment and my healthy bodily state I bolt up the impressive zigzag staircase impatient for that first glimpse of what I know to be the marvel of the cathedral and what fellow Harvard scholar Kingsley Porter considered to be the greatest single achievement in Romanesque sculpture: the famed Pórtico de la Gloria. The carvings fill the narthex in a way I would never have thought possible, surrounding all three doorways in a complexity that at first seems overwhelming. I spend many minutes simply trying to absorb the whole, conscious that I am standing alone

in front of one of the most spectacular entrance statements rendered by human hands (through God's direction, of course, believers would say). There appears so much of such fine detail that I am hesitant in commencing my examination. Then I remember that my early morning solitude here (what a luxury!) will inevitably be shattered by the invasion of camera clicking and guidebook quoting tourists. So to begin.

The first marvel is that I have never seen a tympanum so chock-a-block stuffed with figures. There is the majestic Christ, welcoming hands raised up in understanding and acceptance, and surrounded by angels, evangelists, and the souls of the saved. The archivolt contains, like the one seen back in Estella at the beginning of the Camino Francés, a diversity of bearded musicians of the Apocalypse, their instruments clearly discernible. The jambs beside the doorways contain large statues of Old and New Testament persona that are of great artistic importance, representing as they do, the transition from the Romanesque to the Gothic. It is the birth of vivid naturalism that is particularly evident on the expressions of a smiling Daniel and a flirting, coquettish Queen Esther. My ghoulish side, recognised long ago when like so many I too found Dante's Hell and Milton's Satan to be the most interesting parts of those particular works, draws me next to the right portal and its amazing Last Judgment motif. And so, giving only a passing glance at the angels ascending with the cute child-sized souls of the saved on the left of the archivolt, I concentrate instead on the torments of the unrepentant condemned. Here we have an upside-down drunk unable to consume the contents of his wineskin, a glutton forced to choke down more food, various fornicators and others being eaten by demons, and above all, in the place of dubious honour, Judas still with the noose around his neck. Finally, I focus on the central mullion crowned by Saint James himself, haloed in jewels, pilgrim staff placed prominently across his chest, standing atop a capital displaying Christ resisting his temptations which is itself at the apex of the Jesse Tree depicting the Saviour's genealogy.

It is at this point when admiration vanishes in a second to be replaced by anger. For here at the base of the mullion, a location steeped in history, the placement of a new, metal barrier thwarts me from engaging in rituals that pilgrims and scholars have been performing for centuries. I simply can't believe it! To have come all this way and not be allowed to participate in the most important ritualistic acts of shared confraternity with the thousands, no…millions, who have come before, is galling. There out of reach is the prominent hand depression worn into the stone from the fingers of countless pilgrims who have leaned against the column in prayerful thankfulness for having arrived; and there at the base is the head of Mateo, sculptor of the Portal and

against which scholars have touched their heads hopeful to absorb some of the maestro's brilliance. A sign says the area is closed for conservation purposes but nary a single workman nor any tools are present. Thinking about the glacier-like rapidity of reparations in Venice about which I am familiar, I wonder if the Spanish are any more efficient at expediting this sort of work than the Italians. Otherwise, given the increasing popularity of the Camino, the number of similarly disgruntled, fellow pilgrims will become legion.

Bitterly disappointed at my ill luck and recognising that I am in no mood to visit the sanctuary, I turn my back to the cathedral nave and proceed around outside to study the Puerta de las Platerias, named after the silversmiths who to this day occupy the neighbourhood. The tympana of the two doors and the upper frieze are filled with a jumbled assortment of figures on separate slabs that have been cut and cobbled together after damages to the cathedral during riots in the twelfth century. On the spandrel, the image of Santiago standing between two trees and stepping on a demon shows a realistic expressiveness in facial features that is certainly of the finest quality seen along the Way, very much in contrast to the roughness of the nearby figures of Adam and Eve being banished from the Garden. Interesting features of the left tympanum include the assortment of demons including, my favourite, a monkey-headed one looking like it has just flown out of the Wizard of Oz film. It is the figure

of the adulteress that grabs most of the attention, however. Taking out my monocular I admire the waves of her dishevelled hair and the anatomical features of her left leg, details reminiscent of the past Classical Age and prescient of the future Renaissance. Clutched in her lap is the rotten, decapitated head of her lover, courtesy of her cuckolded husband, who makes her kiss it twice daily. On the right tympanum I also enjoy the thin-lipped and pug-nosed features and Beatles-like bang haircuts of the big-headed soldiers who surround Christ at the flagellation pole.

Finally I admire the elongated and finely worked figures on the columns, sculpted in the round and suggesting that they might have once been freestanding. This calls to mind the statue from this cathedral that I had repeatedly visited back at the Fogg Museum, just a few metres from my office at Harvard, prompting me to wonder about a possible shared provenance. On the chance that it might be so and still livid from being prevented from engaging in the Portal of Glory rituals, I decide to initiate a personal ritual here. I sit down on the steps and forage around in my daypack until I find my wallet and withdraw spent digital photo cards. It takes several minutes of screening them, one after the other in my camera, until I find the appropriate one. Checking about to make sure no one is nearby to observe the lunacy of the act, I stride over to the columnar statues and holding up the camera to their faces with the displayed image from the Harvard museum, show them their long-lost brother. Laughing at the absurdity of the act it is only then that I notice the beggar squatting inside the doorway regarding me in the most perplexed way. I smile, give him some change, and quickly depart.

FOUR YEARS LATER, after having finished the manuscript of the present book, I finally complete my pilgrimage to the Santiago cathedral by visiting the Victoria and Albert Museum in London. There in front of the plaster cast replica of the Pórtico de la Gloria, and ignoring the puzzled looks from tourists and disapproving glares from security guards, I insert my hand into its rightful place at the base of the column and fall to my knees and touch my head to the maestro's image. The long pilgrimage of paces and of pages is finally over.

And I take comfort in knowing that although the structure may only be a plaster cast, its form, captured at an instance of time more than a hundred years ago, is actually a more accurate representation of what medieval pilgrims would have encountered compared to the exposed and eroded original there now. Once more I reinsert my hand into the depression and joyfully wiggle my fingers in a dance with history.

Monuments

I REACH THE SOMBRE CAIRN beside the busy highway outside of Estella. This is one of a handful of memorials to various pilgrims sadly lost to accidents or natural causes along the Way. Both because it is the first such marker that I have seen, as well as being for a fellow Canadian, I am moved. It reads that Mary Catherine Kimpton was killed at 4 pm on June 2, 2002. I would learn later that she was struck by a car that had veered off the road and that the following year her husband and another pilgrim who had been there at the time of the accident dedicated this memorial before the survivors continued on to Compostela in her memory. Over the next month I would learn that there is much sadness along the Way, with many pilgrims walking wrapped up in memories of their dead or of their own once happier lives. At the moment though I search the ground and find a suitable stone to place at the base of the cairn and read the closing words of the inscription: "May she walk forever in fields of gold," before moving on.

✦ ✦ ✦

MANY ARE THE MODERN, metal-cast statues of pilgrims struck in various poses, some defiant, some reflective, and most enjoyably, some intimate, that are scattered along the Way. Standing in the large open square in front of the medieval pilgrim hospital and monastery of San Marcos on the edge of León, I feel myself particularly drawn to the nearby statue and its skilful capturing of emotions and actions with which I can closely identify. Here an elderly and road-weary pilgrim decked in medieval garb is seated at the base of an ancient cross, his head leaning back against the plinth, eyes closed and hands crossed in repose. What is especially endearing is that the pilgrim has taken off his sandals and is dangling his bandage-wrapped feet and toes over the edge of the pedestal. How many times, with hundreds of kilometres walked along the pilgrimage roads of France and Spain, have I seen this same scene repeated by modern pilgrims and have participated in myself? I begin reminiscing about the many times I've watched as individuals, needles in hand, attempt triage on their battered feet by bursting painful looking blisters. After glancing about to see that no one is watching, I bend down and, kissing my fingers, gently place them on the statue's feet as a blessing for continuance of my good fortune in being injury free.

❖❖❖

THE SUMMIT OF MONTE DEL GOZO, the Mount of Joy, is anything but. What it is, is a bitter disappointment. For it is from here where the medieval pilgrims upon racing up the slopes would have caught their first glimpse of the towers of the Santiago cathedral in Compostela, their long-sought destination, the first in the group to do so assuming the appellation of 'King.' Today what had once been one of the most important views in all of Christendom has been obscured by communication towers, large apartment blocks, and other egregious signs of the modern city's sprawl. It is nothing short of sacrilege. So different I reflect from the thankfully still-preserved westward view from the summit of Mount Nebo in Jordan where Moses had his first glimpse of the Promised Land. Incredibly disappointed, I walk back to the enormous, enigmatically shaped sculpture to the Camino that was constructed in the 1993 Holy Year for a large mass held on the hill by Pope John Paul II. Around the pedestal are carvings of some famous pilgrims including, I'm happy to see, one of Saint Francis who apocryphally arrived here early in the thirteenth century. It is the carved inscription however that moves me to tears of happiness in a way denied by the desecrated view of the distant cathedral. For there, without even so much as a little Spanish squiggle over the "e", is formal indication and final proof that this long outward journey along the Way has also been an inward journey along *my* way. "CAMINO DE FRANCE" the writing states. My namesake road. My life.

♦♦♦

I AM STANDING IN ADMIRATION of the statue in Negreira honouring the emigrant experience of Galicians who, like their Celtic brethren in Ireland, have been forced by the thousands to leave their homeland to seek economic betterment elsewhere. Rarely have I seen a sculpture that through capturing a single scene is able to evoke such poignant sympathy for a complex experience. Facing into the town, a mother sits beside a yoke symbolising the hard agrarian lifestyle of rural Galicia as she balances a small infant on her lap. What is at first puzzling is the lower half of the torso of the second figure who is leaning out through the open back window. Only upon circling around to the other side which purposely faces the gateway leading out of the walled town does the full impact of the monument become discernible. There one sees that the window-framed figure is an adolescent boy who with arm outstretched is grabbing hold of his father's trousers as the latter strides away from home, belongings on his shoulder, to seek fortune for his family in the wider world as represented by the globe above him. Leaving the statue behind I, belongings also on my back, follow the footsteps of those past locals and continue westward to the coast.

◆ ◆ ◆

THERE IT IS STICKING OUT INTO THE NORTH Atlantic: Cabo Fisterra, the termination of my pilgrimage and the end of the then-known medieval world. But then it's not really either, is it? For does not pilgrimage, that over clichéd yet undeniably apt metaphor for one's life journey, continue on afterwards? Or at least one so hopes anyway. And for anyone who has ever looked at a map, does not the Spanish coast to the north near Muxía jut out further westward, as certainly does Lisbon also come to think of it, notwithstanding Ireland of course? I smile at the graffiti on a boulder: the inscription "5000 Km ULTREIA" underneath a yellow arrow much like those I've been following for the past month that points ahead. In this case, however, it is not actually pointing west toward its intended destination of North America as many of the geographically challenged pilgrims arriving at this spot suppose but rather it points south toward Africa. Strange. This causes me to reflect on the very last Neanderthals at the end of their own 270,000-year European life-pilgrimage, clustered in their caves near here at the end of the world beneath the massive Gibraltar headland, staring southward back toward the continent from which they had originated, possibly wondering how and why it had come to this for them.

Still, despite the erroneous orientation, I do admire the simple and stark statement represented by the statue of a solitary boot left behind by a long-since-departed pilgrim predecessor, her or his subsequent step (metaphorically in my case as a mixed first and second generation European descendent) on the terra firma of the distant New World of North America. Surrounded by the crashing waves, it is a moving, beautiful, and worthy end-of-the-road sculptural testament. The next day back in Finisterre I emit a belly-laugh when Pasquale admits, somewhat abashedly, that he was disappointed in the boot statue after having glimpsed several foreshortened close-up images of it on postcards for sale in various shops about the town. These had led him to imagine the statue to be a gigantic, person-sized structure as seemed to be indicated in the photos and not the humble, realistically sized replica that it turned out to be! If only all our disappointments experienced at the end of the pilgrimage could be so slight.

On Memories...

CHAPTER 7

PARALLEL ROADS

> "*A reflective pilgrim on the road to Santiago always makes a double journey when he tries to collect his memories – the backward journey through Time and the forward journey through Space.*"
>
> – Walter Starkie, *The Road to Santiago: Pilgrims of St. James*

> "*Along the way,, remember...*"
>
> – David Whyte, 'Camino' in *Pilgrim*

The Road Most Travailed

THE QUESTION OF WHERE TO ACTUALLY physically begin one's pilgrimage is, or at least should, be an important decision. In medieval times of course, this was not an issue. The pilgrim would simply bid his or her family and friends adieu, receive a blessing from the village priest, and head right out the door. Today, it has become customary practice for pilgrims to travel first by plane and then by bus, rail, or taxi to the French mountain town of St.-Jean-Pied-de-Port from where to commence their walk. This despite the fact that there is no historic significance ascribed to this particular location. Being a traditionalist living outside of Europe I decide to leave directly from my house in north Cambridge, Massachusetts and to walk the ten kilometres to the airport in Boston and once in Spain, if possible, to begin to walk from the airport there.

And so it is an early, mid-November morning when I lock my front door and begin to walk through my familiar and much-loved neighbourhood, passing by a pedestrian sign within a few minutes. I soon pass the Catholic church whose priest had refused to return my many calls and inquiries about providing a pilgrim blessing and walk a further five blocks to the Anglican church of Saint James. Here, the female pastor had, in contrast, been particularly enthusiastic about my request. And so now, under a stained glass image of the Saint in his accustomed pilgrim garb, I drop to my knees and am blessed along with my staff and backpack with words from a medieval text to this effect. From here I move a few blocks along the busy road and enter the scallop-shell-emblazoned doors of the appropriately titled *Half Shell* restaurant and have breakfast.

Next, I walk – it never fails to amuse – along Oxford (Street) through Cambridge (city) to Harvard (campus) My office has only days before been emptied of everything save provisions for the upcoming noon-hour *bon voyage* party (Spanish sangria, Spanish red wine, Spanish fried-rice, and Spanish peanuts) and a humorous advertisement poster for a mock-intended book that reads:

114 | ALONG THE WAY

SHELL SHOCK
Hype, Deception, and the Cult of Personality on Pilgrimage from Harvard to Compostela

By Robert L. France
Editor of *Ultreia! Onward! Progress of the Pilgrim*

After ten years and two months at Harvard University, internationally renowned scholar Professor Robert France was unceremoniously informed that his job was to be terminated. Searching for an opportunity to reflect on his Harvard experience, France donned his scallop shell emblazoned hat and began a month-long, 700 km walk across Spain to Santiago de Compostela.

In the tradition of W. Wright's *Harvard's Secret Court*, R. Navarrette's *A Darker Side of Crimson*, and E. Kerlow's *Poisoned Ivy: How Egos, Ideology, and Power Politics Almost Ruined Harvard Law School*

I sit down at my now uncharacteristically clutter-free desk and pouring myself a glass of wine, try not to feel sad about the end of my job. Soon, select colleagues arrive for the party and to wish me Godspeed and write good luck blessings in my pilgrim journal. At one pm it is time to leave and continue the walk to the airport…to Compostela…and beyond. And so I shut my office for the last time and leave Harvard, the self-imagined intellectual centre of the universe, to walk to Finisterre, the once-imagined physical end of the world. Myths both.

♦♦♦

AFTER WALKING ONLY A BLOCK from my office, I step into Harvard's Fogg Museum, something which I have been doing repeatedly for inspiration over the last month while preparing for this pilgrimage. Once again, I circulate around the atrium and closely examine the wonderful collection of Romanesque capitals collected from the pilgrimage routes in France and Spain. I pause in front of two that I have grown to particularly admire: one of the enthroned deity (the *Maiestas Domini*) whose robe-draped torso leaps majestically out of the stone; the other depicting an early-medieval building complete with a cute, miniature capital and also showing a demonic head looming over the structure, possibly forewarning about the impending end of the world in the apocalyptic year 1000.

But above all, the major reason I am here now is to once again view the marble columnar support and its marvellous carvings of the Apostles Matthias, Jude, and Simon, with which I have become so enamoured. There are two reasons for my fascination with this particular piece of sculpture: first, one of the figures – bearded and clutching a book, presumably the Bible, across his chest – bears a striking resemblance to me; and second, amazingly this piece of sculpture actually originates from the cathedral of Santiago de Compostela, the very goal of the pilgrimage I am about to undertake. The sculpture was a gift from the Republic of Spain to Harvard University brokered in the 1930s through Harvard scholar Arthur Kingsley Porter, the leading authority on Romanesque sculpture of the pilgrimage routes. Lifting up my large backpack, I pose, pilgrim staff in hand, and have my photograph taken in front of the column. Lastly, I lean my forehead into the protective glass encasement and, holding up a hand against the pane, give a silent promise to the stone Apostles that hopefully I will be able to give my blessings to their statuary compatriots, still in situ, at the great cathedral in Spain.

Leaving the museum, I chuckle over the suggestion raised by several of my colleagues that, given the miserable way the university has treated me, that I should somehow find a way to steal and then stuff the column into my backpack and repatriate it back to its home. Jokingly, they had also suggested that it is only through the physical act of carrying the half-ton weight along the entire length of the Camino that I could be assured of acquiring enough indulgences to counter both Harvard's well-known as well my own no-doubt copious sins.

♦♦♦

THE MAJOR PIAZZA IN COMPOSTELA is a-bustle with university students dashing back and forth between classes and social gatherings. After a several long months without exposure to such beautiful young women, Pasquale, feeling homesick for his life back in Paris, ignores the cathedral behind him as he watches the female students pass by, safely out of reach of all but his ogling eyes. For me, these lively scenes of urban academic life remind me of those back home in Harvard Square as well as of memories, both good and bad, of my time spent at that noted institution. The pilgrimage was more or less created by the great abbey of Cluny, which in terms of reputation and influence was somewhat akin to the Harvard of its day, both being very much concerned with self identity (perhaps it is no accident that the archaeological excavations of its ruined abbey in the middle of the last century were conducted by a Harvard professor).

✦✦✦

I AM STANDING IN A SMALL PARKING lot in the Galician coastal town of Muxía waiting for the bus to Finisterre after having determined that the walk there would offer few views of the coastline. And I can't believe my eyes. For there in front of me are a series of teardrop-shaped and treed mounds that look more or less identical to those of a well-known project in Minneapolis designed by a famous Harvard colleague of mine. I examine the mounds and am interested to see that at least they do not suffer from the same soil erosion problems that so plague the "dance of the drumlins" project back in America. Like most such landscape confections, however, the present project as well as its United States counterpart are ethically questionable in that they shed rather than collect and treat storm-water runoff, and thus contribute to, rather than mitigate, one of the most serious of all urban environmental problems. Looking at the mounds in front of me, I am saddened to reflect on my decade of time spent trying, often vainly, to instil concepts of environmental ethics in landscape students, faculty, and practitioners. As has frequently been written, as long as landscape architecture remains trapped in championing novel artistry at the expense of environmentally and socially conscious projects, it will continue to remain a marginalised profession in relation to architecture. Thankfully the bus soon arrives to whisk me away.

♦♦♦

FOR FIVE MINUTES I SCRAMBLE over the boulders and bedrock at Cabo Fisterra before finding an appropriate location in which to partake in my own end of the pilgrimage ritual. Due to the strong winds I had quickly abandoned the idea of using any of the exposed fire pits on the rocky outcrop. Besides, not only are these erroneously orientated toward the south rather than westward across the Atlantic but they are also too exposed to the eyes of casual visitors. Because I desire a secluded place for my private ritual I have made my way, using rock-climbing techniques, down from the summit crest to a small ledge that is out of both wind and sight. There, an enormous boulder sits precariously perched on the edge of cliffs that fall hundreds of metres to the crashing waves below. As no one in their right mind would attempt to negotiate such a difficult climb I am confident that I will be undisturbed.

It is customary practice for modern pilgrims upon reaching this final destination to burn their clothes or other personal items in a metaphorical gesture of leaving behind part of their old lives. Indeed, I would later learn that Maria, a pilgrim with whom I had travelled for many days, had burnt belongings from her late husband after having carried them all the way from their home in Austria. Poignantly, traversing the Camino had always being a dream of his, now completed through the actions of his widow. In my case, I withdraw crumpled sheets of paper from my pack and with a cigarette lighter carried all this way for just this purpose start a fire in a leeward crack at the base of the boulder. Then, in chronological sequence I burn the front-end pages from each of my desk calendars spanning my decade at Harvard. Before each page is consigned to the flames I read through and thus relive the most salient academic events of that particular year that I had previously transcribed from the body of calendar to these summary pages. It is as if I am experiencing time travel and catharsis simultaneously. Ritual completed, content with my life's journey so far, bitterness left smouldering in the ashes, I relax and listen to the waves that have blown here I imagine from my much-missed New England home.

Roads to Romantic Ruin

WHILE STARING AT THE ALABASTER sarcophagus in the Burgos cathedral, not for the first time during this pilgrimage do I remember the words, simple yet so apt at capturing so much, from an old Dylan song: "I hardly think about her most of the time." There looking up at me is supposed to be Doña Mencía Condestables. Instead I see the cold features of Mary Margaret on a frigid winter street in Toronto lingering in front of the subway entrance as she says a final goodbye. It had been a tumultuous relationship with her moving closer and then back-pedalling for over a year, struggling with her biological and emotional need for companionship while striving for an unencumbered existence as an independent woman of strong feminist leanings. As she descends the stairs on her way to the airport and from there to Japan, I look at the magazine rack and see a feature cover story about vacations in Spain. Avoiding rather than dealing with the present sadness from yet another "love's labour's lost", I flip through the issue and am surprised to discover an article on the Santiago pilgrimage about which I had read as a child. "Are you going to buy that or simply look at it for free?" barks the newsagent. "No, just browsing," I say putting the magazine down only to forget about Santiago for another seven years. Walking away I look down through the chain link fence to see the rear end of train as it leaves the station. "The blue light was my blues and the red light was my mind," I mumble to finish the lyric from Robert Johnson's classic paean to loss, *Love in Vain*. Now in Burgos I gently touch the sepulchre and move on into the darkness of the cathedral.

♦♦♦

WE FIND THE *ALBERGUE* IN CASTROJERIZ to be locked and so head back to the bar to continue drinking until such time as the manager returns. As the night progresses I find myself staring more and more at the humorous poster on the wall depicting how consumption of junk food is related to differences between the backsides of European and American women. Perhaps it is the many beers but as the evening progresses the shapely woman in the poster looks more and more like a past brief but deep love interest. My first glimpse of Rebecca was, like staring at the present poster now, fuelled by base emotions. There she was standing over the mailroom table in the McGill biology department in Montreal looking like a pin-up model dressed in a skin-tight top, short black skirt, and knee-high boots. Although I would later fall in love with her generous spirit and especially her poetic sensibility, at that moment it was all carnal. It was a surprise to discover after only a few friendly words that we shared interest in nature writers and the Romantic poets, thereby leading us to arrange a later rendezvous to continue the conversation. Much later I would learn more about her tragic background of familial abuse and also be moved, following many intimate times spent together, to formally propose, though by that point I was safe in knowing that the answer I would receive would be a "no." The use of that word "safe" speaks volumes. Looking again at the poster as Amador goes up for another round of beer I think back to a morning of revelation several years ago in a hotel room in California when, setting aside an earlier Camino account that I had been reading, I came to realise just how many of my failed loves seemed to have been touched by Saint James and his pilgrimage. Case in point:

reflecting back again to that first meeting with Rebecca, I remember that as she left the room and my heartbeat began to return to normal, I had glanced down at the pile of unsorted mail on the table and saw a large postcard from the Uffizi of Botticelli's *The Birth of Venus*. Women and scallop shells...the story of my life.

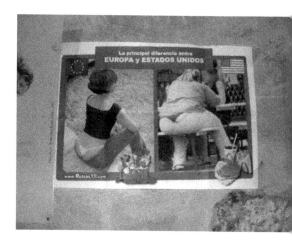

◆◆◆

IT IS NIGHT AND I HAVE BEEN slowly walking around the empty hallways surrounding the cloisters in the monastery-cum-hotel of San Zoilo in Carrión for over an hour when I enter the mortuary chapel. Although there are dozens of sarcophagi, one with a simple surface effigy grabs my attention. It is of a smooth-faced, wide-eyed woman of notable beauty and obvious grace. With high cheekbones and hair tucked back behind her ears the image resembles Laura, the object of a brief and sorrowful infatuation that ultimately led to my present, decadal-long state of going on strike from all things romance related. Studying the face pulls me back in time to when I was lured by the promise of lasting romance but was then used as labour to help with moving materials for the construction of her seaside writing retreat before being abruptly dismissed, my company no longer required for either task. Eventually I would be able to use some of her wonderful writing that emerged from that retreat as a foreword for a book of mine, so that in the end my time had not been entirely wasted. Bothered by my still obvious bitterness about the relationship of almost a decade ago, I sit down on the edge of the tomb in the dark chapel, noting as I do the eerie coincidence that the music now playing on my iPod is a Requiem mass purchased from a monastery that I had previously visited while walking on one of the French pilgrimage routes. Reflecting that If ever there were a time for forgiveness it should be now, I gaze upon the facial likeness and concentrate on remembering my one-time friend's many positive traits, and eventually do reach a state of peace with the past.

I stare again at the funerary image and pull out my photocopied pages from an architectural guide for the Camino in order to determine if the

identity of the woman is mentioned. Suddenly I freeze in remembrance. "Oh for Heaven's sake. Not again," I mumble, shaking my head in disbelief. In a way, however, I am not surprised to recollect that I had met and immediately fallen in love with Laura when she was visiting Cambridge on a book tour. Her emotion-packed lecture on the perceptions of nature had taken place on an evening only a day after my attendance at another book tour lecture given by two New England academics who are the very authors of the detailed guide whose pages I now hold in my hands. Looking about for movement among the shadows in the crypt chapel I am spooked by the convergence and immediately leave for the comfort of my room, hoping that all ghosts have been left behind.

✦✦✦

DETERMINATION SHINES IN THE FACE of the statue of the pilgrim, her walking staff in the form of a cross, scallop shells sewn onto her cloak, and a travel scrip at her side. It is starting to rain as I pause beside the sculpture in the little park leading out of Samos, still unhappy at having found the great monastery to be closed. Glancing at the statue again I am painfully reminded of the fact that as initially conceived I was to have undertaken this pilgrimage eight years before and with Leslie by my side. I remember our first meeting across a lunch table at an environmental conference in Niagara Falls; those penetrating blue eyes and crinkled cheeks when she smiled. A few days later we shared drinks in the hotel bar on the last night of the conference, floating innocent sounding but purposely exploratory questions back and forth as we tried to establish whether the depth of our commonalties would be enough to be worth exploring once we parted ways the next day. She described living through a "dark night of the soul" and finding solace in the words of Thomas More. Only long afterward do I find out that she had been using a catch phrase popular amongst her therapy group that bore no connection whatsoever to the classic sixteenth-century Christian text that I was now carrying with me on this walk, and that the author of whom she referred was not the one-time Lord Chancellor of England and writer of *Utopia* but a New Age self-help guru with a closely similar surname.

Soon other conference attendees came trickling into the bar. Feeling a little sorry for one such, with his affected beret and obvious absence of companions, I beckoned him to come join us, glancing at Leslie first for her approval. The black irony of this gesture of kindness on my part would only become realised months later when I was suddenly informed that the two of them had in fact been having an affair for much of time that she and I had been involved in planning our future lives together. I shake my head in an attempt to prevent a purposeless journey down that too often travelled negative pathway of green jealousy. Instead, as I leave the statue and its painful associations behind, I force myself to go over again that wonderful first evening of falling in love when the three of us and another who later joined our table, each shared plans about how we would mark the upcoming new millennium. At that time I had discussed how that for me such a celebration must involve something to do with both Europe and Christianity given that that was where and what the first millennium had been about; and that, not

being a traditionally devote Christian myself, this problem of identity and purpose could be accommodated by undertaking the famous pilgrimage walk across northern Spain. "What a wonderful idea," the group had enthused at the time. Later, after Leslie and I had became romantically involved, this was to have been the first shared adventure we (or at least I) had imagined in a life of many such. But now here I am instead, alone on the Camino a few days short of my fiftieth birthday, slogging along through the rain toward Sarria, and struggling to prevent solitude from sliding into self-indulgent loneliness.

♦♦♦

THE PAINTED FACIAL FEATURES of the attractive woman — the lipstick-reddened lips and rouged blushing cheeks — are in sharp contrast to the characteristic whiteness of the rest of the stone sculptures in the Santiago de Compostela museum. The resemblance of the statue to an early love is likewise, startling. Suddenly I am wrenched back in time and place to that early morning in a tiny hotel room in southern California several years before where I had spent several hours reading a Canadian's pilgrimage narrative. In the section when she mentions visiting the Cathedral Church of Saint James in Toronto, I reflect backward to the pain experienced during my own visit to the same church. For it was there late one summer evening more than two decades before, while sitting on an outside bench in the lovely landscaped church common, that my fledgling romantic life took its first severe blow, one it could be argued from which it had never completely recovered. Fellow graduate student Sarah, she of the beautifully large expressive eyes resembling those of the statue now in front of me, and with whom I had had a friendship, romantic in every sense of the word except for its formal consummation, slowly and in embarrassment given her behaviour toward me, told of her sudden acceptance of a proposal offer to marry someone else. Decades later, I am unable to recollect any of her apologetic words. Standing now in Compostela in front of this statue, what is most memorable about that wretched Toronto night is of staring up at the profile of the majestic steeple of the Saint James church silhouetted against the surrounding bright lights of the downtown office buildings, and of the sudden irrational feeling, forgotten

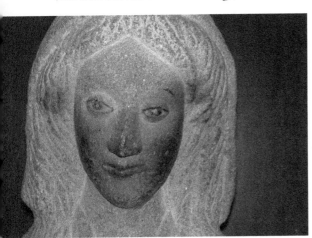

until that moment of revelation years later in the California hotel room, that I hated and vowed to never have anything to do with the Saint, as if it was he rather than my own failings that were at the root of my then miserable state. And yet here I am in the Saint's own museum. I smile ruefully as I leave the statue to seek out the Apostle from whom to ask forgiveness.

The Road to Heaven

MUCH OF THIS EARLY PORTION of the Camino between Logrono and Navarrete closely parallels the busy N-120 highway. I put on my headphones and turn up the medieval pilgrimage music in attempt to drown out the din of the constant stream of large semi-trailers rattling by. A mindset of ambivalence toward the surroundings and impatience at finishing the day leaves me surprised when I encounter one of the most truly inspirational sights along the entire Way. For a distance of more than a kilometre the fence separating the walking trail from the highway is covered with hundreds of wooden crosses that have been interwoven amongst the metal lattice. Whereas some are little more than a couple of twigs, others are comprised of metre-long branches. The effect is most beautiful in those sections of fence covered in green plastic through which the bright sun shines, silhouetting the crosses.

My feelings toward organised Christianity have always been of hesitation and apprehension. Although faith, a belief in hope, that most admirable of human aspirations, has always deeply attracted me, it is the unquestioning certitude with which the dogma is often purveyed that so unsettles me. But here it is undeniably moving to see the humble demonstrations of faith from the many believing pilgrims who have walked before me and especially the manner through which that faith is expressed with such celebratory joy. Foregoing my customary observer status – a recognised safety mechanism to avoid religious disappointment and, it must be admitted, the potentially more alarming possibility of life-altering acceptance – I pause, and looking about the ground and selecting several twigs, construct my own cross high up on the fence of hope. Striding away I cannot but help to reflect upon the obvious metaphor offered by the presence of the fence. Will the physical act of engaging in this pilgrimage with its acknowledged ability to change, for many, affairs of the head to those of the heart, be enough in my case to pull me down from that hitherto comfortable fence-top perch of spiritual ambivalence?

♦♦♦

BURGOS CATHEDRAL, THAT GIANT GOTHIC spiritual ship rising up out of the sea of grain at the edge of *meseta*, leaves me cold. Even putting aside my architectural prejudice that equates pilgrimage to the Romanesque, the sand-blasted newness of the outside façade, the closed-off cloisters, and especially the forced unidirectional flow paths inside has not predisposed me to being in a receptive mood for my present attendance at the evening mass. The absence of song makes me nostalgic for services I'd attended along the various pilgrimage routes in France when the acoustic accompaniments had often leave me on the edge of tears following a hard day of walking. Nothing like that here.

Above all I simply cannot get past the image on the gilded and gaudy Baroque *retablo* that soars up behind the altar. Every time the priest says something that I struggle to translate as being about peace and love, my eyes move up to the incongruous but now familiar image of Saint James, not as the gospel-preaching Apostle, but rather as Santiago *Matamoros*, the slayer of Moors. And there he sits atop his horse waving his sword over his head like a frenzied maniac while below a group of defeated Muslims cower as they are about to be dispatched. All sense of piety is lost while I reflect on this inescapable and unsavoury element of the Camino Francés: its creation by the powerful abbey of Cluny as a vehicle for encouraging the Christian Reconquest of Spain, and their fervent religious intolerance in marked contrast to the inter-faith harmony of Andalusia in the south. Having spent considerable time in the Arabic Middle East and fearful of the rising tide of *Christianism* (a different thing altogether from Christianity) of the American religious right, I feel incredibly uncomfortable worshipping in front of such an image. Never more

so when a few minutes later I notice – certainly it must be my overtired state and overactive imagination or simply some trick of the light – that the facial features of Saint James begin to resemble those of that contemporary crusading defender of the faith and monetary interests: George W. Bush! Feeling suddenly nauseous, I decide to forego receiving communion and duck out of the cathedral.

❖❖❖

ALTHOUGH IT IS JUST AFTER NOON when I arrive at the Hotel Monasterio San Zoilo on the outskirts of Carrión de los Condes, the reasonable off-season price and knowledge that I have yet to treat myself to staying in one of these hotels converted from historic buildings makes me decide to end my day's walk. After all, is not this whole outing supposed to be a celebration of my birthday? I therefore indulge in a hot bath (only the second such during the last two weeks) and have my first sit-down restaurant meal on the pilgrimage. Then trying not to feel guilty about my wayward companions who are still plodding along somewhere out there in the cold wind and spitting rain, I begin to explore the enormous monastery-cum-hotel. The halls are oddly empty of any guests or staff and I admire the spectacular ceiling carvings of the Renaissance cloister, touted to be amongst the best in Europe. At the entrance to the chapel are a collection of capitals whose placement at eye level allows their finely carved details to be closely examined. Opening a nondescript doorway off the second floor hallway, I find a small, simple chapel with rough-hewn benches and an odd little ceiling cupola. I have been listening to choral chants on my iPod, some recorded at the famed San Domingo de Silos monastery located only a hundred kilometres away. The music helps me to sense the age of the building and of the pilgrimage itself. Later in the evening while still in such a heightened mood of historical appreciation I leave my room for another walkabout which will culminate in one of the most moving experiences of the entire pilgrimage and one of most intense spiritual moments I have ever felt inside a church.

For an hour I slowly circle the cloister, listening again to medieval music on my headphones while I move in and out of the shadows cast by the bright moonlight. Again, not a single person is seen. I am alone but for the ghostly imagined steps of monks who for centuries had strode over these same smoothened slabs of stone. In the dark and with atmospheric music in my ears, the whole scene assumes an eerie *Name of the Rose*-esque or Brother Cadfael fantasy as I imagine onetime monks shuffling about after Compline. I find my way to the bar

and enjoy several beers while catching up on my journalling. On the way back, finding the cloisters finally closed for the night, I ascend to the second floor to continue my perambulation. There I once again enter the small chapel seen earlier in the day, and turning off the music, spend a reflective half hour sitting in the twilight. In the enveloping silence an amazing peace descends and all past difficulties as well as future anxieties are swept away. All that matters is the present pilgrimage and my feelings of gratitude in having been able to experience this gift at this time in my life.

It is upon throwing back my head in thanks that I'm surprised to make out the faint outline of a small, 'secret' door closed flush with the unfinished wall of the chapel. Odd that I had not noticed it before, I think, as I slowly make my way to it in the twilight. With an easy twist it swings open into complete blackness. Completely puzzled about where it might lead I ever so tentatively edge forward as if passing through a portal into another dimension or the far depths of space. The latter seems apt for though I cannot see a thing there is an inescapable impression of enveloping vastness, the slight sounds of my footsteps on the creaky wooden floor echoing back from across unseen expanses. I back up to the chapel and crossing it open the hallway door just enough to allow some light to penetrate. Returning through the secret door (will I find Narnia on the other side?) I am amazed to discover that the small chapel whose cupola I had thought to project into the sky is in fact attached to and entirely contained *within* the body of the large church and sepulchre which I had visited earlier. In fact, the portal through which I had just passed actually enters onto the second floor choir. I move to the edge of the balcony and stare into space down the length of the darkened nave. Already struck dumb from the surprise discovery I am overwhelmed when a few moments later as if on cue, the clouds outside dissipate enough to allow moonlight to bathe the distant *retablo* behind the alter in a soft yellow glow as if just for me. My hands clutch the rickety wooden balustrade in emotion. For the next hour while listening to Einhorn's haunting *Voices of Light* on the iPod, I move back and forth between the intimacy of the chapel and the great open expanse of the church, repeatedly going over the physical actions and attempting to recapture the experience of the surprise. Finally, I close and return the secret door back to its occult wall niche and sit once more in the dark chapel moved to tears by the experience before retiring to my room.

❖❖❖

Rabanal is a sleepy mountain village filled with ancient fieldstone buildings, one of which is the twelfth-century church of Santa Maria de la Asuncion. Inside, I, two male pilgrims whispering softly in French, and three local women dressed in black, all wait in the cold for the Compline service to begin. The small, ill-lit church is in a decrepit state. Large sections of the floor are missing through which several broken caskets can be seen in front of a small statue of the crucified Christ. I'm grateful to have brought my gloves but find I have to keep wiggling my sock-covered toes to keep them warm in their open sandals. Outside, the searching December wind can be heard howling down from the surrounding, gloomy hills. Still, a feeling of overwhelming peace permeates the chilled air which I try to draw in through deep breaths as if it could somehow provide palatable sustenance. Which perhaps it can. The tiny congregation respectfully stands as the two Benedictine brothers enter. We wait as they light candles, open their hymn missals, and position themselves facing each other on two wooden chairs in front of the simple altar. And then – there is no other way to describe it – a tiny piece of heaven descends as the monks begin a Gregorian chant, the sad tones of Compline marking the end of another day in this village along the Way. Rarely have I ever experienced such a feeling of complete synesthesia. The intermeshing of the slowly cadenced sound of the beautiful medieval chant, the haunting image of the swirling puffs of the brothers' exhaled breath in the candle light, and the smell of the dank earth and rotten timber beams combine in a rapturous physicality. Following the brief service and after the brothers, pilgrims, and locals have all departed, I linger, sitting in the cold by the light of a single flickering candle. And there, for the first time in years, I pray.

◆◆◆

Suddenly the pilgrim falls to his knees. Alone in the middle of the nave of the cavernous cathedral in Santiago he gently places his wooden staff by his side, and with large pack still on his back, stretches out his arms in front toward the distant altar. I can see his lips move but am too distant to hear what is being said though it is likely, I presume, to be some sort of thanks. A patch on his pack displaying the German flag suggests that he could have been walking for as long as several months to arrive at this destination. Like a frozen statue he maintains this position for over a minute before slowly lowering his head in supplication for an additional minute. He then regains his feet and moves on to the Apostle's shrine.

I'm both moved and disturbed by the scene. Why am I not there on my knees beside this fellow pilgrim? Why must I always maintain this protective status as an observer rather than as a participant, this illusion that as in other affairs of the heart that I am safe as long as I remain distant? Am I therefore a complete failure as a pilgrim? Has the last month then been a waste of both time and effort?

Later, trying to ignore yet another statue of Santiago *Matamoros* trampling heathens to death, I too enter the sanctuary tomb of Saint James. Denied being able to complete the rituals at the Pórtico of Glory I am keen to be able to do so here. Tucked in behind the altar is a little alcove, the *camarin* or image chamber, to which pilgrims and visitors ascend along a narrow stone staircase worn smooth by the multitudinous feet of the faithful. A young priest sits on a stool in the corner reading from a Bible as people file by and reach their arms out to embrace and kiss a small statue of the seated Apostle. I wait my turn as an elderly Spanish woman and her daughter, speaking in hushed tones, perform their ritual and move on. Looking about to see that no one else is coming up the stairs behind me I stare at the Baroque silverwork back of the statue and then at the priest who has not raised his eyes up from his reading. Hesitantly I reach out my hands but simply cannot perform the act, my rationalist's mind unable to purge itself of the knowledge that the entire pilgrimage is ultimately built on fraud, the discovery of the relics of Saint James following his magical…sorry *miraculous* transport here from the Holy Land being at its root really a political creation. Perhaps had this been an individual like Saint Francis, worthy of admiration, and the location been like Assisi, where one could reasonably be assured that the tomb actually did contain the bodily relics of the touted saint, then I would be much more willing to participate. But here, now, the best I can do, more in homage to the historicity rather than the religiosity of the pilgrimage, is to put aside my reservations and reach out both hands and bowing my head but stopping far short of touching it to the statue, offer a simple whisper of thanks…to whom or what, I know not.

I return to the nave and assume a seat in front of the transept and altar and wait for the pilgrim mass to begin. Gradually the pews fill up with locals, visitors, and pilgrims, the presence of large backpacks on several of whom indicates that they have just arrived after spending a last night at the Monte del Gozo hostel. It is a joy to greet one-time companions, some who have not been seen for several days. With much laughter and many hugs and kisses, we are an unruly bunch that have to be hushed several times by cathedral officials. Finally, I sit on a pew surrounded by these individuals with whom I've shared so many wonderful experiences. When the priest, reading out the countries of origin for those pilgrims who like me had arrived and registered the previous day, says "Canada", I cannot hold back the tears. Filled with pride, humility, and above all happiness, moments later when returning to my seat following Communion I reach out and warmly touch my companions in passing, accepting of and comfortable with my own established belief system. Seeing the smiling faces and generous well-wishes in the eyes of those about me, I realise that for me this is enough. This is all that is needed for my outer pilgrimage to have been a success: leaving a positive memory of myself in the heads and possibly the hearts of these, my fellow companions of the Way.

ROUND NUMBERS HAVE ALWAYS SEEMED ATTRACTIVE, seducing us as they do into the belief that somehow they are of greater import than those sad, odd numbers immediately on either side which instead leave us feeling slightly uncomfortable through impressions left of either their unreached or over-shot states. And this is no more so than with respect to that most auspicious of birthdays: one's fiftieth. What better way to mark this important event than through a pilgrimage that would allow the opportunity to reminisce and reflect back on one's half-century of life. It is surprising, therefore, that of the dozens of Camino accounts in my library only a few have been so inspired.

Pilgrimages to Santiago de Compostela really begin long in advance of the first steps ever taken on Spanish or European soil. Day after day I would sit in my home library and accompanied by glasses of full-bodied Spanish wine and listening to medieval pilgrimage music would pour over guidebooks and pilgrimage accounts as I planned my walk. I soon assembled a large spreadsheet of long columns in which the suggested (from the guidebooks) and realised (from the diaries) daily stages and mileages were laid out. My rationale for this was that I wanted to arrive at the destination – which for me had always been

Finisterre, the end of the world, and not Compostela, the cathedral of Santiago – on my precise birth date anniversary in late December. So I spent a considerable amount of time working the Way backward in order to know when to start my walk and book my plane tickets. It was not a straightforward task of planning as the majority of the journal accounts came from elderly individuals or those whom seemed to have had little prior hiking experience. And it was to these that the guidebooks catered in their suggested itineraries. Confident in my own physical and mental capabilities, I planned out an approximate itinerary based on the achievement of much greater daily distances than the established norm.

Once my plans had been made, I had thought that I could settle back and relax until departure. But this was not to be. Instead, preparing for the winter walk I packed, unpacked, and repacked up to a dozen times as I repeatedly placed, removed, and sometimes replaced various items of warm-weather apparel. And through this I became compulsive in my repeated reweighing of the backpack as iteratively it subsumed or ejected certain belongings depending on my mood with regard to their presumed essentialness or luxuriousness.

Like a marathoner just before the race, I grew anxious, eager above all else to simply be off and moving, dreaming of that moment when I could abandon myself willingly to the forward impulse. Throughout, I inquired from friends and acquaintances about what they had done for their own fiftieth birthdays and became surprised by the mostly unmemorable, lacklustre ways that they had marked those occasions. And so, when the morning came for my departure in mid-November it was with a glad heart that I literally bounded down the stairs and out the door for what I came to think of as being my month-long birthday celebration.

Much later, returning home after the pilgrimage, I pay the taxi driver and head back up those same stairs late on the eve of my birthday. Dumping my pack and warmly greeting the cat I settle in with a bottle of celebratory wine and begin to sort through the month of accumulated mail. And there – I had been warned by friends beforehand of what to expect – was my letter from the AARP asking me to become a member. Nowhere in the brochure did they actually spell out what the acronym stood for or what the organisation represented. I smile at the subterfuge. Refilling my glass and stroking my glue-cat who had missed me as much as I did her, I ponder the American Association of Retired Persons, finding it remarkable that anyone could be wealthy enough to be able to retire at fifty.

✦✦✦

With the exception of a very few sections, the Camino Francés is an unchallenging enterprise, more akin to a Sunday afternoon walk than a serious mountain trek. A good deal of the terrain is flat, much of the landscape more sublime than picturesque, many of the structures of perhaps more historical than aesthetic interest. And it is all these reasons, as well as the fact that there is now so much waymarking it is almost impossible to become lost, that make this pilgrimage such a wonderful experience. For in the absence of a constant bombardment of external stimuli it is the inner journey that often predominates. And so, slogging through a wet afternoon and in such a reflective mood I spot the statue.

From the distance there is little to distinguish the tiny village of Atapuerca from others along the Way. The statue, a representation of Europe's earliest humans found nearby, indicates that this is a location of global significance to merit its UNESCO World Heritage Site status. Thinking of deep time makes me ponder the seemingly short expanse of my own little life now past its halfway mark. Staring at the statue of a half-a-million-year-old hominid whose lifespan would have been only three to four decades makes me feel the ephemeral nature of personal time and the relative insignificance of my own accomplishments to date. What might this early ancestor have undertaken and succeeded at during his brief life? What had he hoped for or dreamed of? How remarkably different were or were not his thoughts from those of us today? Would he too have perhaps felt disappointed at a life that might have been only half-way or worse, half-heartedly lived? No replies come from the mute statue and so I pull my hood up over my wet hat and head off to find a refuge from the rain, wondering if my own life at fifty, is half empty or half full?.

❖❖❖

NOT FAR FROM THE PICTURESQUE REMAINS of a ruined church in a hamlet before Burgos I laugh at the cute wayside mural of the ruined pilgrim. There on the side of a building the struggling, over-laden fellow is shown daydreaming about reclining naked in an armchair back at home. How many times along the Way have I too felt the pull of home memories, those often taken-for-granted little idiosyncrasies of comfort that support and shape even the most wayward of lives? Luckily I have been fortunate up to this point to have avoided many of the aches and pains that seem to traumatise so many Camino pilgrims. My feet are free of blisters, something I attribute to liberal applications of Vaseline each morning as well as the use of well-travelled hiking boots. My shoulders do occasionally smart from the jostling weight of a too-heavy pack but that is really more discomfort than pain. Only my hips hurt in a chronic fashion, something I attribute to the rake-thin mattresses in many of the *albergues*. This has necessitated the nightly consumption of Tylenol PM to enable sleep. The few physical health problems I have are those I brought with me: cardio arrhythmia and gastric IBS, symptoms of both ameliorated through the daily ingestion of drugs. Leaving the mural behind I reflect on a life of half a decade ago when I might have not consumed a single pill in an entire month and if so it was likely to have been an aspirin to counter a hangover. How different things are today with the middle-aged body requiring up to half a dozen daily pills in its struggle to maintain a semblance of normalcy. Still, I have been amazed at how easily the soreness felt at the end of a day's walking can be dispelled by the curative power of nothing more than a night's sleep. Each morning I arise eager to be off once more on the Camino.

❖❖❖

THE CARVINGS OF SKULLS AND CROSSBONES on the outside walls of the derelict church of Santiago de los Caballeros are located right along the street in Castrojeriz along which pilgrims have passed for nearly a thousand years. The carvings are there to warn all passers-by of the inevitability of death. As if such were needed in the Middle Ages when death was omnipresent, possibly never more than a single bad harvest away. Today, in our sheltered and sanitised lives, death seems remote. I let my fingers trace the weather-worn outlines of the carvings and think of those friends and colleagues (thankfully no relatives) who had not reached their fiftieth year. I think too of all the risks I have knowingly inserted myself into; those brushes with the Reaper that I have thwarted; those balancing points of delicate dependency while climbing, while Scuba diving, while polar exploring, while living a life of full of adventure and travel at the edge; those activities engaged in that have threatened and thereby enriched my life. I am suddenly reminded of a friend who while awaiting news of whether her cancer was in remission went for a holiday hike during a storm atop a ridge in the Cotswolds and thought that if a lightning bolt were to suddenly strike her in that beautiful location then she would have been content with her life lived up to that point. Looking about me at the wonderfully beautiful town stretching up the hillside, now suffused in an almost unbelievable bright yellow-orange alpenglow from the setting sun, I too realise that if my heart would suddenly stop right then and there in front of the glowing carving, that I too would be at peace for decisions made and opportunities taken. To be here and now was gift enough; no more ever need be asked for; no more ever need be expected; everything else that life may offer, a complete luxury…extra.

Later that evening I leave the *refugio* for a meditative stroll about the town and by happenstance (really?) find myself back in front of the death carving. I stare up at the stars now appearing and am reminded that this pilgrim route has occasionally been referred to as the "Road of the Stars" since it seemed to follow the wide arc made by the Milky Way stretching off toward the west. I reach out to touch the carving and am surprised to find it still retaining warmth long after the sun has set. I also think of the gloomy lyrics from a song by the

fittingly named (given the present circumstances) group, Dead Can Dance: "The stars we see in the night sky have been dead for centuries." So here we have the Road of Stars leading to Compostela, etymologically derived according to some from the Latin *compostum*, or cemetery. The Way of death leading to death. And it doesn't end there. For legends have it that the route had pre-Christian origins as the Celtic death journey of the setting (i.e. dying) sun to the still-named Costa de Morte (coast of death) that overlooked the Mare Tenebrosum or Sea of Darkness/Abyss of Death as the Romans called the ocean which we now name Atlantic after a lost and dead mystical civilisation. And on these happy notes I return to the hostel nervous as I walk through the empty streets that I might encounter the hooded and scythe-wielding character from Bergman's film. That night, struggling to fall asleep in my melancholic mood, I am haunted by Cormac McCarthy's words from his post-apocalyptic novel, aptly titled *The Road*: "Out on the roads the pilgrims sank down and fell over and died and the bleak and shrouded earth went trundling past the sun and returned again as trackless and as unremarked as the path of any nameless sisterworld in the ancient dark beyond." I fall asleep contemplating cheerful metaphysical thoughts of the possible infinity of darkness at the end of life and of what might have existed before the Big Bang.

✦✦✦

THE SIGN ON THE OUTSKIRTS OF Mansila de las Mulas is a joy to see. For two long weeks and hundreds of kilometres I have seen nothing but signs indicating that I have been walking along the "Camino de Santiago", a moniker which, though popularly used today to designate the Way, is of doubtful historicity. But here finally is a sign that accurately identifies the route by its medieval title: "El camino francés" – the way of the French. For it is the French, through the great abbey at Cluny, that largely created the Way. And it is from France where the vast majority of pilgrims originated. The Camino Francés has personal resonance of course as my namesake road. So whereas a handful of books have been published variously titled or subtitled "My Camino", none until now has had such a close affiliation.

Rocky Roads

THE FIELD IN FRONT OF ME IS RIDDEN with thousands of black boulders that had once served as foundations for houses. In the distance lies the receding shoreline of the great lake shimmering in the hot desert sun. These are the much-debated ruins often identified as being those of the Biblical town of Bethsaida in upper Galilee, home to the Apostle James the Greater, he who would later be martyred and miraculously transported to Galicia. Given my long-held dream of someday completing the Camino to the Saint's burial place I had thought it important while in the neighbourhood to come to this location where it all began; to start my future planned pilgrimage – to be at the source as it were. Hopping off the bicycle I wander over the silent ruins and try to imagine the bustling fishing village of two millennia ago when the site witnessed miracles (Christ's feeding of the five thousand and healing of a blind man took place nearby). Historically there is really no support for the contention that James ever left the Levant for Spain, his initial preaching mission and the later transport of bodily remains there, being apocryphal. Scanning the ruins I bend down and pick up a stone from what might once have been a passageway or street between the rubble piles of several buildings. Placing it in my daypack I remount the bike and begin to pedal back to Capernaum hoping that someday I might have the opportunity to carry the stone to Compostela. If the Saint didn't get there himself, I reflect ruefully, perhaps a stone that he might once have walked over can make the journey.

More than a decade later it is late at night when I leave the hotel and make my way through the now silent streets of Compostela to the Plaza del Obradorio, considered together with Venice's Piazza de San Marco, to be Europe's grandest cathedral-fronted public space. I pull the stone out of my pocket after having removed it earlier from a deep recess of my backpack where it had resided during the last month of walking. The slight rain of this

PART II | 137

cold December night is so different from the blistering sun and oppressive below-sea-level heat of that distant day from when the stone was collected on the shore of the Sea of Galilee. Looking about to make sure no one is watching I jump into the small garden at the edge of the plaza and there, underneath the sparkling Christmas-light-adorned trees, bury the stone from Saint James' birthplace. Now finally there is some veracity to the claim that something from Galilee is present in Santiago de Compostela! The 'miracle' in this particular case of 'translation' is that anyone would actually be loony enough to carry a stone for seven hundred kilometres along a route where fellow pilgrims were famous for doing everything possible to reduce their ported weights, some even going as far as to shorten the lengths of their toothbrushes. I turn and admire the bulk of the cathedral silhouetted under a halo of stars and smile before heading back to my hotel room, mission accomplished.

❖❖❖

THE TWENTY-FIVE KILOMETRE springtime walk to the iconic lake from my home in Cambridge, Massachusetts has been lovely. Making my way along the forested shoreline to a set of steps leading down to the water I peel off my sweaty outer clothes and plunge into the clear waters of Walden Pond, referred to by its onetime resident, Thoreau, as being one of earth's eyes, looking into which the beholder could measure the depth of his own true nature. Opting for hedonism over narcissism, I enjoy a refreshing swim and then emerge and dress before continuing along the shoreline to the site where Thoreau had

situated his historic cabin; a site of such great resonance that it can be said to have transformed the way in which we look at and appreciate our non-human world. There beside the fenced outline of the onetime cabin and woodpile is a large mound of rocks and stones that have been deposited over many decades by 'pilgrims' visiting from all over the world. On the hill I turn over rocks until I find several with faded, indiscernible messages scratched on their undersides to their environmental hero; messages from across time and space. The ritual is that an individual would have brought a stone from his or her distant home to add to the growing pile. In this case, instead of depositing a stone, I collect one free of words and of unknown provenance that I will later take for a walk across Spain. Taking a stone for a walk – it sounds crazy but given that there are few writers who have so championed the art of sauntering as Thoreau, I don't think the master scribe would mind the dislocation of one of his many votive offerings in this manner. After all, to "saunter", he believed, was to walk in the Holy Land of saints.

Much later, the ascent up Monte Irago has been somewhat anticlimactic after being spooked the night before by a poster in the hostel which showed the entire Camino in exaggerated vertical scale. Still it is moving to finally reach the pass of Foncebadón, which at over fifteen hundred metres, is the highest elevation on the Camino. My eyes and legs are immediately drawn to the towering iron cross set high atop a wooden stake emerging from an enormous pile of stones and boulders. I approach the pile in reverence for it is one of the oldest monuments along the Way. I have long waited for this particular moment and, dropping my pack, forage into an outer pocket where this morning in preparation I had placed the small stone collected and transported all the way from Thoreau's cabin site at Walden Pond. Celts often marked mountain passes with such a cairn, itself a Gaelic word, a tradition that was also

adopted by the Romans who referred to such stone piles as *murias* after Mercury, the patron god of travellers. Since Christian times, the tradition has been for pilgrims to carry a stone from their home along the length of the Camino in symbolism of the weight of sins carried upon their souls. And at this location, in an act of contrition, the pilgrims would leave their stones behind in much the same way that they would hope to shed their sins through engaging in the act of pilgrimage.

While other, historically illiterate pilgrims relax, drinking from their water bottles after the arduous climb and watch me with puzzled looks on their faces, I scramble up the pile. Then, with a hand placed upon the famous Cruz de Ferro, I gently kiss the stone and drop it on top of the pile, watching it bounce its way downward until it reaches a final resting place nestled amidst a group of large rocks. And so there rests a stone from some unknown location, transported in reverence to Walden Pond by one pilgrim, and then taken from there and carried along the Camino Francés by another, to be partnered now with stones of unknown origin transported by manifold pilgrims from around the world, all in a ritual extending back to ancient times.

◆ ◆ ◆

ALTHOUGH SOME MIGHT THINK it sacrilege, I reach down and select a small stone from the many thousands comprising the pile beneath the Cruz de Ferro and walking down the hill place it in my backpack. Reciprocity, I think; that is when the pilgrimage will finally be concluded: back there at home, not here in Spain.

And so it is that early in the morning of my fiftieth birthday when, still shivering from the ocean plunge of a few hours before and despite still feeling jet-lagged from my arrival home last night, I drive to Walden Pond on a bitterly cold, albeit sunny, New England winter day. As the shoreline trail is treacherously icy I opt to walk across the frozen and snow-covered surface of the pond itself. Only a few birds are my companions; the only other sounds are those of the hardened snow crunching beneath my feet. As I make my way to the cabin site I am excited for this is the moment that I have so looked forward to over all these many weeks. Approaching the pile of stones and dropping to my knees in the snow, I carefully insert the stone collected from Spain but of unknown provenance deep into an interstitial space. I stand up and pulling out a hip flask of single malt, toast that great walker, Henry, and also myself upon reaching the end of this month-long birthday celebration.

It is now over. For a month I have diligently followed my walking shadow westward into the setting sun. Now I leave the historic pond, moving eastward to my home and new life. An hour later, having along the way (now the little "w") bought a fresh-smelling Christmas tree and all the fixings for a grand birthday feast, I enter my house and parroting Tolkien's Samwise at the end of his own adventure, announce out loud: "Well, I'm home."

✦✦✦

It has been raining steadily all day and I am soaked to the point of hypothermia. Behind me rising up into the fog is the O'Cebreiro massif. In front, also in the fog and hopefully not too far away is the destination of today's miserable walk, the valley town of Tricastela. I struggle to keep my eyes open in the blowing rain, scanning either side of the road for an appropriate outcrop. Finally, I spot a section of roadside cut in which the limestone slabs have been exfoliated. I leave the tarmac and slide down into the steep ditch, now flowing with runoff. This is insane I think as I climb up to the cut and grab a largish piece of stone before returning to the road and burying it into my already full and far-too-heavy pack. I begin to shiver and suddenly feel like Admiral Scott, diligently collecting and carrying those heavy Antarctic rock specimens as he slogged off toward his demise after losing the race to Amundsen. I glance up at the ridge paralleling the road but do not see my fellow pilgrims who, without stopping to collect rocks, are no doubt well ahead on their more direct route. But there is a precedence for this act of rock transport, crazy as it may seem. The earliest medieval guidebook of the Santiago pilgrimage advised pilgrims to likewise pick up and carry pieces of limestone from the Tricastela area.

Three days and ninety kilometres later I am at Castañeda, the historic destination for jettisoning the rock. For it is here that the large lime furnaces were once located. Early medieval pilgrims carried pieces of limestone over this interval in order to feed the furnaces. This was an important task since it enabled the production of mortar that was essential for constructing and repairing the great cathedral of the Apostle in Compostela. As all traces of the furnaces have long since gone, I simply find a field and release my weighty companion, flinging it as far away as possible. Shaking my head in disbelief, I cannot but laugh at the absurdity of my own silly bit of historical re-enactment.

♦♦♦

Satiated after the large, celebratory lunch of scallops, octopus, and wine, I leave the terrace and head down to the wonderfully quaint working harbour of Finisterre. There, scouting around the tidal pools I select and pocket a nicely shaped stone from the end of the Old World.

It is more than two months later and I am back at Plum Island, Massachusetts on the edge of the New World. As has been my custom for the last twelve years, it being February 29th, I have decided to be truant from responsibilities and to celebrate this gift of an extra day by doing something special. And so I walk along the beautiful sand beach and spend time staring out at the north Atlantic, reminiscing. Pilgrimage, so it's said, is supposed to help shape the direction of one's life, the outer world experiences providing those talismans of reference to guide the development of one's inner world. Looking back now across the sea of distance and time as I roll the wave-smoothened Galician stone in my hand I continue to realise, as I have done every day since returning, that the month spent on pilgrimage will be a touchstone event of my life, having an impact whose significance stretches far beyond those brief thirty-one days. Finally, I raise the stone to my lips for a kiss of gratitude before throwing it into the ocean and returning home.

On Pilgrimage...

CHAPTER 8

COMMUNITAS

"The social element is vital for those on the Camino…It is commonly said that many people start alone but always end accompanied by others…In the open social contexts of the pilgrimage participants come to trust themselves and others – even all of humanity – to a greater extent."

– Nancy Frey, *Pilgrim Stories: On and Off the Road to Santiago*

ROUTINES

LAUDS/PRIME – Withdrawing my earplugs, I begin the day at 7 am in the dormitory at Navarrete. Already, fellow pilgrims – shadowy figures in the dark – are bustling about their beds, talking in whispers. Shivering in the cold morning air, I throw off the blankets and excavate myself from my woefully inadequate sleeping sack. Putting on sandals I head to the bathroom, my filled urine bottle discreetly hidden under a small hiker's towel. Back at bedside, morning toiletries over, I take my pills and begin to force down a litre of water as I start packing up to get ready for the day. Sleeping tights, socks, and t-shirt removed, I don my loose boxers and stepping on the ice-cold floor, pull on the thin nylon pants. Next comes the long-sleeved sport undershirt whose mock-turtle neck zipper I quickly pull up against the cold. Then the thin pile, long-sleeved sweater is pulled down over my head, over which I put on another thin, sleeveless pile vest.

By this time most of the pilgrims are up and someone turns on the light. A few words of greeting in the form of a friendly *buenos dias* are exchanged amongst those nearest to one another. Overall the mood is quiet and reflective as each pilgrim diligently addresses her or his preparatory morning routines. Sitting back down on the bed I withdraw the tube of Vaseline from the top of my pack and lather my toes and heels before putting on thick walking socks and sliding my feet into the cold boots, carefully pulling the socks up tightly to prevent any folds which could lead to blisters. Continuing to drink water, I next address my pack.

By this time, the first pilgrims – today as almost always Pasquale and a few others – have already finished suiting up and are heading out the door. As it is still dark outside and the most difficult route-finding of the day inevitably involves navigating one's way out of town, I can never quite understand this zeal to get away so prematurely early. Knowing that many of these departing pilgrims will soon be making their way to the nearest café for a morning caffeine fix – something in which I do not partake – I know that I will catch them up in due time. I return to my packing.

Planned and perfected over many days, by now every single belonging has its own precise location within the pack. All the time I struggle to finish the bottle of water, recognising the camel-like importance of the liquid in preventing dehydration on the trail. Finished, I stand up and leave the dorm to complete the final tasks. Returning to the bathroom I refill the water bottle and entering a toilet stall drop my pants and begin to lather on generous amounts of Vaseline to my nether regions, both front and back, to prevent chaffing during the long day's walk. Then passing the small table around which other pilgrims are eating their breakfast I head outside to gauge the weather and assess if any protective rain gear is needed. Back in the dorm I shoulder my pack, slip maps into each leg pocket, don my thin gloves and warm headband, and wishing any present a *Buen Camino*, head outside into the frigid dawn air. It is now about 7:45 am and I stride forward, rising sun at my back, to my rendezvous with Saint James.

✦ ✦ ✦

TERCE/SEXT – Although some pilgrims travel the entire route with a walking stick or hefty wooden staff in their hands, I resort to such only in sections of very uneven ground, preferring instead to let my arms swing freely in order to tactilely encounter the world. Case in point: I approach the village of Carrión de los Condes and walk along the *senda* – that increasingly common and much maligned yet undeniably safe roadside pilgrim sidewalk – and indulge in a silly habit developed from time spent along the pilgrim pathways in France. As I pass each pair of tombstone-shaped waymarks, I reach my arms out laterally and bending slightly at the knee let my fingers lightly glide across the scallop shell carvings as if somehow my digits could be capable of assimilating goodwill particles or positive pilgrim *chi* in the process. Later, in the streets of Carrión, I spend a few confusing minutes wandering about in search of a yellow pilgrim arrow or yellow and white scallop shell waymark. When I finally spot the latter, indicating that I've regained the Camino, I touch the small scallop shell badge on my hat in silent thanks to Saint James.

NONE – I approach the church of San Lorenzo in Sahagún and proceed through my customary visitation routine. Slowly circulating counter-clockwise around the edifice, I pause frequently to study various architectural elements with the aid of my light-weight monocular lens. I then find a place to sit down and reread through my photocopied guidebook pages. Even more important, however, is my exercise of mindful time-tripping, honed to perfection through decades of visiting archaeological and historical sites around the world. With fingers in my ears if, like here, they are needed to block out extraneous sounds, I time-cast backward, trying to imagine the place at the height of the great age of pilgrimage in the twelfth and thirteenth centuries: the bustle of street vendors, the cacophony of pilgrims, the peeling bells of the church, the aura of sanctity mixed with frivolity, commerce with

worship. At times it seems as if I can almost see them all right there in front of me; ghosts made real, if only for a moment; echoes from the past resonating for the briefest of instances in the present. Listening, I can imagine hearing the footsteps of the road-weary pilgrims, their cries of *Ultreia!* as they pick themselves up from the church steps to continue their onward journey to the tomb of Saint James.

VESPERS – As always, I am delighted and relieved to find the door to the pilgrim *albergue* – in this case in the village of Rabanal – to be unlocked at 4 pm. So many hostels have been closed for the winter, including even those that my three-year-old (and apparently completely outdated) handbook states are supposed to be operational year-round. Leaving my hiking boots at the door, I enter the dormitory and select a vacant bed in the most remote corner of the common room. Already half a dozen individuals, most recognised, are present. Cheerful words are exchanged about particulars of the day's walk: "Wasn't that stretch along the side of the highway horrible?"; "Did you stop and visit that church with the interesting carvings?" etc. The most important inquiry, however, is whether the water in the showers is hot. Finding out that in this case the answer is affirmative, I grab my evening wear (sounds impressive but in reality is comprised of a clean pair of underpants, thick socks, a pair of lightweight nylon pants, t-shirt, and long-sleeved shirt) and enter the bathroom. Having become accustomed by now to the need for diminished expectations with regard to the quality of Camino accommodation, I am not surprised to learn that the 'hot' shower is at best really only lukewarm. Quickly stepping in and then out after a rapid scrub, I reflect that at least it's not ice-cold as has been typical in many other hostels. Returning to the dorm I arrange my wet walking clothes on the upper bunk (a luxury possible at this time of year with the always half-empty dorms) and over the back of a chair pushed in front of one of the meagre heaters, hoping that by morning they will have dried. The *refugio* warden arrives and we are signed in, pay our minimal fees and, most importantly, get our pilgrim passports stamped.

It is at this time that I part ways with most of my fellow pilgrims who are usually content to relax in the *refugio,* engaging in social repartee. I fill my small day pack with wallet, camera, writing journal, wrinkled and weathered maps from today and pristine ones for tomorrow, and photocopied pages from several guidebooks, and head out for a walk about the town. I've grown to love these end-of-the-day strolls as a *flâneur*, free from both the unidirectional forward imperative of the Camino and the increasingly reviled, obscene weight of my large backpack. If the town hosts any structures of merit, I scramble about to try to visit as many of these as possible before they close (luckily the otherwise annoying schedule of working hours in Spain whereupon opening hours extend into the early evening is amenable to such sightseeing). And if there are no such sites of renown, as is the case here for the town of Rabanal, I simply wander the streets trying to get a feel of the place, enjoying watching the locals going about their daily routines. During such walkabouts I keep an eye out for a grocery store from which to later pick up supplies such as cheese, sausages, pasta, cookies, and wine to take back to the *albergue* for supper, either to be consumed alone or pooled into a communal meal. Also I am on the watch for a bar in which to settle into a hopefully comfortable chair beside a window or fireplace in order to sip (ok gulp) a beer or two (or three). Spreading out the maps at such times, I begin to write about the day's walk and various experiences and, if time allows, to read up about what is in store for the morrow. Then it is back to the hostel for dinner and companionship, the sustenance of both much needed after a long, cold and solitary winter day spent on the Camino of Saint James.

♦ ♦ ♦

COMPLINE – Nine pm finds me sitting alone at the table in the O'Cebreiro *refugio* finishing the last of several glasses of wine. After catching up on several days of journal writing I have spent the last hour studying the maps and reading about the history and sites to be encountered the next day. Soon I pack up and enter the already darkened dormitory. Several pilgrims are reading in their bunks, books illuminated by headlamps. Quietly I make my way to my bed and change into my sleeping tights and sweater. Luckily, as there are few of us here, each can make use of two to three hostel blankets piled atop our sleeping bags. Already the night-time temperature is falling. I arrange my belongings on the floor beside the head of the bed: my eyeglass case, a hanky, a filled water bottle, and most importantly, my earplugs to nullify the omnipresent rumble of snoring, all placed within easy reach. I apply tiger balm to my upper lip to counter the smell of the mildewed and unwashed clothing and pop a Tylenol PM to help sooth sore muscles and ensure deep REM. Then, nestling into my sleeping sack, I turn on my headlamp and start reading the Spanish mystic Saint John Divine's *Dark Night of the Soul*, a book guaranteed, if ever there was one, to rapidly induce sleep. Dreams when they come are often filled with thoughts of the still-distant cathedral of Saint James.

Pilgrims

Turning my back on the Roman bridge I put away my camera and, procrastination over, shoulder my pack to begin the hundred-metre climb up the Cuesta de Mostilares. The ridge has been visible since leaving the *refugio* in Castrojeriz a half hour before; a steep wall rising up out of the *meseta*. Head down, hands clasped on my shoulder straps, I start to trudge upward ever so slowly like one of those claymation animated dinosaurs in old films. Body hunched over, eyes just a metre above the rocky surface, my world having shrunk to the immediate, I'm startled by Laurent flashing by with a cheerful hello, well wishes, and an encouraging tap on my pack from his staff as if to swat me up the difficult hill. Jealous at his youth and vigour, I return to the slog. Ten minutes later as I'm pausing for a breath and enjoying the fine views back to the improbable bulk of Castrojeriz proud in its towering isolation over the plain, I am greeted by Amador who stops seemingly also to enjoy the view. I wait for him to proceed but he lingers and offers many words in Spanish. Much of this I cannot explicitly comprehend but the overall message becomes clear as he matches my crawling pace for the next fifteen minutes while proceeding to talk me up the hill. Touched by his fatherly concern, I smile and wave him ahead upon summiting and wait until he makes his way down onto the immense cultivated plain spreading out ahead. Alone again, I savour the expansive views of the track – the Collada del Camino Francés – winding its lonely way toward a bright, solitary patch of sunlight caused by a single break in the cloud cover.

And there in the distance can be seen the snail-like movements of my fellow pilgrims, so small against the empty magnitude of the *meseta*, individuals toward whom at that moment I feel such a strong bond of affection. The track winds its way from dark to light, solitude to companionship, and seems in the stark simplicity of a pilgrimage where everything can be interpreted as some sort of sign or life lesson, an important message to heed. With renewed purpose I therefore scamper down the hill and endeavour to keep my companions in view for the rest of the day, drawing energy from their proximity and our shared enterprise.

◆◆◆

AFTER A NIGHT MADE RESTLESS by a rake-thin mattress and my already sore and sensitive hips, I'm the first up. Uncharacteristically, I decide to linger while the others have breakfast so as to lead them out of Ponferrada along the route I had 'recced' yesterday from atop the castle walls as well as from a brief walk about the complicated urban grid. Also, though I am slow to acknowledge it, the idea of having company while walking today seems an appealing change from my normal solitary peregrination. And so, feeling ever so much like Gandalf (I'm the only bearded one in the group), staff in hand, I lead 'my' little fellowship over the Rio Sil near where the original iron bridge (*pons ferrata*) had once crossed. Soon we see a sign for the suburb community of Compost*illa* and joke about terminating our pilgrimages there instead of having to continue for another week to reach the real Compost*ela*. All, however, resist the temptation, and laughing at our collective moment of hesitation, we continue on, me shouting an enthusiastic *Ultreia!* for motivation.

Once we gain the suburbs of Columbrianos and its empty streets, Jean-Olivier, Emmanuelle, Tony, and I can all walk abreast chatting merrily in a combined pilgrim argot of French, Spanish, and of course English, the lingua franca of our times. Passing a series of big mansions I ask in mock seriousness about which *casa* is Tony's summer residence away from his no doubt much grander real home back in Barcelona. Much laughter all around as, playing along, he goes into a long-winded discussion about how he and his wife being unable to decide which among the many they would like had simply purchased the entire street so that they could circulate among all the properties on a weekly basis throughout the summer.

A few minutes later a local resident – a very beautiful woman – crosses the street in front of us and begins to walk in the opposite direction along a side path. Slightly in front of the group at that moment, I suddenly veer off the street upon which we are walking as if making to follow her while the others pause. After a few steps I return apologising for having "a Pasquale moment" in reference to our randy fellow pilgrim who was somewhere a day's walk ahead of us and whose stories about his amorous exploits we all remember. And with huge laughs, loud enough to cause my beautiful quarry to turn around in puzzlement, our fellowship continues forward.

❖❖❖

WHAT A NUISANCE THE GUY HAS BECOME! This section of the Way from Sarria to Portomarin in Galicia is reputed to have some of the loveliest scenery of the entire Camino. Reading the guidebooks and looking at the maps last night I was so looking forward to a contemplative walk through glades of oak and chestnut trees bordering the quiet country lanes that link a chain of sleepy hamlets. But here I am with 'German glue-boy' firmly adhered to my side like a barnacle that I can't shake off. Until now the group of fellow pilgrims I had been around had all respected each others' personal spaces, especially those who have chosen to walk alone. Many were the times we would leap-frog past one another throughout a long day's walk, one stopping for a morning *café con leche*, another for a visit to a church, the others continuing through, all realising that socialising would be saved for the evening in the *refugio* when experiences of the road would be shared. Often, even when walking as a group, we would string ourselves along in a chain, each separated from the other by dozens or even hundreds of metres. But today Carl has been right beside me for the last several hours, stopping right next to me every time I either pause to take a photo or savour a view. Once he even lingered while I took a roadside piss. It would not have been so disagreeable had he been more interesting. Unfortunately there are just so many questions I can ask about the vagaries of computer programming until my brain simply shuts down altogether. How different the experience is, I reflect, from one remembered when walking a pilgrimage route in France when I had spent a wonderful day of incredibly wide-ranging conversation with a newly met fellow pilgrim as we sauntered along almost oblivious to our surroundings, while enthralled in our shared banter. But here I am too timid to be impolite and risk insulting Carl by saying that I wish to walk alone. I also begin to feel sorry for him. So I feign interest and continue the conversation and try to soothe his obvious need for companionship. I try to remember that pilgrimage, though ultimately a solitary experience, should never be allowed to reside exclusively there as an internal journey to the point of ignoring one's external actions towards others, especially one's fellow pilgrims…of *whatever* stripe. "So, Carl," I begin anew,

"tell me again about that interesting program you were working on to synchronise the fire alarms in that apartment block back in Nürnberg…"

❖❖❖

SADDENED AS I LINGER NEAR A SMALL monument to an elderly pilgrim who had died of a heart attack here just thirty kilometres shy of Compostela, my melancholic reverie is broken by the arrival of three pilgrims: Simone, a happy-go-lucky northern Italian whom I had met several times over the last month, 'glue-boy' Carl again after a separation of several days, and another German, Michael. We stroll along together all happy that this is the last big day of walking on the long journey to Saint James' shrine. I'm surprised that Simone is here catching me up since he had passed me several days before. I laugh when, explaining, he recounts having only walked ten kilometres yesterday as he and Michael had stopped off in a friendly bar and spent the entire day socialising with locals until evening at which time they had been allowed to sleep on the floor. What a healthy attitude toward pilgrimage I think, so different from others who are preoccupied with achieving daily distance at the expense of all else. We move through a eucalyptus forest and I marvel at Simone who, taking great interest in his surroundings, frequently pauses to stare up at and sometimes photograph the trees. So different from Carl who I discover, despite this being his third Spanish pilgrimage, still does not know what the word *Ultreia* means! It is hard to resist shaking my head in disbelief. For me, next to kindness, curiosity is certainly the most cherished of all the characteristics that I search for in friends and companions.

Several hours later after emerging from washing my groin as per established custom since medieval times in the frigid waters of the aptly named Rio Lavacolla (the last stream before Compostela) I enjoy a lunch break with my boots doffed to rest my feet in the atypically warm sun. Soon I am greeted by the pilgrim group again who had apparently stopped for a café break. This time they've been joined by a young fellow who I'm told is from Japan and who is surprised and beams with a huge smile when I stand up and greet him with a formal bow saying *"gashi"*, one of the few words I remember from time spent in his country. Then, when he finds out that I've actually visited his home town, he drops his pack and gives me a big hug before scampering off to follow the others. Forcing my unwilling feet back into their imprisoning boots I marvel at the drawing power of the Camino to attract those from many of the world's religions.

Not long thereafter, just as I finish taking photos of the words "Camino de France" on the enormous pilgrimage monument on the top of Monte del Gozo, I hear my name shouted loudly. And there are Emmanuelle and Jean-Olivier, unseen for many days and who I had thought to be well ahead of me and thus had not expected to meet again. Big hugs and cheek kisses as they tell me that they are planning to meet Pasquale, whom none of us have seen for over a week, in a couple of hours' time right in front of the cathedral in the city, all arranged via their mobile phones. Come along they insist. I hesitate as I had always planned to follow the long-established protocol of spending the last night in contemplation in the *refugio* on the hill before the short concluding walk the following morning. Pilgrimage, however, is above all an opportunity to extend one's self into new directions, which for me I had long ago recognised to mean becoming more social and companionable. So putting humanity before ritual, I follow them down the hill and into the city, finishing the official pilgrimage in the presence of others when I had begun it alone. That evening I treat the group to a special meal (as seems to be the case for many pilgrims met along the Way, they are either under- or unemployed and thus quite poor) as a big thank you for their warm companionship over the past month. As we part, they for their various pilgrim *albergues*, me for a pricey hotel as a treat to myself for reaching Compostela, I am so grateful that circumstances have allowed me to share such an experience of a lifetime with such a singular group of cheerful and kind people.

✦✦✦

I HAD BECOME USED TO SPENDING the entire day walking without seeing a single pilgrim. Knowledge that there was always a handful of fellow walkers scattered before and after me on the Camino brought with it a feeling of camaraderie through shared purpose. However, only a very small fraction of those reaching Compostela continue walking to the coast, especially in the winter months. As a result, I feel alone for the first time. After hours of solitude I'm therefore excited to see someone walking up ahead. Not feeling the need for the two-hundred-metre climb up and down Monte Aro recommended by the guidebook, I had left the route and stayed along the level road that skirted the hill. And now I had caught up with someone who had done likewise. We warmly greet each other and spend the next hour strolling along the empty tree-lined road having an interesting conversation about his early days of growing up in rural Galicia and his later work as a sailor on a variety of commercial vessels that had visited several cities where I have lived (Montreal, Boston). Now, retired, he is spending a few days walking from his home in Compostela to the coast, stopping off to visit a series of relatives and former sailing buddies. Buoyed by the companionship I'm sorry to have to part ways with him as I head into the little, ramshackle village of Olveiroa where I will stay the night while he continues on the next town for a rendezvous with his girlfriend.

Soon, my spirits soar and I'm happy beyond belief. For there, stepping out of the doorway of the village *albergue* about a block away, is Pasquale! He freezes and cannot believe his eyes, not yet understanding that although it had taken him two days to reach here from Compostela I had that morning taken a fifteen-kilometre taxi ride to outside the city's suburbs and from there had been able to catch him up with the present forty-kilometre walk. Remembering that he was wont to sing old American popular songs, I throw my arms wide as I stride toward him with a booming: "The first time e...v...e...r I saw your face..." We embrace happy to know that after our long shared travails from Punte la Reina that we will soon be together on the Galician seacoast, at the end of world.

Meals

AFTER A WEEK SPENT EATING SOLITARY meals and privately consumed snacks I'm intrigued by what to expect at the group meal offered later tonight at the private *albergue* in Belorado. Before that, however, I enjoy an exploratory walk about the town looking at the first timber-beam and wattle buildings I've seen in Spain, feeling nostalgic for such from my time spent on France's pilgrimage routes. For the first time, I begin to feel the real age of the Camino and its creation of roadside service towns such as this one. And so it is in this spirit of antiquity that I return to the hostel and sit down for my first communal meal with fellow pilgrims, approaching it as an important experience of the Way. Although the fare is simple and there is not quite enough to satisfy hunger after a long day of walking in the November cold, the esprit des corps amongst everyone clustered around the table, expressed in a Babel of languages, warms our souls as does the nearby fire, our bodies. Later our friendly host gives us a tour of his pet rabbits in the backyard. We return to the table for a dessert of freshly baked cookies, some individuals settling down with cups of tea for their daily journal writing. Can it get any better than this, I wonder.

❖ ❖ ❖

IT IS SUNDAY NIGHT IN CASTROJERIZ and little in the sleepy village seems to be open for business. The first hostel, despite the guidebook stating it to be operational year-round, was barred shut. It is already late in the afternoon when I approach the second *refugio* only to find its door to be locked as well. Stepping back and wondering where I might have to bivouac and how cold and miserable that will be, it is only then that I notice that the door on the upper level is slightly ajar. Thank Saint James! Soon, settled comfortably inside after a hot shower and having the place all to myself, I spread out and attempt to dry my sweat-dampened clothes atop the empty bunk beds. An hour later Laurent arrives and after his shower we begin to scour the village in hope of finding something, somewhere to eat. Nary a restaurant can be found and even the few perpetually open bars do not have any food. Laurent, in his best Dickens' Oliver-like begging imitation, persists and eventually we are rewarded with a frozen loaf of bread of unknown antiquity dug out from the deep recesses of a freezer. Back at the *refugio* we combine our meagre remains of days-old cheese and sausage and, laughing at the absurdity of the situation, resort to using a hairdryer from the bathroom to thaw out each broken-off chunk of bread. Ah, the penitential life of hard done-by pilgrims, we joke, both realising that this will certainly be one meal that will long be remembered.

❖ ❖ ❖

AFTER COVERING NEARLY EIGHTY KILOMETRES of the *meseta* in the last two days I am exhausted as I enter Mansilla de las Mulas but briefly pick up the dragging pace once I spot the sign up ahead for the pilgrim *albergue*. My finishing 'sprint' is broken, however, when I hear my name being shouted out. I grind to a halt and, pirouetting, enter the open door of a bar from where the bellow had emerged and find it filled with fellow walkers whom I have not seen for several days, as well as a new pilgrim, the Austrian, Maria, about whom I had earlier heard. As I'm introduced to her I recount that of course I've heard of her, she being famous on the Camino for shamelessly exposing herself to other pilgrims (the real story I had been told is that she herself had been the victim of such an encounter, resorting to using her walking stick to dissuade a Spanish pervert from attempting anything more serious than exhibitionism). Much laugher as we all sip our beer and wait for the *refugio* next door to open at the top of the hour.

As Amador and Elidae volunteer to cook a feast, we others scatter throughout the town to buy and bring back supplies. Later, Amador, still dressed in his pile walking gear with a Basque toque perched high up on his head, sits hunched over a portable stove on the floor and furiously stirs an enormous pot filled with chicken, rice, and his own special spices brought out from some secret nook of his small backpack. He works like a medieval ironsmith with the flames swirling about the pot and, oblivious of the danger, both to his feet and the sitting stool as well. The rest of us settle down to watch while addressing the important task of consuming many bottles of wine. When the meal is ready, we are hailed and, plates in hand, line up to receive our generous dollop of the hearty and tasty pilgrim stew. We all feel guilty when Amador, stating that he is too tired to eat, collapses still clothed and immediately falls asleep on his bunk, his herculean task of cooking for the sole benefit of others completed. Unknown then to many of us, this will be his last big day on the Camino, as he is to return home to Madrid upon reaching León the following day. As such, our most fond collective memory of him, discussed much later at the end of the pilgrimage, will always be that image of him stirring the magic pot over the open flames, tossing in pieces of meat, vegetables, and mystery spices like some maniacal witch from Macbeth.

❖❖❖

FINISHING MY WALKABOUT and photographing the interesting buildings of Astorga I pop into a bar to share several beers with Pasquale, Emmanuelle, and Jean-Olivier while discussing the latter two's upcoming travel plans to Asia. I also find out that all three are staying at the other pilgrim *albergue* in town which has a discounted relationship with a nearby restaurant provided proof of staying in that particular hostel is presented. Further, it seems that the *hospitaliero* has left for the night and that they know where the *sello* or identification ink-stamp is kept. I hurry back to my refuge and picking up Maria and Elidae and our pilgrim passports we proceed to the other hostel where after meeting Tony, a Spanish pilgrim, sure enough, we are 'officially' stamped before all make our way to what will be the only restaurant meal that we will share as a large group before reaching Compostela. Proudly presenting, depending on the person, either our real or fake *sellos* (if the latter with one's thumb strategically placed to cover the stamp from the other hostel in town), thereby proving our status

as pilgrims (as if our dress, language, dishevelled state, and inescapable odour were not a dead give away!), we settle into an enjoyable pilgrim meal, sharing stories about our personal motivations for being on the Camino. Satiated, it is in fine spirits, due partially it must be admitted to the copious consumption *of* fine spirits, that we make our ways back to our respective abodes, all looking forward to what tomorrow's Camino might bring.

❖❖❖

ARRIVING IN VILLAFRANCA DEL BIERZO early in the afternoon after a relatively easy walk I decide to call it a day and stay at the famous *refugio* run by a family whom have devoted their lives to looking after pilgrims. In this respect, they not only offer the traditional bed and board but also provide healing, prayers, and above all encouragement for the next day's long climb up to O'Cebreiro. We are three pilgrims that night: Sandra from Germany, another young woman from Japan, and myself. We sit down at the table and are joined by two men (brothers?) who are running the place. Soup from a big terrine is ladled out into our bowls and for the first and only time on the Camino I stand and hold hands with others over our food while one of the hosts recites a prayer in Spanish. Incredibly moved, I'm too shy to glance at anyone, instead focusing my attention on the bowl in front of my now watery eyes. Perhaps it is the rising steam from the soup that has caused this?

BEDS

ALTHOUGH I'VE BEEN AWAKE for over twenty-four hours, the excitement of walking these first few kilometres of the Camino have banished all feelings of jet-lag. And there it is: the welcoming scallop shell signage of the *albergue* in Puenta la Reina, my first pilgrim hostel in Spain! It's a bit of a wait until it opens but once inside I and several French fellows quickly sign in and have our passports stamped before laying claim to our respective beds. Alarmingly, it is much colder inside the old stone building than outside. Soon, we conjoin efforts to build a raging fire around which we and several other late-arriving pilgrims will cluster for warmth during the hours ahead. Later, it is difficult to leave the fire room and return to the still frigid dormitory. I nestle into my worrisomely thin sleeping sack and watch in a semi-awake state as the others begin to trickle in. I smile at the behaviour of one of the Frenchmen as he converses with and ogles a young and pretty Canadian cyclist who unabashedly practises her yoga stretching exercises in her underwear. Even this

interesting sight, however, cannot keep me awake for long and I soon nod off. Unfortunately, despite the tiredness I spend a fitful night shivering with little sleep. An inauspicious start I reflect in the morning as I hurriedly dress and leave the *refugio*, anxious to get moving so as to warm up.

✦✦✦

IN WHAT WILL BE A COMMON occurrence along the Way, I find the Azofra municipal *refugio* closed for the winter. Checking my map to see that the next place for accommodation, Santo Domingo de la Calzada, is fifteen kilometres and three to four hours walk away, I pray for the first but by no means last time to Saint James for the other hostel in the tiny hamlet to be open. I'm soon at Nuestra Señora de los Angeles, a church used for pilgrim burials during the Middle Ages. Tucked against its flank is a small lean-to building that houses the *albergue*. A modern wall plaque states that the hostel is dedicated to a Dona Isabel de Azofra who founded a pilgrim hospital on the Camino in 1168. Appreciating the history of the place, I nervously approach the door and twisting the old knob am happy to find it opens into the simple habitat: little more than a common eating room, several small dormitories housing a handful of bunk beds, and a decrepit-looking toilet. But it is open and right now, shivering in my sweat-dampened clothes, that's all that matters.

I claim a lumpy bed and twiddling with the antique heaters soon have them chugging away like miniature steam locomotives. I spend several peaceful minutes warming my hands and then, discovering that there is no hot water and thus a shower is out of the question, head outside for an exploratory walk about the hamlet. After half an hour, the cold, biting wind drives me back to the *albergue* where I find others have arrived. Later, we are given a tour of the adjacent church by the warden, an elderly woman missing many teeth and much of her hair, neither of which, however, in any way hinders her overt enthusiasm as she points out the statues of the famous pilgrim saints Martin, Roche, and James. Back at the *albergue* we find that a friendly ginger cat has also fled the cold and joins us for part of the evening. Writing up my daily journal as I sip tea, stroke the cat, and look over my notes, I am struck with a sudden realisation about how absolutely blessed I am to be here in these wonderfully rustic accommodations which one guidebook refers to as being some of the most peaceful of the entire Camino. When the warden comes

by to stamp our passports and collect a *donativo* I give not only the expected five euros but as I'm so grateful, an additional fifteen euros as contribution toward ensuring that the place is kept open during the cold winter months. I'm rewarded by a beaming smile and kind blessing from the old woman. Happy that my largesse has been so gratefully received, I climb into bed content with the day's activities.

The next morning I awaken scratching from bed bug bites.

❖ ❖ ❖

IT HAS BEEN THE MOST MISERABLE weather encountered yet. During the walk down from the summit of O'Cebreiro I opted to take the open road to avoid the slippery rock and mud trail but in so doing exposed myself to the full force of the brutal wind and driving rain. Absolutely soaked and becoming alarmed that I'm starting to shiver I decide to truncate the day's walk by seeking shelter in the little town of Tricastela. I'm happy to see that the *refugio* is one of the new Galician ones. The buildings are situated on a grassy slope at the edge of an attractive valley of small copses and patchwork fields and filled with slate-roofed dwellings. The scene bears an uncanny resemblance to the English Lake District. Up ahead I see Jean-Olivier and Emmanuelle enter and in a few moments I too am inside and out of the rain.

The *refugio* is designed as a long corridor off which are a series of small rooms, each entered by a set of half-height, western-style, swinging saloon doors. I take advantage of the present emptiness of the place and in having a room to myself and spread out my soaking gear on all four bunk beds and over a drying line stretched in between them. Later, when I realise that the

clothes will not be dry by the morning under such a regime, I take more deliberate action. I move a chair into the hallway and plunking it down in front of a big heater proceed to sit there and alternate holding up different pieces of apparel against the radiator. It is both a challenge to avoid burning anything as well as to avoid choking on the noxious clouds of steam that arise: a reeking mixture of many weeks of body sweat and dirt.

The *refugio* begins to fill up but never the point that anyone has to share a room, unless of course they really want to. Case in point when four days later at a celebratory meal in Compostela Jean-Olivier and Emmanuelle – the former smiling proudly, the latter blushing profusely – admit that, when they found out that I was resting in bed in the Tricastela hostel with my iPod headphones on, to warming themselves up with an evening of amore in their adjacent room. Pasquale, who never met a story with a promise of ribaldry that he didn't want to learn more details about, leans over the table and in a conspiratory voice asks them if the open salon swing doors leading out to the hallway filled with pilgrims walking back and forth past their room, added to the experience. He is satisfied with the broadening smile and deepening blush that he receives in response to his query.

♦♦♦

IN AN ATTEMPT TO SHAKE THE annoying German 'glue-boy' pilgrim who has been beside me all day I decide to push on alone from Portomarin Palas de Rei and several hours later arrive at the *albergue* in the little hamlet of Gonzar, a name sounding as if from *The Lord of the Rings*. Once again the stark building is one of those former schools that Galicia has transformed into pilgrim accommodation. In such establishments one appreciates the modern, functioning facilities even if they come at the expense of historical ambience. I sign myself in, pay the voluntary *donativo* in a box, and throw myself into a super hot shower. It is soon dark and I realise that this will be the first time I've spent a night alone on the Camino. Relishing the solitude, I cook up a packet of emergency pasta and tin of tuna that I've been carrying for weeks. Oddly, despite a big shiny kitchen there is only a single small pot in which to accomplish all this.

Following supper, I huddle myself into a small room in which the heater is turned up to maximum. Can I, as a camel does with water, somehow soak up and store this heat to draw upon the morrow? I settle down to write my journal and scrutinise maps and plan out a schedule for the few remaining days to Compostela. Flipping back through my journal I realise that with today's effort I've walked more than six hundred kilometres since starting three and a half weeks ago. More significantly, this means that sometime today I would had crossed over the two-thousand-kilometre mark in total distance travelled along the pilgrimage pathways of Europe. With feelings of accomplishment tempered with acknowledging the sin of pride, I reflect on the passion that has so consumed my life over the past three years.

Afterward, I read through the warden's log and find out that as many as thirty individuals a night stay in this *refugio* until as late in the year as mid-October, and that during the summer peak there are days when almost a hundred people are checked in. Shocked at this revelation I go upstairs to the dormitory and count a total of only twenty beds. Later, as I settle into my corner bed in the big empty room I realise with a thrill that this will be the only night that I do not have to get my earplugs ready to mitigate the loud snoring. I count my good fortune to have decided to undertake this pilgrimage in the winter rather than summer. How do they fit thirty or a hundred people into a place that only has twenty beds and limited floor space all around? What madness! One hears stories of course about the nightmare that the Camino has become during the summer (and it now seems even the fall and spring as well): people leaving their *refugio* at 3 am and walking the route in complete darkness to be assured that they can obtain a place to sleep for the next night even if that means having to line up and wait (and I suppose get caught up on sleep) for hours and hours in front of the locked door at each new location, nothing of the town ever being visited; fist-fights that develop among pilgrims who use their elbows and shoulders to muscle their way into dormitories; and ultimately, the increasing numbers who simply get

sick of the entire circus, give up, and head north to walk along the much-less-travelled coastal pilgrim route there. But here, now, in the quiet and peace, I thrive in the solitude, grateful for the opportunity to explore myself in a way that is only possible far from the hustle and bustle of the 'madding crowd.' Alone with only the ghostly echoes of frustrated and fractious summer pilgrims for company I fall into a deep and peaceful sleep.

❖❖❖

I AM BACK IN COMPOSTELA after finishing my walk to Muxía and pause and look up at the ornate Plateresque carvings that adorn the entrance to the Hotel de los Reyes Católicos in the cathedral plaza. Built in the early sixteenth century as a pilgrim hospice and infirmary, since the mid-1970s it is the most famous (and expensive) of Spain's *Paradores* (luxury hotels in converted historic buildings). After a month of staying, with few exceptions, in hostels that ranged in quality from the Spartan to the decrepit, I'm excited at the prospect of indulging myself. Stepping gingerly with my oversized backpack past the parked limos and frowning chauffeurs I enter and quickly sign in, not for a moment second-guessing the exorbitant price. It is not every day after all that one reaches the Galician seacoast after walking eight hundred kilometres, much less having the good fortune to approach one's fiftieth birthday in more or less sound body if not mind.

My suite is filled with dark-stained wood on the floors, cabinets, and headboards. I sit in an uncomfortable but atmospheric chair upholstered in faux medieval tapestry that is pushed up against the lead-paned window and begin to sort through the contents of my pack one last time. It is a joy to be able to finally bag my hiking clothes whose exuding aromas hint at their near toxic waste status. Then in the bathroom, not able to decide among the selection of various bath products, I pour them all into the tub as it fills up with steaming hot water. Cupping my hands over sensitive body bits I settle deep into the frothy cocktail of bubbles. Then, while listening to medieval pilgrimage music on the iPod, I go through slowly – ever so slowly as there's absolutely no reason to rush any more – a complete review of each and every night's accommodation along the Way since leaving Puneta la Reina in what seems like a lifetime ago.

Later, I wander about the complex network of corridors that surround a series of gardened cloisters. The hallways are oddly empty of people yet filled with much antique furniture and furnishings: elaborately carved wooden chests set atop wrought-iron tables, wooden icons shining brilliantly with their gold-leaf backgrounds, comfy plush chairs and couches about which I wonder if they are ever used, paintings whose gilt frames do little to enliven the sombre subject matter enclosed therein, richly embroidered tapestries of obvious age and diverse subject matter, and all number of shapes and sizes of lamps which cast an atmospheric amber glow over all.

Eventually I find my way to the chapel and marvel at the columnar carvings of leaves, vines, cherubs, and animals, all of such a delicacy as to suggest plaster but which are in fact finely worked stone. In niches various saints stand clutching their bibles, and there in the middle, walking staff in hand, scrip at this hip, and floppy pilgrim hat with its scallop shell atop his head, is Saint James himself.

In the evening I meet up with Pasquale one final time, treating him to a tour of the building and several cups of crème-de-menthe-flavoured hot chocolate in the lounge before presenting him with a gift of a small fridge magnet in the shape of the yellow arrows which we had followed along the Way. Then, on the steps of the hotel we take leave of one another. Both on the edge of tears, he fondling the cheap fridge magnet and saying how special I am, I thanking him for his cheerful company these many long days, we embrace. I watch him make his way across the dark rain-washed plaza beside the bulk of the cathedral and silently wish him a heartfelt Godspeed for the rest of his life's journey.

And so it is in a melancholy mood that I re-enter the hotel and go into the nearly empty dining room to partake in a sumptuous dinner by myself. Toward the end of the wonderful meal the piano player commences two of my most favourite and certainly most wistful and bittersweet of songs, *Moon River* followed immediately by *Somewhere Over the Rainbow*. I finally lose it and start to cry. "Was something wrong with the food, Señor?" asks the concerned waiter a few minutes later. I reassure him that all is well and I'm just simply relived that "It is all over." For a moment he pauses, a puzzled look on his face. Then, "Ahh…*peligrino*," he astutely surmises with a knowing nod of his head before discreetly backing away, no doubt having seen many such emotionally overwrought individuals before.

Locals

I AM RELAXING IN THE COMMON ROOM of the pilgrim *albergue* in Navarrete after my third full day of walking along the Way when a pretty, middle-aged Spanish pilgrim sits down at the table with a book in her hand. I offer her some of my wine to break the ice and identify my language. We begin chatting and soon establish that we have both walked the pilgrimage routes in France. When learning that I am certainly no greenhorn and after looking about in a conspiratory way she leans forward and begins a diatribe about the rampant abuses on the Camino. Through repeated excursions along the Way over the last decade, this *peregrina* has reached the opinion that most of those present are not "true pilgrims" or at least do not engage in behaviour that one might expect to be "worthy of a pilgrim." As she explains, most individuals never volunteer to donate any money when they stay at the hostels, some even going as far as to rob the kitty of cash. And hardly any pilgrims bother to attend mass, even if requested to do so by the clergy or nuns who are sometimes providing them with their accommodation and board. And finally, as for the esprit de corps or camaraderie that one might expect or hope for among pilgrims, "forget it....at least during the summer period these days," she remarks. And that is why she will now only walk the Camino in the middle of winter when the harsh weather has screened out the serious from the frivolous, the spiritual from the superficial, the seekers from the see-ers. Alarmed about where I myself might fit into this rigid dichotomisation and what she might think of my own motivations, as yet unknown even to myself – and thankfully she never asks me about them – I discreetly slide my photocopied guidebook pages about the architecture of the Camino underneath my book by the Spanish mystic Saint John Divine. Giving a perception of complete empathy, I nod in agreement and pour more wine into our glasses.

♦ ♦ ♦

IT IS MID AFTERNOON and as the municipal *refugio* in Frómista is still closed I agree to join Amador for my first – and given the events that unfold, last – *comida* as the Spanish call their big, mid-afternoon meal of the day. The only table available to us in the small family restaurant is one that looks as if it was hastily placed right beside the doorway entrance to the dining room in order to provide extra seating. All goes well until the time comes when the elderly woman who has been serving the half dozen tables begins to clear away the plates. Finished with my simple but filling meal, I have been sitting cross legged for the last half hour with the woman making dozens of trips back and forth from the kitchen to the dining room. Now, however, with her hands filled with stacked plates that block her forward view, she stumbles over my legs and goes into a slow-motion fall in which, as one of my legs is trapped against the other by her falling weight and I am stuck in place, I can do absolutely nothing to prevent. She crashes to the floor scattering plates every which way. Immediately, once free of the intertwined legs, I stand up and bend down to help...and am met by a dragon! Swatting aside my hand, she commences to scream at me in rapid Spanish and starts waving around a large knife that has somehow suddenly appeared in her hand. Apology frozen in my mouth, I am at first struck dumb and only when the deluge of verbal abuse continues unabated into its second full minute, do I become angry and wave her away with a dismissive flick of my hand in annoyance. This of course sets her to screaming at me even louder. By now other customers have left their tables and gone to the side of the woman in support, which consists of picking up the dishes and glowering at me. Amador, sensing an ugly scene about to unfold, grabs me by the wrist with one hand and his wooden walking staff with the other. He throws a bill on the table and pushing me behind him and talking up a storm with the antagonists while gesturing at them with his protective staff, we back out of the room, collect our packs from the hallway, and quickly exit the restaurant. Although I'm too shaken to see the humour in the encounter, Amador laughs, dismissing – if my limited comprehension of his Spanish is accurate – the woman and threatening patrons as crazy idiots from Palencia. Luckily, seeing the gate to the hostel located across the town square to be finally open, we flee for sanctuary. Glancing backward at the crowd of patrons now gathered in the doorway to the restaurant, I think that never has the term *refugio* seemed more apt.

❖❖❖

EVEN THE SHORT DISTANCE of walking along the pilgrim *senda* beside the busy highway leading out of Frómista is more than enough to convince me to opt for the much more pleasant, albeit slightly longer, riverside route to Carrión de los Condes. The Rio Ucieza turns out to be a lovely stream left relatively undamaged by agriculture, its water plants displaying a brilliant russet colour. The Way alternates between a narrow riparian trail and a small, tyre-rutted track. The only noise is the fierce wind blowing in the trees and the sound of my steps and walking stick hitting the frozen, rough ground. Once the sun disappears into the clouds the temperatures plunge and I am forced to put on my wind shell and pants. Soon the clip clop and tip tap of my boots and staff are joined by the swoosh, swoosh of my swinging arms and striding legs as nylon rubs against itself. After an hour, the pastoral beauty is broken by the sight and sound of a small white truck bouncing toward me along the rutted track. Frowning at the intrusion upon my reverie – is there nowhere along this Camino free of damned automobiles? – I move to the side to allow the vehicle to pass. Perplexingly, however, it slows down and veers right up to me. "Now what?" I wonder, prejudicially expecting the worst;

perhaps chastisement for trespassing or some such. The driver rolls down his window and abruptly thrusts his fist out at me. I am chagrined when he smiles and, opening his clenched fingers, presents me with two wrapped candies. Then, wishing me a *"Buen Camino"*, he immediately drives away. Totally stunned by this kindness and unexpected generosity, I shout several loud *"Gracias"* at the retreating truck and am happy to see him raise his arm in acknowledgment before withdrawing it inside and rolling up his window. I stand frozen to the spot and watch the truck until it disappears into the distance, at which point my moistened eyes start to freeze. *"Gracias,"* I mumble softly once more before turning back to the Camino.

❖❖❖

LATER IN THE EVENING while over dinner, Emmanuelle states yet again that I displayed considerable reserve and that had it been her whose honesty was challenged in such an offensive way she would have grabbed the bitch's hair and slammed her head into the counter several times to knock some sense into her obviously only half-filled brain...

Earlier: Arriving in front of the Santiago cathedral, I move off to the side to let Jean-Olivier and Emmanuelle embrace and have a private moment. Staring up again at my long-sought destination, I force myself to resist succumbing to immediate feelings of anti-climatic melancholy. Soon Pasquale, unseen for many days, greets us with hugs of congratulation, his big smile and boyish enthusiasm raising my spirits. He guides us around the corner to the cathedral office where we can be registered and obtain our official *compostelas* or certificates that since the fourteenth century have been awarded to arriving pilgrims. Today the distance needed to be walked to receive the certificate is a meagre hundred kilometres and the proof is presentation of your pilgrim passport that has been stamped in the various places of accommodation.

I let Jean-Olivier and Emmanuelle be processed first and then move to the counter myself, proudly presenting my passport filled with a month's worth of Spanish stamps or *sellos*. I also show the woman attendant colour photocopies of more than two months of stamps garnered from walking portions of not one but all four of the feeder pilgrimage routes in France. The woman nods but looks unimpressed. She refocuses on my Spanish passport and looking up curtly states that she cannot issue me my *compostela* certificate. In the background I see Emmanuelle and Jean-Olivier pirouette and stare, shocked, and puzzled looks on their faces. In disbelief, I control myself and politely inquire why. Like a robot the woman points out that I have only a single stamp, from Gonzar, that is within the magical hundred kilometre zone. "I have walked over two thousand kilometres to get here as you can see," I patiently state, shaking with emotion. "I don't care about any of that," she replies dismissively, "Only the last one hundred kilometres count." With the office closing in just a few minutes time, I suppress the mounting panic that if this is not immediately sorted out, I will not be one of the successful pilgrims whose arrival is announced at the mass in the cathedral the following day. Looking at my companions with whom I have shared so much over the past month and who have now moved beside me at the counter, I fear that I will be unable to share with them the final acknowledgement of our joint accomplishment in the cathedral.

Resisting the temptation to verbally blast the pin-headed bureaucrat (God, they're same the world over!) I enter into a negotiation with the woman. I explain that I had spent the previous night in Arzua having walked there from Gonzar the day before. "Not possible," she states, "Eight-six kilometres from

there to here in two days. It is too far. You must have taken a bus or auto." Look at my passport I tell her and you will see other days of similar walked distances along with the bracketed stamps at each end to prove it. Begrudgingly, she does so. By this point, Pasquale has returned to the room and all three of my fellow pilgrims, in a flurry of English, French, and Spanish, lobby my case, bearing witness to having seen me walking such distances during the past month including walking with me yesterday (a lie) and today (true).

"Where is the *sello* from Aruza then?" she barks. I explain that I had been exhausted when I arrived after walking nearly fifty kilometres that day and had been unable to find the *refugio* open and had consequently stayed in a small hotel that did not have a stamp. "Humph," she snorts, "You could have gone into cafes and gotten stamps there." When I explain that I don't drink coffee and given that I had not entered a single café during the entire month in Spain, why would I suddenly do so on the last day? She finds it hard to believe that anyone does not partake of coffee. Regardless, I should have in any case simply gone in to ask for a stamp every now and then. Reiterating, slowly as I struggle to keep the anger out of my voice, that, firstly, given that I had never entered a café in Spain how was I ever to know that they gave out stamps, and that, secondly, in not a single guidebook I had read had there ever been mention of the need to obtain such stamps; and, thirdly and finally, why would I, after having spent three years walking such distances, have cheated at the very end given that she can see that I am in no way incapacitated by injury and that indeed I plan to continue walking to Finisterre in a few days time. Seeing an opening, the dragon pounces. "So Santiago is not your *real* destination," she concludes with a triumphant smile. "Perhaps you are not even a Christian." This is finally too much. Grabbing my journal I thrust it into her face and ask her if she'd like to see what I had written about attending masses at every opportunity along the Way. "OK, OK," she holds up her hands and without any shame, proceeds to silently copy down my particulars before finally issuing me the certificate. I mumble a barely audible thank you, and gathering up my belongings depart without once meeting her eyes and acknowledging her presence. "Bitch," one of my companions behind me states loudly for all to hear as we exit the door. "F~~king bureaucrat," I say upon reaching the street. And also: "God, I need to get drunk as soon as possible to forget about all this shit so that it doesn't ruin my stay here." And so we agree to meet up in an hour's time after everyone is checked into their various places of accommodation.

◆◆◆

THE DECREPIT CHARM of the windy streets and ancient fieldstone homes in the Galician village of Olveiroa is alluring. I'm happy to spot and enter a small, family-run bar. It is so good to get out of the cold. Taking off my gloves I order and quickly consume a hot chocolate before picking up my glass of red wine and moving into the dimly lit adjacent room. There I am greeted by a scene straight out of a Van Gogh painting of nineteenth-century country life. It is an image that is so powerfully haunting I know from the first glance that it will be with me for the rest of my life.

In the orange glow thrown out by the enormous stone fireplace, sit two wizened old men. They are dressed in raggedy wool overcoats, each with his hands crossed atop the handle of a snarly wooden walking cane. At their feet lies a sleeping dog. They sit across from one another, knees just about touching, on two twisty wooden chairs that have been pushed up so close to the fireplace as to almost be inside it. I pause at the doorway, soaking in the rustic atmosphere and warmth, before moving to take a seat a small table in the corner. I am halted by gestures from one of the old men that I should join them beside – actually *within* would be more accurate – the fireplace. Nodding, I pull out one of the chairs and careful not to disturb the dog, place it down on the large stone hearth between them with a "*Muchas gracias señor*" acknowledgment. Seeing the scallop shell on my small day pack, one points a finger, asking "*Perigrino?*" From Canada, yes, I state, also explaining in halting Spanish that I do not speak Spanish, adding quickly as an afterthought, nor local Gallegan as well. They smile, one tapping my knee in understanding, the other tapping his chest proudly stating that he too did the pilgrimage to Santiago de Compostela in – if my translation is correct – the year 1965. Unwrapping the scarf about his neck he pulls out a small medallion to show me. "Santiago," he whispers reverently before kissing it and burying it again within his voluminous clothes. Staring at the flames, we settle back into a peaceful silence that seems to emanate from another time.

PART III

Becoming the Way

"You cannot travel the path until you become the path."

– Guatama Buddha *in* Cousineau, P. *The Art of Pilgrimage: The Seeker's Guide to Making Travel Sacred*

PRO-LOGUE

> *"'El camino es un druga' (the way is a drug), the Spaniards say. It enters the body, it fills the veins, it floods the heart and mind."*
>
> – Nicholas Luard, To Santiago de Compostela; A journey of remembrance.
> *In* Fladmark, J.M. (Ed.) *In Search of Heritage as Pilgrim or Tourist?*

Santander, on the north Spanish coast, is a beautiful city used by the wealthy as a summer retreat from the intense heat of the central plains. It was June 2005 and I was there to give a series of lectures on environmental restoration. This was my first time in Spain and I was using the excuse of an expenses-paid and salaried teaching appointment to finally activate that long stillborn pledge to walk the Camino. With more and more research, however, I had come to realise that there was no historical precedent for starting one's pilgrimage in St.-Jean-Pied-de-Port and that the pilgrimage route to Compostela had really as much or more to do with France than it did with Spain. As a result, in a few days time I was to begin my walk far 'upstream' in the town of Le Puy. There was no hurry; I still had a couple of years to make my way to the Apostle's shrine and perhaps beyond to Finisterre in time for my fiftieth birthday.

Morning lectures over, I left the beachside luxury of the resort hotel and wandered through what remained of the old city. From my reading I knew that Santander was an historically important stop on the northern pilgrim route to Compostela. A few days earlier I had been driven to the nearby town of Santillana del Mar to see the exquisite carvings on the capitals in the acclaimed cloister of the collegiate church, another pilgrimage stop. Now I was visiting the twelfth-century Santander cathedral. And it is here where I met my first true foot-weary pilgrims on their way to Compostela. The two elderly French gentlemen, who had started their pilgrimage in Tours, were patient enough to tolerate my questions as we whispered back and forth while seated in the nave. They seemed so confident, so happy, so enthused in what they were engaged in. Radiant almost. I bristled with eagerness and a deep-felt longing to be able to join the august confraternity of which they were members.

A week later, on the evening of the fourth day of my own pilgrimage, I was sitting on the ground outside my small tent in a riverside campground in the French town of Espalion. I was writing my journal while sipping wine and nibbling cheese when approached by two backpack-toting French lads asking for directions to the campground office. My broken French and Spartan belongings caused one to suddenly ask: "Vous êtes le pelerin?" Realising even at the moment or the next when replying and not feeling in the least embarrassed about acting out such a cliché, my heart filled with pride, I straightened my back, assumed a self-imagined aura of profundity, and replied with gravitas that "Yes, I am a pilgrim." After lingering for a few minutes to exchange stories of the road, the fellow pilgrims left. I returned to journalling, brimming with the spirit of being recognised as being one of the community.

Once the Camino Kool-Aid has been drunk the first time there is often no going back to a normal, pilgrimage-free life. During my Spanish steps in 2007 I wrote the following in my journal: "I was born a *Homo sapiens*. Then I became a pilgrim. Then I became the Camino. In the end, because I became the Camino, I became a human being."

One hears stories about and occasionally meets individuals along the pilgrim routes in France and especially in Spain who are repeat or even sometimes perpetual pilgrims. And though I can understand the drug-like hold that the Camino can exact upon susceptible individuals, I am left bewildered and saddened by the manifestation taken by their intoxication. In the Middle Ages, repeat pilgrimages to the same location, if not penitential in nature due to fresh offences, were considered to be either dishonourable or arrogant. The world is such a big, richly diverse place, and pilgrimage is such a universally held trait of human existence, that one could spend a lifetime of walking to sacred loci and never set foot down on the same hallowed ground twice. But then I tell myself that there are all kinds of people, sadly many whose spirit of exploration and adventure has been so beaten out of them that they eagerly return year after year to the comfort and predictability of the same loved and familiar vacation spot. But can a pilgrimage based on comfort and predictability, obtained through familiarity, ever really be a true pilgrimage?

Before I took my first step in Spain I determined that I needed a flavour of all four French 'feeder' routes. As such, I walked fourteen-hundred kilometres along them over a period of several years. And following my time on the Camino Francés I have spent a considerable amount of time, money, and effort in planning and then walking to Assisi, Canterbury, and other medieval pilgrimage destinations in Europe. My book shelves are filled with research material and maps for future pilgrimages in England, Ireland, France, Italy, and Ethiopia, to name a few dreams. It is disheartening to realise, of course, that my ever-growing pilgrimage 'bucket list' will never be completed given whatever time I might have remaining. In such instances, I am reconciled somewhat by reminding myself of the ultimate lesson of Bunyan's *Pilgrim's Progress*, namely that which matters most is how one traverses the inner pilgrimage of one's own earthly life. The number of steps and the direction and destination of travel out of the front door are in the end, of secondary importance. But then I remember too, the compelling words of Tolkien's magical poem giving voice to the promise of travel and spirit of adventure: "The Road goes ever on and on. / Down from the door where it began. / And now the Road is far ahead …" And once again I am saddened.

In between physical pilgrimages I sit content in my sun-room discovering, dreaming, and planning future pilgrimage endeavours, surrounded by Camino memorabilia and an ever-expanding library of pilgrimage-related tomes. If you were to visit me, it would be easy to find your way to this room. A series of familiar yellow-on-blue stylised scallop shells or arrows on replica ceramic plaques purchased in Compostela would direct you from the driveway to the front door, through the twists and turns of the rooms in the house, to the secular pilgrimage shrine in the back sun-room. There you would find a variety of scallop shells on strings dangling from nails tacked into the wooden bookcases or window frames. Your attention would also be grabbed by the diversity of sparkly replica pilgrim badges and insignia lying or hanging about: Saint Francis' beautiful Tau cross, Saint Thomas astride his horse on way to his martyrdom, Saint Winifred standing beside her holy well, Saint Peter's crossed keys, Saint Brigit's star-wheeled cross, Glastonbury's Chalice Well cover, Axum's Arc of the Covenant, etc. Had you walked in southern France or perhaps visited his gilded tomb in Venice, you would recognise and admire the replica plaster cast hanging on the wall of Saint Roch, pilgrim *bordon* in one hand, lifting up his robe with the other to allow his trusty dog to lick his plague pustule. You might then notice the colourful, replica eighteenth-century map showing the European pilgrimage routes to Compostela and reflect back to your own memories of various locations along the Way. Near it on the wall you would see my own framed *compostela* certificate indicating that I too, like you, had completed the pilgrimage.

Eventually you would make your way to the bookcase and I'd ask you to select one of a dozen CDs of medieval pilgrimage music found there to play as you browsed through the collection of books. I'd leave you at this point, to pour a glass of French or Spanish wine from a region through which you had walked. Meanwhile, head a-kilter, you would be scanning the spines of several dozen works of Camino fiction before moving down to the middle shelves to scan more than five dozen contemporary pilgrim narratives. On the lower shelves you'd find many books about the history and global diversity of pilgrimage. Finally, you might wander over to the other bookcase and there find books about my current research and writing projects, recognising such famous locations as Holywell, Glastonbury, Canterbury, Walsingham, in addition to Assisi, Clairvaux, Rome, Jerusalem, Axum, and Lalibela. Finally, you'd make your reading selection, sit down, sip the pilgrimage wine and nibble on the *tapas* snack, and, depending on the subject of the chosen book, either reminisce about past pilgrimages or dream of future ones. And in this act you would be sharing an activity engaged in daily by thousands of one-time and as-yet-to-be pilgrims, the world over.

On Literary...

CHAPTER 9

INVENTING SANTIAGO

Mystery

Dead End on the Camino by Elyn Aviva (formerly Ellen Feinberg) is an unpretentious, occasionally unbelievable, and otherwise largely unmemorable self-published effort by a first-time novelist who has considerable knowledge and experience about the Camino. The latter, however, becomes a problem in that, like many works of Camino fiction, there is a tendency for inexperienced authors to create characters whose major literary purpose seems to be as authors' mouthpieces for didactic lessons about the legends and history of the Camino. Often, here as elsewhere, these lessons do next to nothing to advance the plot and do nothing for character development. That criticism said, Aviva can write well and does handle the task of managing convincing, though often for the reasons noted above, stilted dialogue, a task that many academic scholars dabbling as fiction writers (myself included) find difficult to accomplish.

The novel beings with the protagonist, Noa Webster, who like her creator, is a cultural anthropologist, doing research in the National Library in Madrid. Inside an antiquated volume, she finds a five-hundred-year-old letter by a member of the Knights of Santiago, an organisation whose role had been to protect pilgrims on the Camino. Soon, an old librarian dies under suspicious circumstances, a mysterious scholar arrives to assist Noa, and 'the game's afoot' as it were. The pair begin a journey by car from Roncesvalles to Compostela following clues obtained from one piece of statuary to the next, all leading to a treasure that is hidden somewhere on the Milky Way, as the ancient, pre-Christian Camino is sometimes called. Along the way, they encounter reappearing and disappearing cloaked figures who seem intent on thwarting their plans.

A problem faced by many contemporary crime novels concerns how to make the unexceptional, Joe-and-Jane common (wo)man characters react to the exceptional events surrounding death. Unfortunately, in this regard, the present book contains far too many unbelievable responses in relation to, for example, the police and especially to the subsequent death of a major character, to allow one to suspend one's disbelief and become engaged in any significant way with the story. Aviva, through her protagonist, seems preoccupied with describing, often in off-putting detail, regional food and her naïve belief that the trait about women that men first notice and fixate on is the colour of their hair. The reader does learn about the Camino, but again, like the retelling here of the legend of the crowing cock in Santo Domingo, it is in the form of a mini-lecture rather than a piece of information that has anything really to do with either plot or character development.

A major challenge faced by all fictional works about the Camino is trying to tell a unified and building story where the physical setting is constantly shifting as the characters slowly make their way to Compostela. David Dickinson attempts this, to somewhat mixed results, in his Edwardian period mystery *Death of a Pilgrim*. The well-written novel (part of a series) begins in 1907 with Michael Delany, an American robber baron of Irish ancestry, who decides to bring members of his dispersed family together to undertake a sponsored pilgrimage in thanksgiving for the miraculous survival of his son, James, from terminal cancer. In due course, a cast of eccentrics gather in Le-Puy-en-Velay in southern France, one of the four traditional pilgrimage assembling points. Soon a cousin is found dead under mysterious circumstances, and to circumvent difficulties from local authorities, Delany's lawyers bring in the British detective Lord Francis Powerscourt to smooth things over.

Powerscourt informs the group that he expects there to be further murders and that it is his belief that one of them is the murderer and, as a result, he would strongly advise them to abandon the pilgrimage, separate, and go home. He is met with arguments, one pilgrim stating that such an escape would be giving up and that pilgrimage is supposed to be hard. At which point the detective gives up, realising that he is dealing with an irrational group. To him, such a judgmental belief seems to make sense since "no rational person would set out to walk the thousand miles from Le Puy to Santiago de Compostela."

Bribes are paid and the group of suspects is allowed to proceed on their pilgrimage, travelling by carriage, train, and walking. Along the way the individuals share their stories and motivations for accepting the offer of undertaking the pilgrimage, many of which have a distinctly medieval feel to them; i.e. praying for healing for oneself or a spouse, redemption from bad behaviour, etc. And occasionally glimpses are revealed of the pilgrimage psyche: "As the days have passed I have come to realise that it is not all despair and guilt, that the process of pilgrimage itself, the rhythm of the day, the aching feet at the end of journey, the deep sleep that comes with so much exercise, is helping me toward some kind of understanding." Dickinson does a good job of subtly inserting just the right amount of history and local descriptions to provide the novel with authenticity, yet wisely stays free of overwhelming the story with tangential didacticism.

And so the cavalcade of death begins, with both kilometres and the body count increasing as the group nears the border with Spain. The unbelievable part of the story is that local authorities find one unconvincing reason after another to justify why their chief suspects should be allowed to leave their town and continue ahead, the murder *du jour* always being left unsolved. The story reaches its dramatic conclusion at the running of the bulls in Pamplona with the death of the murderer. Powerscourt leaves the group, promising to return in a month's time to greet the survivors in Compostela. There a humorous scene enfolds wherein the priests in the cathedral temporarily lose control of the *Botafumeiro*, the giant swinging incense burner, which almost kills Powerscourt, leading one pilgrim to remark that thankfully the murderer didn't know of the "smelly monster on the rope" or he would have used it to kill half the congregation.

One way to get around the difficulty of a constantly shifting location for a Camino murder mystery is to set the novel in the Middle Ages when after a death and burial of a victim it is much easier to believe that the remaining pilgrims could continue forward in the absence (or limited presence) of any effective legal system to detain them. In short, in such times acts of violence and death were much more commonplace and the pilgrimage along the Camino in particular was widely recognised to be an extremely dangerous undertaking. As Sharon Newman describes in *Strong as Death*, a volume in her mystery series featuring the twelfth-century former novitiate Catherine Le Vendeur: "Pilgrimage didn't stop long for death. Once a body has been cared for and prayers said, it is necessary to move on. When a vow has been made to visit the saints, it cannot be broken and might not be delayed."

After a series of miscarriages and stillborn births, the heroine and her husband are advised to go to Compostela to pray at the shrine of Saint James for a child. The story beings in Vézelay, another pilgrimage rendezvous point in France where our protagonists meet up with the improbably yet authentically named Astrolabe (think Moonbeam Zappa or Prince Michael Jackson), the son of the famous star-crossed lovers Héloise and Abelard. A ragtag ensemble of characters of various classes with all the classic motivations head out toward Le Puy and things seem fine, so much so that Catherine beings to feel guilty: "She felt so content that it seemed wrong. A pilgrimage shouldn't be so pleasant." But then of course things take a turn as several unsavoury characters join the group and the murders begin.

The tone of novel at times seems confused, mixing good period insights about pilgrimage in general and the Way in particular ("Pilgrims, traders, imposters and thieves, sick and well, rich and poor, speaking in a dozen languages, everyone heading in the direction of Santiago.") with anachronistic sensibilities ("Perhaps by the time I reach Compostela, I will have found the answer.") and sayings ("By the callused palms of Santo Domingo the bridge-builder."). On a positive note, chapters are entitled for specific locations and times ("Seventeen: Just outside Cirauqui, heading down the hillside toward the Roman bridge, Thursday, June 5, 1142, the Feast of Saint Boniface…") which makes interesting reading for Camino veterans. And Newman's descriptions of the idiosyncrasies of various locations and sights demonstrate her research and intimate familiarity with the Way.

Murders solved, culprits dealt with, the survivors continue onward. And the protagonists come to realise that their own quest for fertility is in the end trivial compared to the more weighty concerns and hopes of other pilgrims, as Newman ably concludes:

> There were many others now; the road was clogged with those limping, carried on litters, lepers with their wooden clappers of warning, the aged hoping to die at the feet of the saint, parents with children ill or born with deformities, and those that appeared whole but were bent under the weight of their sins. Among them were also those who came on pilgrimage of thanksgiving, who had left their crutches and chains behind. Their joy gave the others hope.

Another strategy to circumvent the difficulty of blending a crime novel with a road trip is to focus on a single location, as accomplished by Sister Carol Anne O' Marie in *Murder Makes a Pilgrimage*. The author, herself a septuagenarian nun, has her Miss Marple-ish alter-ego, Sister Mary Helen, heroine in a number of novels, win an expenses-paid 'pilgrimage' to Santiago de Compostela as part of a promotion from a local Californian restaurant. Sister Mary and a group of other winners are flown to Compostela and as their taxi approaches the Plaza del Obradorio one shouts out "*Mon joie*" in order to be the 'queen.' The pilgrims are accommodated in the pricy Hostal de los Reyes Católicos and early the next morning while everyone else is still jetlagged and asleep our sleuth enters the cathedral to visit the shrine of its saint: "Eyes closed, Sister Mary whispered a prayer and touched St James' coffin lid. She didn't expect it to feel wet and sticky…What in heaven's name could be leaking down here?" And of course, coming as no surprise to readers, it turns out to be blood and we have our murder.

This unassuming novel, a throwback in spirit and style to Agatha Christie, has the group of pilgrims driven to other Galician locations such as the Roman lighthouse at La Coruña and includes many atmospheric descriptions of the seemingly perpetually rain-drenched streets of Compostela around the cathedral where most of the events transpire. Following a good description of the *Botafumerio* ceremony in the cathedral, the incense burner almost does in the heroine when she is pushed in front of its swinging arc. And finally, as in many improbable Christie-esque mysteries, a confession is neatly extracted from the culprit in a final group setting.

Michael Jecks, in *The Templar's Penance*, part of his well-received series featuring medieval knight-sleuth Sir Baldwin Furnshill, uses the same rooted-in-place strategy for his take on murders and pilgrimage. The novel opens with a youth running up Mont Joie to become the 'king' through being the first to see the pilgrimage destination of Santiago de Compostela. But almost immediately the party of pilgrims are set upon by a band of brigands and are in turn rescued by our protagonist. Baldwin, on pilgrimage as atonement for killing an innocent man (as described in an earlier novel), is later awestruck at the carvings on the Pórtio de la Gloria: "He found himself gazing up into the eyes of the statue of Saint James. Then he felt a curious sensation and a tingling along his spine, not at all unpleasant, and he became aware of a conviction that here he not beg forgiveness: it was offered freely. In Saint James' eyes there was compassion and kindness – and understanding."

As the Saint's feast day approaches more and more pilgrims from all of Christendom arrive and Jecks does an admirable job in enabling readers to imagine just what the bustling of heterogeneous pilgrims might have been like in the year 1323. And amidst all this celebration, a young woman is raped and murdered and the investigation begins with many interesting details provided about the differences in medieval laws between Galicia compared to Baldwin's home in Britain. Layers of complicated intrigues, one involving the theft of relics and another concerning Templar history, are teased open, interspersed with exciting descriptions of chases and scuffles about the twisty alleyways surrounding the cathedral, all working toward a satisfying whodunnit conclusion. Along the way there are some humorous anecdotes that modern pilgrims can relate to, such as the overly devoted and self-righteous who become quickly annoyed at the "sacrilegious" behaviour exhibited by the latest arrived batch of excited and jabbering pilgrims hugging each other and gawking at the cathedral and thereby interfering with the prayers of the former.

History

WITH *THE RAMSAY SCALLOP*, FRANCES TEMPLE has written an engaging story that convincingly portrays the Middle Ages for young-adult readers. The year is 1300 and fourteen-year-old Elenor Ramsay is waiting nervously the arrival of her betrothed, twenty-two-year-old Thomas, who has been away on the Crusades for the last eight years. Thomas is emotionally shattered from his experiences abroad and is himself apprehensive about assuming his duties as a lord managing a large estate as well as at the prospect of marrying someone only vaguely remembered from his youth. The local priest decides that the best thing is to send the young couple on the pilgrimage to Santiago de Compostela during which time they can get to know each other (preserving a vow of chastity, of course) as well as exposing these two members of the ruling class to the sort of commoners who they will later have to manage on their lands. At the same time, the Father wishes them, upon arrival at the Saint's shrine, to pray for the collective sins of their village, located near Peterborough. Details about the legend of Saint James are nicely revealed through a series of fireside lessons given by the priest to village children. And soon the young couple are on their way, encountering and learning about the wonderful diversity of European humanity as well as each other as they gradually fall in love.

Temple's maturity as an author comes through the gradual and subtle presentation of information about the art, architecture, and history of pilgrimage, as well as revealing details about what it was like to travel in medieval times, and the small and mundane trials of the road such as the need for drinkable water, adequate accommodation, sustaining food, and safety from wolves and wolf-heads, etc. Some of these issues will be familiar to pilgrims of today, as reflected by the protagonists being greeted upon entering a town by a series of criers brandishing signs advertising their various lodgings: "No fleas, no vermin, just good home cooking!" and "Had enough of hard abbey floors? Come to my house and sleep on a feather mattress!" Never does the author succumb to the all-too-easy and thus frequently adopted method of simply inundating the reader with pages of didacticism that can overwhelm the story.

Unfortunately, the same cannot be said for *Walking the Way: A Medieval Quest*, self-published by Neal A. Wiegman, whose back-cover boldly states that the book "reminds readers of Ken Follett's *The Pillars of the Earth*", one of the most popular historical novels written about the Middle Ages. Nothing could be farther from the truth. Wiegman is a retired Spanish professor with three books about Spanish culture and literature to his name, and he simply cannot resist giving what amounts to a long, drawn-out history lesson that is so boring as to make the book, his first novel, nearly unreadable.

The novel's protagonist is young Xavier, who lives in his parents' inn in twelfth-century Pamplona and upon visiting the nearby abbey at Roncesvalles is given a quest to recover a relic of a piece of the Crown of Thorns that has been recently pilfered by a knight from León belonging to the newly established Order of Santiago. The problem with the novel begins almost immediately when we are informed that Xavier, who has a desire to be a jongleur, has a remarkable (today we would say 'photographic') memory that enables him to memorise and then recite huge pieces of narrative verse after only a single listening. As a result, the bulk of the text is composed of a series of long passages, some up to several pages in length, of Xavier directly quoting medieval sources. In between is squeezed the meagre story of the quest to recover the relic. Even much of that fictional text is about quoting documents rather than about anything that advances the storyline. Chapters are named after towns along the Way just as in a modern narrative and the reader is inundated by mind-numbing details that should have been much better placed in a straightforward scholarly account of the literature of the Camino rather than this dismal attempt at a novel. The book provides a recitation about the Camino's sights and history but gives no indication of the mundane, about what it might have been like to walk the Way in medieval times. It is as if Wiegman had read several modern guidebooks about the Camino, fused these with historical information gleamed from Gitlitz and Davidson's (2000) seminal cultural handbook about the Way, and inserted literally hundreds and hundreds of quotations from medieval literature (about which he knows a great deal), around which he sprinkled a few words of dialogue and a lame attempt at creating some sort of story to tie it all together. It simply does not work, and proves, as few other books have ever done so convincingly, that university professors, no matter how accomplished and well-published they may be, should think very carefully about writing fiction.

In contrast, one university professor of history who *is* capable of crafting a good novel is Bernard Reilly. The *Secret of Santiago: A Novel of Medieval Spain* is the first of Reilly's two works of fiction about the Camino, both of which succeed everywhere Wiegman's effort fails. The year is 830 at a time when most of Iberia is under Moorish rule. In the tiny north-western Christian kingdom of Asturias, the childless king Alfonso II is closely watching his three young nephews to see which would be most suitable to inherit his throne. One, Aurelius, is banished to nearby Galicia after he is framed for a rape in order to discredit him and soon takes up with a 'mad' hermit who prophesies that an event of great spiritual significance is just around the corner. Descriptions of early medieval life feel believable and the dialogue is crisp and focused. Lots of historical details are presented but never at the expense of the gripping story.

At a time when all travellers were regarded with suspicion and a belief that they were somehow abnormal, Aurelius' problems are exacerbated by having had his uncle's signet ring stolen. Essentially a prisoner at court, he meets and falls in love with the daughter of the ruling count and continues his visits with the hermit who has settled in the nearby woods. Eventually an enormous storm slams into the area coincident with the hermit's insistence that excavation begin at the ruins of an old Roman building. A marble coffin is uncovered, emblazoned with scallops and other sea creatures. The hermit, later supported by the bishop, declare the remains to be those of Saint James, and the king, visiting from Asturias, declares that he will endow an abbey to be built upon the spot of their "deliverance" from the Muslim threat, hoping it will become a place to where many will come to worship.

The novel ends with a fast-forward synopsis of the later history of the site that provides a sense of temporal connectivity between the distant, medieval events and the modern, reading pilgrim:

> The voice of King Alfonso II has died away. The voices of the bards who sang his praise have perished. The little church that he raised over the sarcophagus of marble has vanished. But in the place of that church one larger grew, only itself still later to yield to a Romanesque cathedral of heroic proportions. And that cathedral, in turn, has been clothed and cloaked over the centuries in the gold-hued stone of addition after addition whose spires glisten yet in the sunlight of afternoons…For five hundred years the great pilgrim hospital of Ferdinand and Isabella, raised in gratitude to the Apostle for the final victory over Muslim power in the peninsula in 1492, has sat next to the church of Santiago. For the pilgrims did come. By tens, then by hundreds, by thousands, and by tens of thousands they came – and come still. The earth groans with the weight of the pilgrims and the stones sink under their burden.

Bernard Reilly's second salvo into the Camino literature, *Journey to Compostela: A Novel of Medieval Pilgrimage and Peril*, is a gem, not only being the most exciting of all novels that have been written about the Way, but also being one of the best works of fiction to portray the Middle Ages. The book, a masterpiece of nihilism, is a refreshing anecdote to the cheerful and uplifting spiritual claptrap that defines most modern pilgrimage accounts and which often also characterises many novels about the Camino. The reality is that any middle-class person of today lives a more luxuriant life than any member of medieval royalty; and there is absolutely no comparison between the respective dangers faced by modern, compared to medieval, pilgrims. Reilly's harrowing tale is a departure from previous idealised presentations and provides a wonderful glimpse of the dismal feudal relationships of the time, when upper mobility was simply unthinkable and where the lives of the masses were controlled by the capricious whims of a few.

The protagonist, Martin, is a farmer who is press-ganged into tending the horses of a group of pilgrims who have been marshalled together with cruel domination by a sadistic and violent knight, Rainald. Descriptions about actual locations along the Way are limited; instead the story focuses with building intensity on the psychological battle of one-upmanship between these two individuals in a sort of microcosm of medieval class struggle, the knight always toying with the farmer as he voices his dilemma of whether to kill him before or after the group reaches Compostela. The novel includes an exciting battle and would make a wonderful period film should it catch the eye of a capable screenwriter and director.

The contested relationship between the two is played out on a tableau of the difficulties of medieval pilgrimage. As one character explains: "And there were two more, a man from Poitiers and a woman from the Touraine, who died. The usual sort of thing – in their sleep. There was no sign of foul play. Likely it was just the heat, too little food, and exhaustion. We made the usual distribution of their goods and buried them." The group faces so many hardships that the pilgrimage begins to resemble Scott's retreat from the South Pole or the Bataan Death March: "This routine was now predictable. They had repeated it so often, and suffered its oppression so regularly that its burden and their endurance of it were largely mechanical. Unless someone in the column fell, and died where he fell, the apathy of the pilgrims ordinarily went unbroken."

The apathy leads to disillusionment at the act of pilgrimage itself. One pilgrim, for example, challenges the concept of finding peace at Compostela as "the kind of miracle that little children and the very simple of mind dream about." In one memorable scene, the jaded knight voices a suite of rhetorical questions:

> The world is mad, Martin. Here we are, the whole company of us, walking half way to the end of the earth. For what? When we reach Santiago de Compostela, if we do, what shall we have accomplished? Will our sins be washed away? We will be quick enough to commit new ones, won't we? Will we be cured of gout, rheumatism, the pox? Won't we be visited by new afflictions soon enough to replace them? But we walk. Well, you common folk walk anyway, and strain your guts, and accumulate your blisters, and cadge swill for food from one another and from the farmers we pass along the way, which sours your stomachs and gives you the trots at night. But this very night, some bandit may steal into the camp and crush your head with a rock while you sleep your more or less innocent sleep…You could sicken, swell, and die. Or one of our fellow pilgrims may find a way to poison you for his portion in the sharing out of your miserable goods. Who then is sane, Martin? Those who drag themselves from day to miserable day afraid to live – whose most noble hope is to put off dying for yet another moon? No matter the pretense, even the dullest of them knows that they are dying. No one can elude that certainty for more than a moment or two at a time. Are these sane beings, Martin, who crawl about the world in such fashion?

As one might expect from such a demonstration, possibly anachronistic, of existentialism, the arrival at Compostela of the survivors is filled with disillusionment due to the absence of immediate cures or attainments of peace of mind, both of which lead to crises of faith. Some pilgrims, facing the dim prospect of a return home to their former empty lives, realise that they have been changed by the pilgrimage experience and would rather settle into new lives in Galicia.

During repairs of Worcester Cathedral in 1986, remains of a pilgrim were found, recognisable by his boots, walking staff, and especially a 'cockleshell,' his treasured symbol of having reached Compostela. Later research suggested the remains to be those of Robert Sutton, a fifteenth-century dyer and a man of enough wealth and influence to be buried in the cathedral. In *The Cockleshell Pilgrim: A Medieval Journey to Compostela*, historian Katherine Lack has scripted what is quite possibly the most accurate description of what it must have been like to be a pilgrim in the Middle Ages. Aided by thorough research (as indicated by the copious endnotes, enumerated, and identified in the text) Lack creates a weird, almost unique, hybrid of history and proto-fiction in which she traces Sutton's journey from the Welsh Marches through

France to Compostela. No dialogue is present but Lack's skill as a writer is evident in her imaginings of Sutton's thoughts and emotions along the Way.

It is in the powerful descriptions of pilgrims walking through familiar landscapes that the book registers most memorably, and leaves a reader hoping that Lack will attempt to script a full-fledged novel in the future:

> From the comfort and cacophony of Burgos, out across the long arid plains, it was late afternoon before they came down into a wooded valley between steep limestone scarps, to the San Antón Convent, a monumental Antonine hospital whose arches spanned the road so loftily that their detail was lost in the shadows. The familiar Tau cross emblazoned in the windows and the bread and wine set ready for them in the hatch beneath the arch, where they gathered in the welcoming shade to rest, were signs and gifts from heaven. Then, doggedly on the road again, it wasn't long before their eyes were drawn to the strange conical hill of Castrojeriz far ahead, but distances were deceptive on these shimmering plains, and it was a full hour before the little hill grew into a great summit, crowned by a fortress, with the convent of St Mary of the apples at its feet, and the town and its hospitals nestling on its flank.

And:

> And so the party set off again, up the valley, pacing their progress to each other's needs, some slower up the steepest parts, some more cautious crossing the frequent streams. As they went up higher, the valley narrowed and it began to drizzle. Wet and muddy, dripped on by interminable oak and pine woods, through towns and villages, still they ascended, past hospitals large and small, until suddenly they were so high they were walking in the very clouds, their sodden clothes clinging to their limbs, feet slipping at every step. After what seemed an age of uncertain progress, a shape loomed close beside their path. There was no time even to be afraid, before they heard a human voice, unintelligible but warm, inviting and friendly, and then, repeated like a holy incantation, the name of 'O Cebreiro'

And finally:

> Up there, beside the cairn of stones and the great cross, Sutton and a hundred other pilgrims like him took off their hats, and stared in reverent awe at Compostela, city of their longing, etched in the evening light in the

valley below. The vespers breeze ruffling their hair, choking with emotion and blinded by sudden tears, they sang a *Te Deum* of fervent gratitude. Then in the last light of day Sutton took off his boots and walked barefoot down the hill to St James' city.

Esoteric/New Age

Walking Home on the Camino de Santiago, self-published by Linda L. Laswell, is one of those odd books (see next section on contemporary novels) that resides somewhere in the uncomfortable middle ground between fact and fiction. From the back cover we read, confusingly, that the book is "the fictionalised account of Laswell's on-again, off-again pilgrimage", and that "this story is based on true events. Some realities have been altered. Some characters have been invented." A handful of standard, though relevant, passages are presented concerning the nature of walking and pilgrimage, with chapters being unimaginatively crafted to simply follow daily journal entries. The fiction element comes through the introduction, à la Shirley MacLaine, of an inner voice called "Simon" (an angel perhaps?) whose role it appears to be to chide Laswell to keep at it and not to quit. And so, Laswell moves forward, often resorting to driving large sections of the Camino, to arrive at the end and come to her big realisation: "It occurred to me that the road never really ends." Yawn.

Elyn Aviva's self-published *The Journey: A Novel of Pilgrimage and Spiritual Quest* begins promisingly with the heroine, Gwen, crying in the cathedral of Santiago de Compostela after having walked the Camino but feeling great emptiness and sadness with her realisation that "there was nothing in Santiago for me, nothing at all." Frustrated and disappointed, she cannot bring herself to hug the Apostle's statue. This is a welcome and refreshing anecdote to all those gushing narratives by modern pilgrims which seem to always end in an epiphany at the cathedral. Readers learn that Gwen had undertaken the pilgrimage for purposes of a transformative rebirth following her painful divorce. So far, so good. But then almost immediately readers are asked to believe that someone who has walked the entire Camino would never had heard a single mention of an older route continuing on to Finisterre. And so, the didactic lessons begin.

The heroine soon falls in with a group of neo-Druids and begins a quest for self-enlightenment that has her, accompanied by spiritual guides, one with the name "Santiago", revisiting the Camino and venturing farther afield to the cathedral at Chartres, a forest in Brittany, the Dordogne, and even Istanbul. Aviva does do a good job at providing esoteric information about the pre-Christian underpinnings of the Milky Way, as the route used to be called in Roman times, including such topics as the Costa da Morte at Finisterre and the 'game of the goose,' an ancient board-game. Most of this information is provided in the form of mini-lectures that do little to advance either the meagre plot or character development. During Gwen's trips we meet a hotchpotch of all the usual New Age suspects: Templar knights, Druids, the Kabbalah, the Grail, labyrinths, Merlin, freemasons, King Arthur, Sufis, energy fields, and Rumi poetry. All this interspersed with chapters about the protagonist's recurring visions of a previous medieval life. By the time the novel is finished, the reader is frustrated and confused by it all, and wants nothing better to do than to simply sit in a cathedral and escape into the sonorous simplicity of a Gregorian chant.

The Prophet of Compostela: A Novel of Apprenticeship by Henri Vincenot tells the story of Johan, a young forester from Burgundy who is intrigued by the construction of an abbey and becomes initiated, under the guidance of a self-admitted heretical prophet, into the mysteries of symbolic geometry related to Celtic myths and Freemasonry. The back cover likens the book to Umberto Eco's *The Name of the Rose*, itself a wonderful fusion of adventure and allegory. Unfortunately, the reality does not support this optimistic marketing.

Johan helps with the construction of the abbey but again this is not *The Spire*, *Cathedral by the Sea*, or even *Pillars of the Earth*. Instead we have a thinly disguised and incredibly boring lecture that goes on and on for pages. These digressions completely overwhelm the story with a cluttered array of complex geometric drawings presented as gems of imagined insight into grand truths about the universe, using that overused metaphor from dozens of science fiction novels: God, the cosmic mathematician, symbolised as pi.

Things do pick up when two-thirds of the way through the lecture-cum-novel, the story reasserts itself when the pair set off on a journey of discovery along the ancient lay line of the Milky Way toward Compostela. And it is here where Vincenot displays that he can pen an atmospheric scene:

> They always walked in the direction of the sun, like the ant on its apple, to impregnate themselves with the rhythms of the earth and the universe, following the road of the stars across northern Castile. A Castile that an iron sun rendered grey and ochre with the cold veins of blue and umber earth. Vast spaces where the pilgrim traveling ahead, all alone a league away,

became a looming giant. No villages, but only piles of gray stones closed at the north against the cold, at the south against the sun, at the west against the rain, and at the east against the wind.

And in a vein similar to that used by Luis Buñuel in his iconoclastic film *The Milky Way* (see Chapter 10), Vincenot, through his curmudgeon prophet, gives voice to his disdain of naïve, Christian pilgrims addicted to the cult of relics: "And they decided to quit the company of these lechers of God, these compromisers of the faith, these gainers of paradise, and to travel alone." After several adventures, the heroes return back home to learn about the recent destruction, through a lightning strike, of the old Chartres cathedral. The novel ends with Johan and his newfound comprehension of the mathematical perfections inherent in the Gothic arch and vault, deciding to go to Chartres to aid in rebuilding there that wondrous and enigmatic cathedral that we so admire today.

Tracey Saunders' *Pilgrimage to Heresy: Don't Believe Everything They Tell You: A Novel of the Camino*, is, as one might surmise from the strange sub-title, a self-published work. The book is based on the reasonably well-known (at least to historians and those historically inclined) theory that the remains buried in the cathedral of Santiago de Compostela are not in fact those of Saint James (it must be noted that hardly anyone except perhaps the blindly devote or egregiously jingoistic Spanish really believe the established dogma today) but rather belong to Priscillian, a fourth-century former Roman senator from Galicia who became a bishop and who has the dubious distinction of being the first Christian to be martyred by fellow Christians for his heretical beliefs in Aryanism. Despite such an interesting and promising concept, one becomes immediately nervous by the back-cover which states that this is a book containing questions about which "the Catholic Church would rather you didn't learn answers!" and then in the mention in the author's Afterword likening the book to *The Da Vinci Code*. The novel suffers from a confusing and distracting text layout in which most but not all paragraphs are without indentations and separated by blank lines as well as a perplexingly inconsistent system of formatting for quotations.

The book contains chapters concerning a present-day pilgrim, Miranda, who meets mysterious characters on the Camino who lecture her about the roots of the early Church, alternating with chapters set in Priscillian's time dealing with the momentous events that ultimately culminate in his execution. These jarring leaps back and forth in time, shifts from first to third person, and excerpts from various texts, make for a confusing jumble of prose. The problem once again with many such self-published efforts is that the interesting material that Saunders has assembled would have been much better presented as a straightforward work of non-fiction than packaged, as it is here, as a loosely masqueraded piece of fiction. In short, description of the over-familiar journey is hackneyed and the conversation-cum-lectures, which at first are interesting, soon become tedious.

Still there are some sections that modern pilgrims can identify with: "The refugio was dirty. The mattresses were lumpy and old. The pillows were musty, and the blankets better avoided." But these succinct and apt truisms are interspersed with other, trite comments such as: "'You should know that you do not choose the Camino. The Camino chooses you.' It was not the last time she was to hear this, and it became more and more profound every time she heard it." Saunders does have the ability to script moving scenes, as for example, the arrival at the cathedral:

> The Cathedral of Santiago, its two Baroque towers, the spires of her dreams, reared up in front of her with unapologetic majesty. It was a physical state of Grace, impelling, imploring her to recognise what it stood for, what she stood for – all those dusty miles, all those self-doubts, all those tortured dreams, all those hopeless yet tenuous hopes which had never really either taken root, nor died. All those who had come before her, or not made it. The group in front of her let out a cheer. Someone threw a hat in the air. And Miranda sank to her knees and cried and cried. 'I'm home!' she said.

Unfortunately, the weight of the jumbled, multi-temporal storyline, filled to the brim with didactic lecturing, buries the occasional good prose. And then there is the odd choice of the cover – a close-up of the Jesse Tree topped by Saint James in the Pórtico del Gloria – when the question remains of whether the Apostle is even buried in the cathedral. But perhaps that is the last teasing message of purposefully designed confusion left by the author.

Paulo Coelho's huge bestseller, *The Pilgrimage: A Contemporary Quest for Ancient Wisdom,* more so than any other book, has become regarded by many as *the* work of fiction that encapsulates the modern Camino experience. Reputedly a realistic account of Coelho's journey with his master and guide, Petrus, in search of a powerful sword that is hidden somewhere along the Camino, much of the book is made up of a series of instructional "exercises designed to free him from the burdens that have been created in his life." From these exercises the reader is supposed in turn to glimpse his or her personal devils and so be guided on the path to spiritual rebirth. Designed therefore as a modern *Pilgrim's Progress*, mixing adventure with allegory, the novel contains chapters with titles such as "Cruelty", "Love", "Death", and "Madness", and is really a self-help manual based on the typical New Age repackaging of elements of Christianity and other sources. Unfortunately, the fact that millions have bought the book and that today one cannot escape meeting while on the Camino some well-meaning pilgrim who feels it to be her or his purpose in life to go on and on about it, does in no way raise the literary merits of the book.

As a supposed work of fiction, the adventure element is extremely weak. The recurring battles with an ominous black dog are just silly and superficial and do nothing more than make one want to cast aside the book in order to reread a real masterpiece of psychological depth such Ian McEwan's *Black Dogs*, in which the characters also confront their own personal demons in the form of sinister canines while on a similar long-distance walking trip. And as a spiritual allegory, the enlightenment offered is banal beyond belief: "Even if the I were not able to find my sword, the pilgrimage along the Road to Santiago was going to help me to find myself", "You don't have to climb a mountain to find out whether or not it's high", "The ship is safest when it's port, but that's not what ships are built for", and "The Road to Santiago was walking me", etc.

And then there are the puzzling spellings that grate, as for example, "San Tiago" (San Iago?) and "El Cebrero" (O Cebreiro or El Acebo?), and the odd and repeated referral to the "medieval route known [to whom other than Coelho?] as the Strange Road to Santiago." No wonder that some have questioned as to whether Coelho ever set foot on the Camino given that the book is supposed to be a loosely fictionalised account of true events. Indeed, the author's ignorance on the subject is profound: "The Road to Santiago has made only one mark on French culture, and that has been on that country's national pride, gastronomy, through the name 'Coquilles Saint-Jacques'". This despite that fact that many have identified the Way of Saint James with nothing short of creating medieval culture throughout much of Europe, and for this reason had it designated as the continent's first Cultural Itinerary Route. In the end, if a New Age reader is interested in reading a proto-fictional work along these lines, he or she would do better to search out Carlos Castaneda's Don Juan series which reached similar popularity a generation ago among wisdom-seeking and drug-infused hippies.

Contemporary

MARGARET K. BROWN'S SELF-PUBLISHED *A Pilgrimage Story* is a mystery, not because there is anything particularly mysterious taking place within its pages, but rather because it is unfathomable as to why it was written at all. Faced with the task of weaving together the experiences from several repeated pilgrimages – as has been successfully accomplished before (see discussion of the narratives of Wallis and of Ward in Part I) – here the author opts instead to fuse those experiences into a single fictionalised journey. Then, rather than taking advantage of the freedom offered by fiction – detailed introspection from a variety of characters, nonlinear sequencing, subtle or exaggerated events working toward some resolution, etc. – Brown simply regurgitates her various diaries into this barely fictional product. Chapter titles simply follow those of any number of Camino narratives, as for example, "Day 10 – Tosantos to Atapuerca", and various scenes or structures described in the text are accompanied by photographs. Can it really be a novel as it purports to be?

Then there is the other problem with the book, as witness the banality illustrated by the closing lines:

> On the way to the airport at Lavacolla, we drove through areas where previously we had walked. I thought to myself, that I was glad not to be walking in the rain. Still on the *camino*, there was always anticipation – what was around the next corner? Then I understood that the *camino* – the pilgrimage – was still going on. Each corner you turn has a new experience, a new challenge, a new opportunity, and each person you meet may be the next friend, or the one that enlightens you, or the one you can help. The *camino* is forever. *Ultreya!*

Yawn, again.

Ten thousand Ways to Santiago: A Pilgrimage Novel, by E.C. Curtsinger, suffers from the exact opposite problem to Brown's effort above. Although ostensibly about the Camino, the novel presents one run-on, directionless, fictionalised conversation amongst a muddle of forgettable characters that goes on and on and on, for more than four hundred pages, and which has little or no reference to the pilgrimage. Right from the start, one becomes nervous about this self-published book. The cover, by someone having the same surname as the author, resembles a child's simplistic crayon drawing; the front flap contains dubious English; and the rear flap's description of the author certainly does not inspire confidence: "Gene Curtsinger is Texas country, a novelist and literary critic-mostly Melville and Henry James – and a professor of English at the University of Dallas. He's an army veteran. 'They didn't want me to come ashore at Okinawa, and shot me in seventeen places'…He 'had to go to Spain a dozen times' to research the Camino." The book presents a cacophony of dialogue, too-cute word games, strange appellations ("C*a*mpostela"?), illogical and inconsistent uses of italics, all buried in a dog's breakfast of meaningless events that jumble together with neither structure nor purpose. This book, more than any other reviewed here in Part III, comes the closest to being totally unreadable.

Cecilia Samartin in *Tarnished Beauty: A Novel* mixes a modern story about a beautiful Mexican girl with a large birthmark across her back and top of her legs who has illegally crossed the border to find work in a California mental hospital with a story told in flashback by one of the patients, a mysterious individual about whom the staff warn her not to trust but who seems to have some sort of power over everyone and who goes by the assumed name of Señor Peregrino. Antonio (the patient's real name) steals her identification documents and insists her illegal status will be revealed to the authorities unless she sits patiently, day after day, and listens to his tale of his pilgrimage along the Camino undertaken decades before.

Antonio and his friend Tomas were Spanish seminary students sent on pilgrimage by their superior in order to clear their heads and cleanse their souls of lustful thoughts about young women. Samartin does a fine job at describing the feel of the mid-twentieth-century Spain, the food, dance, class structure, etc., and creates an intriguing story wherein our two friends become rivals for the affections of a beautiful young fellow pilgrim they meet along the Way. Tormented by lust, love, and guilt, Antonio seeks reprieve by entering and praying in churches whenever possible:

> I stepped out of the room with my blanket wrapped around my shoulders, and made my way to the outer courtyard where it was bright with the blue light of the moon. I was drawn toward the small church across the square. The moon shadows created by the rough-carved statues of saints and the pilgrim saint himself seemed to beckon me. He looked down upon me from his concave perch with his staff held high, as though he might knock me over the head with it. I welcomed the beating if it would earn me a moment's peace.

Samartin is a critically acclaimed author and her descriptions of the Camino have an authenticity lacking in many other fictionalised accounts of the pilgrimage, as for example, "The main via was teeming with pilgrims from throughout Spain and Europe. It was exhilarating to hear so many languages mixing about like a delicious stew, its aroma delighting our sense at every turn", and "On the *camino*, my heart and mind had, along with the plodding of my feet, found a peaceful rhythm. Life's irrelevant distractions were gone. We had all that we needed, and every moment was complete in the present knowing of ourselves and our companions", and finally "And at the very crest of the tallest spire stood the statue of the Apostle Santiago, with his pilgrim's staff and wide-brimmed hat, welcoming all who were as he had been – a pilgrim of faith, a courageous and wandering soul, a child of God…Rosa and I entered the main doors of the sanctuary, feeling as two drops in a vast river of life."

It is commonplace while on the Camino for spiritually minded pilgrims to ascribe even the simplest of natural phenomena to exhibitions of deliberate intent and message, as for example that experienced by Antonio:

> The other pilgrims had left hours ago for León, and all was quiet. Tomas and I sat together watching as pigeons gathered at the fountain for a brisk bath. And then they started to flutter and hover about with a synchronised purpose, much like a swarm of bees. Before my eyes, they shaped themselves into a white, undulating form that evolved, stretching and condensing until I clearly saw the image of Santiago himself floating over the fountain while pointing his staff toward the road, urging us to leave the square immediately.

During the recounting of the pilgrimage experience, the patient and the caregiver become ever closer, each contributing to the other's healing, their stories, past and present, finally conjoining at the end of the novel in a dramatic flourish across time.

Due to his lifelong interest in the act of pilgrimage as attested to in numerous scholarly articles by literary critics, David Lodge is certainly the most famous novelist to have written about the Camino. In *Therapy*, Lodge creates an endearing character, Laurence "Tubby" Passmore, who at the start of the novel seems to have it all going for him: a successful and personally enriching career as a writer of a popular sitcom, lots of money, a beautiful and seemingly doting wife, close relationships with his grown-up children and a female friend, etc. But then a perfect storm of blackly humorous events causes his life to unravel. Passmore, at first gradually and then with increasing anxiety, begins a mid-life crisis that leaves him physically wrecked and emotionally bereft. Becoming neurotic, he seeks solace through a smorgasbord of therapies: physiotherapy, aromatherapy, acupuncture therapy, massage therapy, psychotherapy, etc. He becomes obsessed with Kierkegaard's angst-ridden writings and sad love life. Nothing seems to work. Convinced that all he needs is the redemptive love of a woman to heal him, Passmore goes through a series of amorous escapades that do not work out. Reflecting back four decades to a time in his youth when he imagines he was most happy, he decides what he needs to do is to track down his very first love. From her husband he finds out that she is presently on the Camino, recovering from the sudden death of her son. And so our protagonist heads off to Spain in the final chapter of the novel, where he drives back and forth along the Camino searching for his old flame. The pair reunite near Astorga and Passmore undertakes the daily task of ferrying her backpack in his car while she, suffering from injuries, hobbles forward until they meet up at the end of each day, he walking back along the Way to meet her after checking into a hotel.

At first, Passmore is suspicious of the intentions of the pilgrims: "I found it hard to understand why millions of people had walked halfway across Europe in times past, often under conditions of appalling discomfort and danger, to visit the dubious shrine of this dubious saint, and even harder to understand why they were still doing so, albeit in smaller numbers." Feeling an outsider, he brings an objectivity in his appraisal of the varied types of pilgrims he encounters: the young Spaniards out of their parental homes and eager to meet others of the opposite sex, the "much despised and resented" cycling clubs, those taking an alternative and adventurous holiday, those with personal motives like fundraising, those marking birthdays, job loss, or retirement, and those with whom he most identifies, the walking wounded in recovery from some trauma.

Eventually Passmore admits to himself that the pilgrimage, "even in the bastardised, motorised form" in which he was doing it, is beginning to lay its spell upon him. In particular, he appreciates the gift of pilgrimage in enabling a distillation of the complexities of life into a bare-boned, existential purity. Interviewed for a British television documentary in O Cebreiro, Passmore insists that he is not a true pilgrim, but then when pressed about just who is such, he replies: "Someone for whom it's an existential act of self-definition…A leap into the absurd, in Kierkegaard's sense." He then continues with one of the very best explanations of pilgrimage, linking

Kierkegaard's three stages in personal development – the aesthetic, the ethical, and the religious – with corresponding pilgrim typologies: the aesthetic pilgrim focused on having a good time and enjoying the picturesque and cultural pleasures of the Camino, the ethical pilgrim competitively concerned with the Camino as a test of stamina and self-discipline and preoccupied with who is or is not a "true pilgrim", and the religious pilgrim who like Kierkegaard accepts the coherent absurdity of Christianity and recognises that if it were an essentially rational act, then there would be no merit in believing:

> The whole point was that you chose to believe without rational compulsion – you made a leap into the void and in the process chose yourself. Walking a thousand miles to the shrine of Santiago without knowing whether there was anybody actually buried there was such a leap. The aesthetic pilgrim didn't pretend to be a true pilgrim. The ethical pilgrim was always worrying whether he *was* a true pilgrim. The true pilgrim just did it.

Where all the other therapies had failed, Passmore returns home healed by his experience of pilgrimage, accepting his lot in life and becoming the best of friends to his old flame and her husband. Still, he remains bothered by the jarring dissimilarity between the pomp and circumstance and arcane rituals of the cathedral of Santiago in contrast to the small, austere room dedicated to Kierkegaard that he had visited earlier in a museum in Copenhagen. The book concludes teasingly with: "We're going off together for a little autumn break, actually. To Copenhagen. It was my idea. You could call it a pilgrimage."

The two novels that devote the majority of their text to events along the Camino are both exceptional works of contemporary fiction and are both, interestingly, authored by Canadian women. *Step Closer*, by Tessa McWatt, is in the spirit of Conrad's masterpiece, *Lord Jim*, a complex tale of forgiveness, redemption, sacrifice, and salvation, in this case, played out along the Camino to a dramatic climax at Finisterre. Two timelines are described: the story of Emily, a Canadian writer living with her partner in Santiago de Compostela who is deeply affected by watching the disaster of the Boxing Day 2004 tsunami unfold on the television; and the back-story of mysterious and tragic events that transpired on the Camino a half decade before that involved two friends of hers, Gavin and Marcus, when they all lived in Pamplona. Emily attempts to confront the past through the act of writing about it as a novel, asking the intriguing question: "Can you disinter the past and re-examine it by writing about it?" When not dealing with tumultuous events in Emily's present life, the bulk of the book is based on an intriguing deconstructionism of a-story-within-a-story: "I need to consider what I have just written. The last paragraphs have taken me by surprise and flowed comfortably for my fingers." When Emily herself goes on pilgrimage and arrives at the famous Cruz de Hierro stone pile, referring to as "the most intimate rubbish site in the world", there is a subtle interlinking of the two timelines "Here, at the highest point in the narrative structured by the pilgrimage to St James himself, a reader might expect something to change for Gavin Lake or for me. But no. Every story takes its own time. Another step."

McWatt, with great restraint, ever so slowly, as in the best Barbara Vine novel wherein mysteries from the past remain mysteries for much of the book, releases tantalising snippets of information about what had previously happened on the Camino and how her two friends, one wrapped in a cocoon of guilt and pain, the other recovering from a previous and grievous injustice, might share a common background involving a crime. The unifying theme of the book is that the "Camino de Santiago is a path towards meaning, a navigation forward that is not frightening whose only purpose is to force one to keep moving as an act of doing something in a random world filled with tragedies, both personal and global."

Step Closer, shortlisted for one of Canada's top literary awards, excels in its nuanced descriptions of great emotional intimacy brought to the surface by both mundane and momentous experiences on the Camino, as for example:

> The rising mist made him want to cry. He had to keep walking because something was taking place. The valley to his left was wide and lush, but the mist seemed to be getting thicker. He was walking into clouds like someone already dead. Maybe he had died, he thought, or at least all this walking had been the equivalent of death and he no longer had to enlist Marcus to help him. What was there now? Ancients had walked in search of redemption, and so could he. He suddenly suspected that his old companion, Hope, might be lurking between the steps he took.

And, ably capturing that disappointment felt by many at the end of their pilgrimage when facing the "dreadful horizon" of arriving at the destination city:

> Where do you go to in the end, Gavin wondered, catching his breath, his hands on his waist. Santiago de Compostela? Santiago felt like it would be

a line crossed over into a whole new way of caring for life. Would he get that far? He stood at the top of Monte del Gozo. Mount of Joy. Of course. Claire had primed him that this was where pilgrims got their first rapturous view of Santiago's cathedral spires. What he saw was suburbs: bungalow bunkers, like the Lego he had played with as a child; an aloof plaza, self-serviced canteens, sad shops with bagpipe music ringing out from their tannoys. He eased the cramp in his side by bending over his face to his knees, his pack feeling like it would pitch him forward. Straightening up he looked back to see if he could spot the others anywhere in the distance. As Claire raced towards him, he wondered if perhaps he should have shared this mount of sorrow with Marcus.

And, from the fictional novelist at the completion of her own pilgrimage:

I didn't gasp the way I imagined a good pilgrim, like Claire, would. I entered the cathedral from the Plaza del Obradoiro, climbing up the imposing double staircase to the dramatic baroque façade. I looked at the carved saints and gargoyles the way one does a family tree, wondering which branch might be the one you really sprang from. Where was the joker, the outcast? I searched for my father here, but saw only why he had abandoned his Catholicism. It was like the theme park where my grandfather had once taken me. I squeezed past the pilgrims and other worshippers and sped through each of the cathedral's important stations…I walked quickly towards the altar but looking up, I finally did gasp at the huge, vacant angels like obscene dolls hanging from the ceiling of the nave. I proceeded to the high altar and still higher up the narrow staircase that led to the thirteenth-century jewelled statue of St. James. St. James had his back to me. Appropriately. I deserved that snub. I patted the cold, jeweled-inlay shoulder, forgiving it, and retreated down the stairs.

Simone Caput's *Santiago* contains no mysterious murders or even untimely deaths, no far-fetched New Age guides or fantastic angelic companions, no boring historical tangents or esoteric mystical mumbo-jumbo. What the novel *does* contain is the most raw, most heartfelt, and most honest portrayal of the contemporary pilgrimage experience captured in fiction to date. The book's heroine, Dominique, an interior designer in her early forties living in Winnipeg, is fearful that she has squandered the miraculous gift of life, her best days being behind with only tired re-runs waiting ahead. Empty of purpose and ambition to confront such a future, she is chomping at the bit, looking for an inspiration to escape the drudgery, to perhaps see the sea for the first time. And that inspiration comes in the form of reading a table placemat while eating in a seafood restaurant where she learns the history of coquille Saint-Jacques: "And as she read about seashells and reliquaries, of refuges and monasteries, of the long and lingering journey through the mountains to the edge of the world, her heart began to slow down, and her breathing, and the frantic scrabbling of her fingernails. And all at once, everything had fallen into place." *Santiago* describes the journey of a handful of interesting characters to the eponymous city. But it is the internal journey of the heroine where Chaput's novel shines brighter than all others.

Early in the pilgrimage, Dominique is still filled with excitement and expectation about what lies before her. Chaput does a good job at conveying the hopes shared by many pilgrims at the onset of their journeys when speculating ahead to their imagined arrival at their destination:

> For these people, it was the end of a journey accomplished in faith, a glimpse of eternity caught in the stone and glass of time. As Dominique squeezed into the middle layer of a triple-decker bunk bed, she listened to all the different voices and foreign accents build a church out of myth and miracle and allegory, and it occurred to her these men and women from every nation of the world were as hopeful and wonderstruck as the pilgrims of old. And yes, she thought, she, too, wanted to see the great Cathedral of Santiago. Sure she'd stop a while and sit in quiet mediation with the bones of the old saint. But what she really wanted, what she was really hoping for, was the gift of a chance encounter with a long-lost love.

And by that she means her youthful dalliance, long since abandoned, with Faith.

Although Dominique had expected to deal with disappointment on the Camino, realising that it could never live up to all the hype, she is shocked at the degree of her negativity toward the cyclists she encounters along the Way: the "two-wheeled dervishes" who have "no regard for the real pilgrims and no consideration whatsoever for the spiritual dimensions of the journey." Indeed, she can't restrain her disdain for all that they represent: "Their loud and gaudy circus make a mockery of the pilgrims' hushed tones, their speed ridiculed the slow and measured pace of each painstaking step. They did not belong on the camino and Dominique had to repress the urge to yell obscenities every time they whizzed by her on the road."

For much of the pilgrimage, Dominique feels the outsider, content, like a field naturalist, to categorise and identify the types of pilgrims she observes based on their plumage, behaviour, or pedigree, as for example, one New Age couple who brag about having visited Machu Picchu, Stonehenge, Ayers Rock and Easter Island, the Camino being simply another experience to check off their "bucket list." All the while, she maintains an aloofness, recognising as she progresses that it is that emotional distance which has become her own particular albatross. She feels a jealousy for others who have structure, focus, and meaning in their lives: "As she walks along behind these men and women who pray out loud, in unabashed, unembarrassed voices, Dominique sometimes wishes to be touched by the grace of their certainty. Their faith. Their joyful, unquestioning surrender."

Eventually, like many pilgrims, she 'hits the wall,' to use an analogy taken from marathoners' vocabulary, in the case of the Camino, this being more a wall of internal rather than external exhaustion:

> Dominique would be at a loss to explain how she came here, how she made the long hours pass, what thoughts carried her through each day from dawn to dusk. But now, with the rain pouring down on her rubber hood with noisy abandon, she wishes she had never come to this place. Interior monologuing, it's obvious, is not her thing. Let her life unfold as it will, in all its bitter loneliness, its unrelenting sameness, its unraveling, and its decay. She has not come, she reminds whoever is listening, to hurl her questions at the sky.

Pessimistically, she continues in the same vein, stressing her disinterest in connecting with the Spirit supposedly infusing the universe, or at least the Milky Way and its Camino key lines. She simply wants to get on with her life, believing that there will be no great revelation waiting for her in Compostela nor anything she will learn about herself from walking the Camino that she didn't already know.

The heroine continues on, slouching ever closer to Compostela. Readers are rewarded with the author's wonderfully crafted reflections on homesickness and on the intimacy of contact to the road through the physicality of the simple act of walking. In one particularly memorable instance, Dominique, conscious that she now possesses a "lingering fever in her blood that has made her so susceptible" is struck by the sadness emanating from some beautiful Roman ruins. This leads to ruminations about the fleeting nature of beauty, our only salvation being that we have been given the grace to be able to depart from the world without truly knowing all that we've missed in its munificent rainbow held in place, as Pynchon would have it, by gravity.

Many books about the Camino, either fiction or narrative, build to a crescendo when the protagonist or self finally arrives at the cathedral of Santiago. Few have captured this life-etching moment with more astuteness than Chaput. Here, for example, is demonstration of that singularity:

> As Dominique moves away from the door, she knows the last kilometres of the pilgrimage won't be much different from the first. Her life is strewn, after all, with broken promises, unfinished prayers, and half-hearted commitments. And she hopes that God, whoever He is, has a pretty clear recollection of what it is to be human. She would hate like hell to get to the end of the road and discover He has no patience at all with the feckless and irresolute. With the weak, the hopeless, the very, very small. With the poor, hapless creatures he made of dirt and spit.

And with such a recognition of her own delicate frailties of spirit and character, the protagonist reaches an acceptance of what it is to be a pilgrim: "If a pilgrim is a constant traveller who nowhere feels at home, a passing stranger on the way to Jerusalem, then for me, Dominique thinks, for all the weary walkers come at last to the end of the road, this church, this shrine, this field of stars is as close to home as we're likely to get."

POETRY AND INSPIRATION

HALF OF THE POEMS IN NEIL CURRY'S *Walking to Santiago* deal, in a linear fashion, with his own pilgrimage, most being titled after Camino locations ("Roncesvalles", "Pamplona", "Puente La Reina", "Santo Domingo", "Fromista", "León", "Villafrance del Bierzo", "Samos") and personalities ("Francis Xavier", "Césare Borgia", "El Cid", "Saint James"). Though of course this gives a focus to each offering, it also restricts the freedom and imagination that is the great gift of poetry. It is in the other poems where Curry believably captures elements of the Camino, as for example, "A long quiet walk over the meseta; / Frost crisp underfoot; the sky an unbroken blue; Larksong; watching my shadow slowly shorten / And edge towards the north; feeling my shoulders / Warm to the sun, and hearing that first cicada." The instances in the collection where the inner journey is described resonate most deeply: "There are destinations which demand / That we ourselves have been the journey;" and: "We set out and we return. And we set out / for something which never / has been reached, because to do so is to go beyond it, / and we return / to something within us which has never come into being / nor ever passed away."

Howard Nelson's self-published chapbook *Trust and Tears: Poems of Pilgrimage*, based on his eight-year staged pilgrimage to Compostela is an insightful gem. With a poet's eye he is able to capture in a few words the underlying truths of pilgrimage, walking being defined as the "fragile craft" that links us to our forebears, "And to others for whom we too, / One day, will be those / Who have gone before." Nelson recognises the beneficial purity of silence: "Go lightly, pilgrim, on this ancient earth, / And when you can, alone. / In wind and rain find all your mirth, / And in silence make your home." And he acknowledges the hardships through which pilgrimage can triumph: "High in the hills of this suffering land, / Where pilgrims seek, through sorrow / - The dark evergreen of our souls - / To live their pain more vividly, / And find joy's spring."

The poem "Ending" is the best in the collection, exposing the mixed feelings of gratitude and guilt felt by many upon arriving at Compostela and facing the realisation that the most important elements of the pilgrimage had occurred earlier along the Way. In this light, the true miracle of wine is not the sacred blood of Christ at the Mass in the cathedral but rather a humble glass shared with a fellow pilgrim, and the act of hugging the Saint's statue is not as significant as that of hugging another pilgrim, one "Whose miracle he'd seen, / And to whom he had confessed."

Ultimately, Nelson tells us, the resonance of our time spent on the Camino is our footsteps that will soon be effaced or blown away, leaving behind as an imprint in the stones a bit of ourselves in the form of "Passion, and pain." Finally, the author does a good job at dealing with the nervousness and uncertainty that many pilgrims face when returning home: "I went on pilgrimage to find my home, / But will it be the one I left?" and "Leaving home's a journey / And coming back, a pilgrimage."

The chapbook *Peregrina* by Karen Temple focuses on the day-to-day nuances of walking the Way which she likens to being a rosary wherein one can experience "purgatory and paradise / in a single day". Poems are arranged in temporal sequence of her own pilgrimage, and are actually dated, something that provides no benefit with the sole exception of the 'entry' for September 11, 2001 when she watches the horrors unfolding in New York City beside a print of Picasso's *Guernica* hung on the wall in her B & B. Otherwise, it the loving details of the commonplace where Temple comes off best, as for example, going through customs at the airport "with an / undeclared payload / of anticipation", or her arrival at a *refugio* where "the past is present" wherein she lays claim to a bed "that has waited for me / for a thousand years", and her treating of blisters by using a "needle and thread / to darn my feet / like an old sock."

Pilgrimage and haiku poetry go foot in hand, as exemplified best by that inveterate long-distance walker and scribe extraordinaire, Basho. *Compostelle: A Spiritual Journey* combines haiku poems by Guy Dutey, presented in English, French, and German, with atmospheric colour photographs by René Gastineau. Whereas this accompaniment generally works well, there are instances when one struggles to try to find a connection between the words and images. But then one purpose of haiku poetry is to be mysterious by design. Haikus are also of course short and sweet and are often equal parts cute and whimsical. And in all this, Dutey succeeds, providing an intriguing addition to the Camino literature: "Where could it have been? / I have no memories, / except that of my step", "The walker's soul / joins the secrets of the world, / mysteriously", "The call of the path / I've been hearing for a thousand years. / Winter is over", and "Along the way / I make up stories / a cock crows in the distance".

Walking Life: Meditations on the Pilgrimage of Life, by Michael Metras, also, though less effectively, mixes words and photographs. Cringing and flipping quickly past the "Forward" (a sure sign that the book is self-published and has not been proof-read), the reader is greeted with a series of paragraph-long responses to self-help questions along with corresponding black-and-white photographs of generally interesting subjects both on and off the Camino. Unfortunately half of these are of only marginal quality due to the choice of paper and type of printing. Some of the meditations provide useful guidance about little-discussed subjects such as encouragements to break free of the regimental need to follow the yellow arrow waymarking and the worrying preoccupation as to what is or is not the "right road", the need to occasionally go back to see something again as one might never be that way again, the need to abandon unproductive worry about the imagined difficulties of a forthcoming particular section before it is actually encountered, and the need to live the experience of the pilgrimage existentially in the here and now.

Two books, published almost simultaneously, compile writings of others as inspirational accessories for the Santiago pilgrimage. The creativity, or to use the vernacular of the present chapter, the "invention", in such works resides in their packaging and arrangement. In *Ultreia! Onward! Progress of the Pilgrim*, I compiled over two hundred quotations from more than thirty modern narratives, packaged them into a small, round-cornered and tough-covered format, and arranged them to be read like a Book of Hours, corresponding to the medieval clock, for motivation at breaks while on pilgrimage,. The book has been well-received, garnering positive reviews from the pilgrimage societies in Canada, the United Kingdom, and the United States. One review – by M. Burriss in the August 2010 issue of *La Concha*, the magazine of the American Friends of the Camino – was particularly gratifying as it summed up perfectly just what I had in mind when I pulled together the best of the best quotations: "I can vividly imagine sitting down on a rock or on the side of the path looking at the horizon before me, taking my *bocadillo* and fruit out of my pack, saying my blessing, eating the day's provisions, and then letting some of the quotes from this book motivate me for the rest of the day's walk."

Roads to Santiago: A Spiritual Companion was published to celebrate the silver anniversary of the Confraternity of Saint James and appropriately (numerically so) contains brief reflections by twenty-five pilgrims. Accompanying these words are lavish colour photographs, most obtained from the Confraternity's archives, in addition to selected Biblical or inspirational quotations. The whole product is an odd amalgam that doesn't quite seem to know where it wants to go, intended direction being difficult to judge due to the extreme brevity of the volume. In the end, it seems that the main purpose was to provide a brief overview of the Camino for an audience of the uninformed and of course to introduce the manifest benefits that the Confraternity can provide to prospective pilgrims. And at this it does succeed.

On Visual and Auditory...

Chapter 10

CAPTURING COMPOSTELA

Photography and Art

Given the effusive prose that has been foisted on the Way of Saint James, it is surprising that so few of the narratives have included visual accompaniment to their texts. Of late, attempts to fill the void have been made by a series of large-format, coffee table books about the various routes to Santiago de Compostela. The audience for these books is invariably armchair travellers and all books share a common goal of presenting a visual overview of the Way. This results in a striking similarity amongst them in that frequently one encounters the same objects or vistas photographed in the same aspect and light from the same vantage point. Even mundane scenes are not immune to this repetition. It is possible, for instance, to see one image, say for example of a doorway upon which are hung a string of pilgrim shells and against which are leaning a group of pilgrim staffs, occur on the cover of one book and then come across the near identical image a few years later in another book. Maybe, however, this is to be expected.

As I peruse my collection of Camino books and recognise scenes that I too have taken and included in this book – as for example, the westward view from the top of Cuesta de Mostilares outside of Castrojeriz of the pilgrim path winding its lonely way across the unfolding vastness of the meseta (Part II, page 149) – I wonder about all those different sets of eyes and shutter fingers that have been drawn to the same scene, and I think about Japanese garden design.

I remember sitting in my office and flipping through several books I had just signed out of the Harvard Design School library about the gardens I had recently visited on a trip to Kyoto and being struck by how many of my own photographs were of identical scenes. A landscape architecture colleague of mine who had stuck her head in my office nodded knowingly and seemed surprised that I was surprised given that those very views filling the pages in front of us had been specifically designed hundreds of years ago for just that very purpose of capturing interest. And thus it was no wonder that later visitors with an aesthetic eye should capture the same scene again and again with their cameras, easels, or heart's memories. With respect to the Camino, the devotedly religious would likewise be surprised at my surprise of the repeated publication of similar images. For in their minds cannot all nature – rather Nature – be explained deterministically? Has not, they would argue, the Almighty Himself designed the landscape that I and others walked through in just such a way so as to inspire and give confidence to the struggling pilgrim when s/he, weary after the climb up Cuesta de Mostilares, is greeted by the beauty of the *meseta* leading westward to the destination of the Apostle's shrine at Compostela?

Be that as it may, putting aside such comforting/unsettling teleological thinking, it is the published photographs of the distinct rather than the familiar to which I find myself most attracted before and after my own pilgrimage.

Many are the beautiful colour photographs of the familiar that fill Derry Brabbs' coffee-table overview *The Roads to Santiago*. But it is the penultimate, double-page image at the end of the book that most captures my interest. There, marching across the centre of the photograph from one side to the other is a row of thirteen elegant cypress trees near the town of Belorado. Their dark green colour and columnar verticality are contrasted strikingly with the horizontal expansiveness of the rolling fields that appear to be layered, each one of subsequent further distance atop that of the more proximal field. The colour patterns in the field layering are most engaging: the brown-grey soil into which the trees are planted, the immediate field behind which is of light yellow wheat stubble, progressing in the middle distance to a series of fields that roll upward in dark brown or black-green tones, until the most distant field with a return to the light yellow that forms the skyline beneath the bright blue heavens. With the exception of a few telephone lines situated behind the row of trees, the landscape is empty of all save its overt demonstration of careful agricultural tending. In my mind's eye, it is kilometre after kilometre of just such rolling fields broken only by the occasional copse or row of trees that echo most loudly in my own pilgrimage memories.

It is often easier to find quirky photographs of idiosyncratic scenes in books that double as personal narratives than in coffee table, overview books that have to appease a general audience of armchair travellers. For the first few years after my pilgrimage I would seek out a single image in Kim and Malcolm Wells' *Camino Footsteps: Reflections on a Journey to Santiago de Compostela*. There, two pilgrims are seen walking into the mists as they descend toward Tricastela, each saddled with too large a backpack, his blue, hers red, their hands conjoined and fingers gently touching. The tenderness of the young lovers always reminded me of my fellow pilgrims Jean-Olivier and Emmanuelle and how much I now missed them and how they – as was later confessed (see Part II page 161) – celebrated that day of our own rain-sodden walk down from O'Cebreiro to Tricastela.

I empower a single image in Knud Helge Robberstad's *The Road to Santiago* with a metaphoric significance far out of all proportion I'm sure to what had been the original intent of the photograph. It was a bitterly cold morning when I walked up to the monastery of Irache outside of Estella. The doors were still locked and no one was stirring at this early hour. Worse, the famous fountain of free wine had been reduced to an unyielding frozen red icicle. The best I could do was to chip off a piece of wine-laden ice and placing it in my mouth head off toward the beckoning castle glimpsed on the horizon. Always I had wondered about what might have lain beyond those bolted doors. Robberstad shows a double-page photograph of an inner courtyard of the monastery undergoing restoration in the mid-1990s. The scene is one of palatable melancholy: missing windows and chipped plaster of the surrounding buildings, scattered bricks and piles of sand on the isolated patches of scruffy grass of the courtyard, a forlorn and weathered fountain filled with refuse from which one just knows no water has issued for many years, and a lone, spindly palm tree cropped of its canopy of fronds. The only glimpse of animated life is what looks like a black cat seen scrambling over a pile of debris in the background. I find it hard to resist the temptation to identify the feeling of physical abandonment and desolation shown by the photograph with being an inflated trope for the withering away of the onetime inherent religiosity of the Camino: the spiritual abandonment and soulful desolation of so many of those undertaking the modern pilgrimage to Compostela, such that their walk has no more special resonance than had they engaged in any long-distance hike, as for example, the Appalachian Trail or the Pennine Way.

When I pick up Brian and Marcus Tate's *The Pilgrim Route to Santiago* it is not the usual scenes of colourful sunsets, impressive churches and the like from photographer Pablo Keller that draw my eyes; rather it is of several of his black and white images of intimate village life in the mid-1980s, captured just before such scenes would disappear forever beneath the veneer of Camino popularity and Spanish modernisation.

In one photograph, an elderly inhabitant of the tiny village of San Juan de Ortega is shown leaning forward, his left hand on a stout walking stick, his right hand, knuckles down, against the top of a stone wall attached to the stuccoed house behind him. The man wears a dark sweater and has a Basque-style beret on his head. A large stone mallet lies beside his hand, and leaning against the side of the house are an assortment of other farm implements. It is his posture and expression that grabs the most attention. It is as if all his many weary years can be encapsulated into that right hand holding his weight upright while his wrinkled face reveals a grimace at the effort of it all. It is a candid moment of lasting resonance.

Another of Keller's small black and white photographs is of the narrow, muddy main street in the village of El Acebo, downhill from Foncebadón. Buildings on either side are composed of rough stone rubble with slate roofs and wooden balconies that lean out over the street and look so ramshackle as to tempt the fate of anyone brave enough to venture onto them. In the foreground a middle-aged farmer stands proudly beside his double ox-drawn cart filled with branches. He is wearing knee-high galoshes and sports a beret perched at a rakish angle while he firmly clutches a three-metre-long pole. In the background, a child is seen darting across the street. Other than the electricity lines, one can imagine the scene to have changed little since the first pilgrims passed through the village centuries ago.

The single published image of most lasting import and impact on my aesthetic consciousness is found within the only Camino book I possess of serious photographic artistry: Joan Myers' *Santiago: Saint of Two Worlds*. The full page black and white image is of restoration work in the Colegiata of St Mary in Villafranca del Bierzo. A towering, eight-metre high *retablo* in a corner apse is shown draped with a voluminous white sheet to protect it. From the upper left side diffuse light shines through a gothic window onto the white cloth with some light spilling down to illuminate the stone wall below the window. And, as is the nature of artistically composed black and white images by professional photographers, the atmospheric shadows assume paramount importance. On the left side of the blanketed *retablo* elaborate fluting rises up toward the ceiling vault, while on the right side the edge a tomb is seen covered with detailed bas-relief family crests. On the floor in the foreground of the photograph lies a twisted, corrugated length of industrial vacuum hose that looks ever so much like a giant and coiled annelid monstrosity. The unease in viewing the powerful photograph is further heightened by the enormous, draped *retablo* that looms ominously over all. For, as is characteristic of such structures, the main body of the *retablo* is bordered by two triptych-winged side panels and is topped with a narrowed apex panel. Imagine if you can covering the entirety from ceiling to ground in a single white sheet. The result is the creation of an incredibly eerie giant ghost-like shape – the Spectre of the Camino – lurking in the shadowed, seldom-visited corner of church, posed there at the ready perhaps to do away with any disingenuous or otherwise unworthy pilgrim should they have the misfortune to wander within its grasp!

The ease and inexpensive nature of digital photography has led to a camera-clicking mania of seeing the world through the lens rather than through the eyes. Why pause to reflect, savour, absorb and try to comprehend a scene when it is so much easier to simply click-and-shoot and save before quickly moving onto the next subject a few metres ahead. In such a culture, it is the artist, either sitting patiently with brush or pen in hand while preparing a rendering in situ, or synthesising an experience or memory of the Camino while back at home in the studio, who has become the rarity. There is also something appealingly subversive about such hand-crafted artistry just as there is about choosing to undertake a pilgrimage by walking.

Mark Hoare's *A Painting Pilgrim: A Journey to Santiago de Compostela* contains fine watercolours accompanied by thoughtful text. Above all, it is the interesting back-story behind several of the paintings that makes the book so memorable, providing as it does a glimpse into the creative process during pilgrimage. One's opinion of an otherwise unassuming streetscape in Navarrete takes on a whole new appreciation through learning that the wind had been raging so fiercely that Hoare was constantly buffeted by dirt and the painting itself had been whipped out of his hands twice, while about him metal street signs quavered and the stained glass of a nearby church rattled ominously. Another painting of the wattle and timber panels of an old house in Atapuerca is made more special with the knowledge that while he worked on it a dressing-gowned señora brought him coffee and biscuits along with a motherly admonition that he could get ill sitting out so long in the cold. My favourite painting is of the most commonplace and ephemeral of subjects illustrated in the book: Hoare's own boot-prints in the mud. The mundane is made memorable by the text: "The rain returns, the puddles change colour, the footprint softens and gradually erodes; but I persevere and no tractor rolls by. I spend three hours huddled under the brolly painting something I had thought would take me half the time – for the air is so damp and the paint slow to dry."

In spite its non-promising title, *The Artist's Journey: The Perfumed Pilgrim Tackles the Camino de Santiago,* by Marcia Shaver, is an above average and interesting narrative. The real strength in the book, however, is in the more than fifty ink drawings scattered throughout the text. In addition to renderings of landscapes and famous buildings, Shaver has an eye for capturing warmly endearing scenes of the commonplace that register with many pilgrims. One such is of old tile-rooftops of neighbouring buildings and a road enticingly stretching into the distance as glimpsed through the upper-storey window of an *albergue* in Hontanas. Many times I have stood or lain on a bed and stared past the intimacy and comfort of the worn stone walls and wooden shutters of such a window to similar views of rolling hills which would be met the following day, while imagining what adventures might there ensue. Another drawing catches a heart-warming scene of intimate urbanity in a León plaza: elderly men and women, each dressed to the nines in their Sunday best, the former sitting on a bench, the latter standing nearby, with both groups nonchalantly pretending to ignore the other. As a voyeur, one can imagine that such a dating game has been going on in that exact location in the plaza for centuries.

Cecilia Gossen's doctoral thesis, *Place-Making and Meaning-Making in the Pilgrimage to Santiago de Compostela*, is based on defining a modern "Camino identity" in terms of a sense of place and shared community. Throughout her thesis (as well as a gallery exhibition in her native city of Calgary), she uses sculptures, largely made of wood, to imaginatively symbolise architectural, environmental, and human qualities that transform the pilgrimage to Compostela from a nondescript space to a special *place*. One piece, called *I Pilgrim*, consists of three free-standing arches constructed of laminated plywood and decorated in either Christian or Moorish geometric patterns representative of the architecture of Spain. Along the edges of the arches are the names of the towns that Gossen walked through along the Way. Inside surfaces of the arches are covered in gold leaf symbolising the rich inner journey made by pilgrims. Another creation, *Sellos*, is a long, rectangular box decorated with the *credencial* stamps Gossen collected from the various *refugios* along the Way. Additionally, a sequence of cutouts of her footsteps transit from one side of the box to the other, being indicative of the nature of movement as a place-making activity on the Camino. Intriguingly, the box is designed to be a modern reliquary holding treasured memories of a pilgrimage, infused as it is with the symbolised artefacts of her collective experiences.

The reach of Santiago can be long indeed and not without a certain amount of serendipity and surprise along the way. During 1957, while I was swimming about my mother's womb, impatient to begin my own life-pilgrimage, an eccentric, fifty-three-year-old artist was involved in painting what would become the greatest modern image of the pilgrim Saint. Salvador Dali is certainly one of Spain's most colourful and recognisable artists and his enormous three-by-six metre *Santiago El Grande* is a cryptic masterpiece that has both amazed and puzzled critics for more than half a century. Imagine my surprise to discover that the painting is located only a three-hour drive around the Bay of Fundy from where I now live. And so, with little ado, I undertook a quick 'pilgrimage' to view Dali's surrealistic gem. Arriving at the Beaverbrook Gallery late on a Sunday afternoon I had the remarkable painting all to myself for over an hour while outside residents and tourists alike recreated in a summer heat wave.

The centre of the canvas is filled with the Apostle, apparently naked, mounted astride a rearing white horse while holding aloft a smaller image of the crucified Christ from which emanate radiant beams. On the bottom is a coastline scene calling to mind the rocks and bays of Finisterre upon which a tiny figure – Dali? – lies dreaming the image that rises above him. In the bottom corner, Dali's muse, Gala, resembling Mary, is dressed in a shroud. And linking all is a complex lattice of cathedral vault beams whose intersecting bosses are carved scallop shells of the Camino.

It is the overt and mysterious symbolism that has captured the imagination of so many. Located between the lower legs of the horse is an atomic mushroom cloud at whose centre is found a small jasmine flower, the symbol of purity and harmony. It is thought that the entire subject may be an attempt by Dali to show the similarities between nuclear physics and religion, both particles and souls ascending to a heaven portrayed at the top of the painting with much less clarity than that of the earthly landscape at the bottom. All is held together by the cathedral lattice, possibly signifying Dali's belief in the unifying importance of Christianity. Perhaps this explains why the Apostle does not lift a sword as he so often does in similar iconographic poses but instead brandishes the radiant Christ. Then there is the sequence of small angels that ascend to the ceiling/heaven and which look like one shown on the horse's neck. Go figure. But more than anything, it is the raised naked foot of Saint James, jutting out at one, 3D-like from the canvas, that resonates most with gazing pilgrims. Here, Dali appears to be instructing us, that it is only through undertaking the act of an arduous pilgrimage that we mortals can ever hope to follow in the footsteps of Christ, guided along by that most dedicated of his wayfaring intermediaries, Saint James…Santiago.

Awestruck like so many who have viewed the masterpiece for the first time, I succumb to Caminophilia (see later section) and purchase a t-shirt and pen from the shop, both emblazoned with reproductions of the famous painting. I go to the lavatory, change my shirt, and exit into a heatwave worthy of the *meseta* in its scorching intensity. And just as so often happens in that city in Spain, Santiago de Compostela, no one here in Fredericton, New Brunswick pays the least attention to the starry-eyed pilgrim in their midst.

Films

THE FRENCH FILM *SAINT JACQUES...LA MECQUE* (cryptically translated as 'Start Walking' rather than the literal 'Saint James...Mecca') is an accomplished and beautifully realised undertaking, sensitive to the humour and pathos of the pilgrimage experience. The film begins with the reading of a will at which three estranged siblings – a stressed businessman, a jaded teacher, and a welfare drunk – learn that in order to inherit the million-euro-plus estate from their mother they must complete the Camino together by walking and staying in the same accommodation. Their reactions are wonderful. The businessman flips out, railing that he is not a Christian, pilgrimages leave him cold, and that the bats can have all the medieval buildings. Further, he has an ulcer, high blood pressure, and cholesterol so that he cannot walk for more than fifteen minutes, and besides, humans invented machines and engines so they wouldn't need backpacks. And then of course he has a business to run with lots of responsibilities. And so "You can stuff your pilgrimage," he concludes. The teacher states that she has always worked in the secular school system and her life has always been in opposition to the prejudices, priests, pilgrimages, and "all the Church's underhand ways." What is she to tell her employer: first, this pilgrimage; next, a Muslim head scarf? She then gives a litany of all the important household chores and decisions she has to take care of, including her unemployed husband and children, etc. Finally, why should she give up her already arranged summer vacation to go on "this rotten pilgrimage?" The welfare drunk merely asks if there are any bars on "this Tompohilla [sic] thing?" But of course, all want their share of the inheritance, and so…

Soon the teacher is seen disembarking from the train along with dozens of other backpacked, shell-strewn pilgrims in what turns out to be the town of Le Puy. The businessman brother is helped with his enormous backpack by his chauffeur but its weight is such that he is sent toppling backward. Then the drunk brother shows up with no gear and immediately needs to borrow two hundred and ten euros to pay his taxi fare. The siblings are met by their guide who is holding up a company sign reading *Cheman Faisant*, translated in the subtitles as "Along the Way." Soon they are joined with the other pilgrims of their group: a middle-aged woman with a headscarf that it takes little imagination to predict will be shown to be covering hair loss from cancer treatment, two young French girls and two young French-Arab boys, one of whom announces, to the puzzled looks of the others, that he is proud to be on a pilgrimage to "Santiago de Mecca!"

In the wonderful cathedral and in front of the famous black Madonna, the teacher refers to the Catholic Church as nothing more than being a huge club for paedophiles and submissive women and through whose ban on condoms has been responsible for the Aids-related deaths of millions of Africans. Despite this, she hypocritically lingers behind and also leaves a written prayer just like the others. The youngest Arab boy, mumbling "*Allah Akbar*," confesses to his friend that he is worried about his mother.

The film slowly unfolds with our fellowship struggling along oblivious to the gorgeous scenery about them. Lunch breaks are occasions where the pilgrims walk about trying to catch a satellite signal for their mobile phones and then engage in heated conversations with their spouses back at home. A humorous scene involves several of the characters, on the pretence of slipping away from the group for a pee, ditching belongings (books, clothes, cosmetics, a hairdryer, etc.) from their overloaded packs. And as expected, as the days progress and shared hardships are met and surmounted, the disjointed collection of individuals, including the perpetually squabbling siblings, become one. They begin to share their lunch, spontaneously break out into song, prepare communal meals, and playfully tease each other. Meanwhile, their interrelationships develop: the jaded teacher finds new purpose in helping the youngest Arab boy to learn how to read, the drunk and sick woman have a fling, and the older Arab boy and one of the girls begin a dance of romance.

For Caminophiles, the film has much to offer in terms of showcasing many familiar landscapes and buildings in addition to well-known pilgrimage experiences. One night, for example, they find the only available accommodation to be an abandoned school where they have to share a single outhouse, sleep on the cold floor, and have almost no food. Still, by this time in the journey they are happy. That is until, however, a group of other pilgrims join them and a hilarious scene develops with our French protagonists cursing as they are unable to sleep due to the deafening snoring emanating from the three Dutch pilgrims. And then, when the fellowship reaches St-Jean-Pied-de-Port they encounter another of the famous pilgrimage plagues: the arrogant and opinionated know-it all. Trying to chat up one of the young girls, this individual insists from what he has heard that the route in Spain is much better than those in France, that he starts earlier in the morning than others, groups of pilgrims should be dismissed since the Way should be a solitary challenge, and of course one needs all the latest in high-tech outdoor gear. The next morning, sure enough his alarm goes off at 4:30 am and turning on the lights, he starts his race to the next hostel, chiding the others as "idlers." Later, as the fellowship struggles up over the Pyrenees, they enjoy passing the boasting pilgrim collapsed on the side of the road, head hung in shame as he waits for a taxi to take him back since he states, "pilgrimage is shit."

The businessman brother gradually becomes engaged in the pilgrimage experience to the point when the group arrives at Roncesvalles and a priest denies accommodation to the two French-Arab boys and Mediterranean-looking guide, he states that having already travelled five hundred miles together they are all a family and that he is sick of "moralising preachers who act like pigs." He then pays for the group to stay in a nearby expensive hotel.

After many interesting and occasionally funny experiences, the penultimate scene is an extremely beautiful and moving sequence showing a distant view of the two French-Arab boys walking along the beach at Finisterre with the setting sun behind them while the older pilgrim breaks the news to his young friend that that he has just received a phone call informing that the latter's mother has died. The sudden collapse and then supportive embrace communicates more than words could ever convey. The film closes on a positive note by showing the other pilgrims back at home, their lives all improved by the Camino experience.

The Way, written and directed by Emilio Estevez, is a loving tribute to both his Spanish heritage and to his father, Martin Sheen, who assumes the lead role and who has stated that he considers it to be his best film performance in decades. Estevez has said his film is about loss, memory, regret, reconciliation, and the wonderfully imperfect, beautiful wrecks that we all are.

While on a Californian golf course, Tom (Sheen) receives a mobile phone call to inform him that his only son Daniel has been killed in a storm in the Pyrenees at the start of the Camino. Refusing to pray with a priest in his seldom visited neighbourhood church, Tom leaves for St.-Jean-Pied-de-Port to claim and return home with his son's remains. There he disembarks from the train with a suitcase on rollers in sharp contrast to the many doing likewise with their backpacks. Flashbacks set the tone of a strained father-son relationship encapsulated with Tom driving his son, played by Estevez himself, to the airport to begin his pilgrimage walk. "You don't choose a life, Dad. You live one," the son retorts to a disappointed father who simply cannot comprehend why anyone would opt to go on what he considers to be a holiday instead of getting along with life.

A kind *gendarme* at the morgue gives Tom his son's ashes, backpack, and *credencial* passport, the latter shocking in the stark, unfulfilled blankness of only a single stamp, and gives a mini-lecture on the Camino. Later, in a touching scene in his hotel room while he sorts through his son's belongings, Tom decides to complete his son's last planned act by walking to Compostela while carrying and distributing the ashes along the Way.

Throughout the film, scenes of humour alternate with those of gravity or pathos. For example, the first day Tom heads out the door of his hotel looking uncomfortable in his raingear and backpack and proceeds after a few seconds of uncertainty to exit out of the side of the camera shot only to reappear moments later following a large group of cheerful pilgrims walking in the opposite and correct direction. Later there is a touching scene when he approaches the cross high up in the mountains marking where his son died and has the first of many glimpses of his son's ghost waiting there for him. Here he places some of the ashes and continues on to Roncesvalles where he displays his ignorance by asking for a private room only to be guided to a dormitory filled with snoring pilgrims.

As always happens, a little fellowship of those with similar momentum develops and viewers are introduced to the happy pilgrim in the form of a chunky Dutch fellow undertaking the pilgrimage to lose weight but who gorges himself on Spanish food and drink, the troubled pilgrim in the form of a snarky Canadian woman whose professed purpose on the Camino is to stop smoking but who takes every opportunity to surreptitiously light up, and the exuberant pilgrim in the form of an Irish journalist who hopes to break his writer's block by penning the definitive work on the experience, yet fearing that all he will produce is "another bloody guidebook on the Camino."

Aided by stellar camera work and effective accompanying music, Camino veterans will savour the lovingly filmed sequences of the familiar: the excited bustle of getting ready in the morning, the trying encounters with hateful priests and speed-crazed pilgrims, the recognised landmarks and landscapes of grandeur contrasted with images of the mundane, the far-ranging discussions about comparative politics and aspirations, the painful tending of foot blisters, the reflections about why there are so many lapsed Catholics on the Camino and what really makes a true pilgrim, and the warm camaraderie of shared meals filled with laughter and music while a cute cat, oblivious to all, sleeps nearby.

Yet always just underneath the surface is the haunting, resolute sadness of the entire undertaking. The repeated glimpses Tom catches of his son's spectre quietly sitting at the table amongst the happy pilgrims, or waiting patiently for him beside the trail, thereby partaking vicariously in the dream that he would not live to complete, show a tenderness unmatched in other films of the Camino. The metaphor of the weight of the Way, in this case of unresolved family baggage, becomes realised through Tom's transport of his son's ashes. Along the Way, Tom's growing yearning for transcendence means that the journey begun for his son becomes by the end truly his own path. Deep pilgrimage is thus a movement of the heart just as much as it is a movement of the body. Also, allegorically, the shift in the character of Tom from lonely isolation to a recognition that he is part of a larger community that is an extension of his self can be viewed, Estevez and Sheen have said, as a metaphor for the positive shift and reintegration of the America of Obama back into the global village of mutual citizenship, from the isolationism of Bush's years.

The Spanish film *Al Final del Camino*, directed by the appropriately named Robert Santiago, is an irreverent confection filled with much humour and little depth. Here the Camino plays a secondary role as mere backdrop to a comedy about modern, largely dysfunctional relationships. The film begins with a scene of men in a shower bragging about past sexual conquests and moves to a scene in a restaurant in which a woman is being dumped by a cad with whom she has recently had sex. The following day, this distraught woman is sent by the editor of the woman's magazine for whom she works on a new assignment. She, accompanied by a photographer who is to pretend to be her boyfriend, is to investigate and write a feature article about a self-help guru who charges a whopping twenty-thousand euros per couple to fix their relationship while they undertake a week-long walk along the Camino.

In a small, countryside town before Sarria, couples rendezvous and are immediately told to dress themselves in t-shirts blazoned with the words "In Crisis." Among the participants is a perpetually horny Korean couple and two Spanish men, cousins, who are pretending to be a gay couple when in fact they are cruising the Camino since it is rumoured to be filled with girls in crisis who will "screw like rabbits." As the group moves along, they participate in a set of exercises designed to strengthen their relationships, such as having their feet tied together, being blindfolded, etc. This is accompanied by a corresponding shift in the group t-shirts they wear: "I'm Not Perfect", to "On the Right Track", to finally "I'm a New Person." What transpires is a harmless, humorous, and largely forgettable sort of 'Carry on Along the Camino' type of film that has an odd preoccupation with oral sex. The film builds to a climax – literally – with all couples humping away in a *refugio* near Compostela. The final scene is a close-up of the heroine and her new photographer beau lying in bed talking about how she has become multi-orgasmic while located near her are a scallop shell and a poster about the

Camino representing the cultural identity of Europe. Besides the obvious funny and incongruous juxtaposition, perhaps there is some deeper message here about European sexuality.

Two hundred years from now, when our descendents voice-activate the miniature computer chips embedded in their brains at birth, as they travel aboard the Camino mono-rail, hermetically protected from the climate-furnace outside while on their way to the flood-threatened coastal city of Compostela, they will be able to access and watch a single film, deemed a classic, about the olden days when people actually walked the Way and a few even believed in miracles of salvation. That film will be Luis Buñuel's 1969 profound and surrealistic masterpiece *The Milky Way* (*La Voie lactée*).

Designed as an episodic Spanish picaresque novel, the film focuses on two tramps who, while on pilgrimage, wander through a surreal landscape, shifting back and forth in time as they witness the history of heresy, yet always remaining on the edge of a series of significant encounters as observers, à la Rosencrantz and Guildenstern. Only a theologian can understand all the allegorical religious references. Indeed, when first shown, critics were given a set of crib notes about the main reference points. The DVD of the film is the only such I have bought that comes with a thirty-six page booklet of interviews and explanations.

The events in the film are superficially funny and told in a fantastical, disjointed fashion that many, not used to art-house films, will find disarming. On the outskirts of Paris two tramps, reminiscent of Beckett's everymen Vladimir and Estragon, are hitching a ride to Compostela. While continuing along they meet a well-dressed, Bible-quoting stranger who might be the Devil. In a restaurant they overhear a conversation between a police officer and a priest discussing Christ's miracles, including transubstantiation, and the nature of heresy. White-coated medics suddenly arrive and cart the priest off back to the lunatic asylum. Later, while camping out in a forest the heroes slip through time to witness a Latin service by Priscillian, Bishop of Avila, that ends with half-dressed men and women pairing off for sex. In another scene, waiters and a maître d' engage in a heady conversation about heretics while they set up a restaurant. The flipping back and forth through time continues with the Marquis de Sade making an appearance in a prison cell. In the present time, while the tramps sit listening to a recital about religious dogma by a group of girls on an outside stage, the younger tramp daydreams about a firing squad executing the Pope. Humorously, the fellow beside him somehow hears the rifle shots. In the past times, the tramps encounter a heresy trial that leads to the exhumation and burning of the corpse of a previous bishop who had written sacrilegiously about the nature of the Trinity. One of the memorable scenes involves two, seventeenth-century fellows in fancy garb, a Jesuit and a Jansenist, who argue about predestination versus free will as they fight a sword duel in the ruins of an abbey, all initiated by the heretical statement that "In the fallen state of nature, inner grace is irresistible." In another scene, two Reformation heretics flee an angry mob by stealing the clothes of modern bathers and thus escape into the present time. Other scenes are of a rosary being shot upon an apparition of the Virgin Mary followed by a discussion about her virginity, and a mysterious automobile crash. Finally, the tramps arrive at the cathedral in Compostela only to be told that the enshrined headless body is not that of Saint James but of the first heretic Priscillian. The film ends with a flashback to Jesus and his disciples and the healing of a blind man. But has he really been healed? As a bird flies overhead, he says to Jesus: "Lord, a bird just flew over. I *heard* its wings beating." And the closing scene of the film, acknowledged to be one of the very best such in all cinema history due to its ambiguity, is a close-up of the blind man's cane feeling out the presence of a small ditch as he follows along after the group whom have previously comfortably stepped across. And so we're left with the great enigma of whether or not Christ is a miraculous healer or an unscrupulous charlatan.

The film deals with the basic mysteries of Christian faith such as God being both One and Three, which is of course an absurdity that is impossible to comprehend and thus for that very reason must be accepted on faith as only being possible through God. The film also focuses on heresies such as Priscillianism, Gnosticism, and Manichaeism, which challenged early Church dogma and authority. The point is that heresy is closely linked to mystery. The lunatic priest states, just before he is carted off, "A heresy that denies a mystery can attract the ignorant, but it cannot blot out the truth." The multi-storied narrative in which the heroes walk into and out of one story after another all centres around the idea of what beliefs mean and why some are deemed acceptable whereas others are designated heretical. The message is that Christianity is not solely about being nice to those who are unfortunate but also about its ruthless side in setting man against his brother. Most of the dialogue is taken directly from Scripture or modern and ancient works on theology and ecclesiastical history. It is a remarkably unsettling film due to its overt opacity: we are never quite sure why the two tramps have undertaken the pilgrimage and there is no simple interpretation at the end. Viewers are left to their own opinions about whether or not the blind man was actually miraculously healed by Christ. Rather than giving answers, the film raises doubts about every answer the Church has ever given. The underlying question in the film is about what constitutes faith and the fact that faith can never be arrived at through reason. Was the blind man cured by Christ at the end of the film or was he merely being polite to Jesus so as not to hurt his feelings? Or perhaps he was cured and was, like many of the rest of us, so used to his actions that he cannot easily change his behaviour. How many of us are blind to miracles seen on and off the road to Santiago?

Because he considered the world to be irrational, Buñuel thought films should be so too. He loved the inherent absurdity of faith as reflected by his comment that "My hatred of science and my loathing of technology will one day lead me to the absurd belief in God", as well as his oft-quoted statement: "Thank God I'm an atheist." And he valued the mystery that lies at the root of both life and faith. He was very moved when learning about one such mystery in Demark. When the film was shown there, a group of twenty or so gypsies who spoke no French or read no Danish, saw the film each day for a period of a week. Sometimes these were the same people, sometimes they were different individuals. Moved by the dedication of the gypsies to the film, the owner of the theatre then informed the group that henceforth they could all see the film for free. The gypsies never came back. When told, Buñuel said that it must never be spoken of again as it was a mystery and mysteries must be respected.

DOCUMENTARIES

IN *LAS PEREGRINAS: THE WOMEN WHO WALK*, New Age self-help coach Sue Kenney works with themes from her previously published book, in particular the concept of sorrow stones that are to be picked up along the Way, carried for a duration before being discarded elsewhere, having through the process supposedly absorbed the angst of the transporter. Although there are pleasant scenes of the group celebrating dinner and participating in various established rituals of the Camino, for the most part the documentary is quite amateurish. Many scenes consist of little more than the women walking past waymarkers amiably chatting away. These are interspersed with overly sincere daily testimonials given directly to the camera. Zoom-ins are shaky, editing between scenes is jarring, and sometimes it is impossible to hear conversations above the sounds of crunching gravel and nylon rubbing against nylon. Not that there is much insight offered by the dialogues one can hear above the usual tired and trite 'insights' of pilgrimage being a metaphor for a life journey, walking the Camino being the way to find one's inner path, the lesson that one doesn't walk the Camino, it walks you, and pat advice about the importance of not being judgmental, etc. After only the first few days of walking, already some of the group are rhapsodising about their various life-altering epiphanies. It is all so affected, so forced, and ultimately, so foolish.

It turns out that the group actually walked for less than two weeks, covering daily distances of rarely more than twenty kilometres. This allows ample time for scenes showing the group talking about 'energy' this or 'energy' that, to be found in stones, in scenery, and even in one case, in the soup; or pausing for breathing exercises, communal meditations, and sunset chants. Intriguingly, after only a single day, one of the women bows out of the documentary, refusing to be filmed though oddly remaining part of the entourage. There is a cute and incongruous scene of the women, all decked out in their rain gear and backpacks, clustered around a shop-front window, staring and pointing at the jewellery on display. If only the rest of the documentary had focused on such simple, endearing, and beautiful moments of humanity that bubble up while on pilgrimage rather than dwelling on overly earnest pretensions. As the group approaches Compostela, they suddenly become preoccupied with the distance to their destination. Much discussion and many disagreements arise between those who wish to quickly complete the hike, whereas others wish to drag it out for as long as possible through walking less than seven kilometres a day.

The film does conclude with nice, inter-cut scenes of the stilted and sombre mass occurring inside the Compostela cathedral contrasted with the revels taking place in the square outside where more than a thousand recently arrived Italian pilgrims are wildly dancing to the beat of drums. One is suddenly reminded that long before the Christian Church laid down their own indulgence/purgatory palimpsest upon this landscape, the Celts – and no doubt others even before them – were traversing the region on their way westward, celebrating, possibly also with dance and music, the celestial heavens.

From the very onset we know that *The Way: One Man's Spiritual Journey Along the Camino de Santiago* will be different. The opening scene shows an early middle-aged man, Mark Shea, sitting on the ground in a cemetery (which we soon learn is in St.-Jean-Pied-de-Port) and talking into a large feather duster-like microphone. He greets us with a big warm Aussie "G'day" followed, as he explains himself, by frequent "ums" so one knows immediately that the dialogue is unrehearsed. We are informed that he is carrying ten kilos of camera and recording equipment and that he is not a physical exercise type of guy and that he expects that this upcoming walk along the Camino will be the hardest thing he has ever done. Within a few minutes what soon becomes obvious is that this is a well-meaning individual who is undertaking something that may be way over his head, not so much from the physicality of the act of pilgrimage but rather from the professionalism required to produce a documentary film. That criticism said, what viewers are presented with is a demonstration of such raw amateurism that it would otherwise be barely watchable had it not been for the remarkable naivety, honesty, and above all, positive enthusiasm, that shines through. Simply put, the ineptitude of the production – the jerky zoom-in close-ups, the over-repeated format of the videographer simply walking up to and soliloquising before a placed camera, the frequent interspersed segments of unidentified photographs resembling a PowerPoint presentation accompanied by the incongruous sound of marching footsteps, and many other glitches and gaffs – are forgiven in the unpretentiousness of an individual struggling with a new (to him) technology in an attempt to document the novelty and possibly (he hopes) transformative nature of his undertaking.

Harsher criticism is also tempered by the self-effacing nature of the Shea who confesses his fears about his performance and personality: his being repeatedly passed on the trail by old-age pensioners, his recounting of an ongoing litany of each day's minor ailments, his boredom at the daily grind of walking and filming, his uncharitable opinions of those pilgrims who wake up at 4:30 am in order to rush to the next place, his guilty pleasure of being able to temporarily escape from fellow pilgrims in some of the big cities, etc. Only when he films within several *refugios*, seemingly unaware that those being interviewed as they lie in their beds or prepare dinner are merely humouring or poking fun of him or, in one case, even going so far as to make faces behind his back as he asks his over-earnest questions about their motivations, does one feel uncomfortable and critical about Shea's pushiness. But again, to his credit, these few scenes that reflect somewhat unfavourably upon his character, or at least upon his awareness and sensitivity of others, have been left in the film.

Of course there are the usual platitudes offered up as insights. On only his second day of walking, for example, Shea tells us, while the words "First Camino Metaphor" run across the bottom of the screen, that – yawn – "El Camino is like life with its ups and downs and that when the going gets tough, it is necessary to take a break and catch your breath." Later he learns – double yawn – that "the Camino provides when you need it", and that one can appreciate God by savouring Nature, etc. One nice scene, however, leaves viewers with the impression that perhaps Shea, himself, may not even believe such platitudes. While effusing to the camera about the life-changing nature of the Camino, he loses his train of thought and confused, just laughs at the overall absurdity of it all, letting slip out a momentary and knowing smile of collusion directly at the camera as if confessing to us, the viewer, that it is all, if not an act, at least something that is to be expected of anyone walking today's Way, before he regroups and continues on with more superficialities. One cannot help but like the guy to keep such a little gem of honesty in the film. But this underscores a difficulty faced by many modern pilgrims; namely, the desperate need to have something transformative happen along the Way. One empathises with Shea when at one point, he recounts a wonderful story of serendipity that he had heard earlier in the day from another pilgrim, and confesses to being worried that nothing like that will happen to him and that, in consequence, the pilgrimage might be a complete waste of time.

In the end, the film is rewarding in showing, without being preachy, that internal growth can in fact happen through the bodily act of pilgrimage. Early on Shea informs that he had been initially attracted to the Camino through reading Paulo Coelho's novel and that he attributed his fortitude in overcoming the numerous physical ailments brought about by walking by being receptive to the energy along the Milky Way. Much later, sorer in body but wiser in spirit, Shea discovers that he doesn't need Coelho's New Age "mumbo-jumbo" mysticism in his new-found spirituality. He is happy with just himself and his God. And interestingly, he comes to realise that it has been the act of making the film that will be more important for him than the act of reaching Compostela.

In *Naked Pilgrim: The Road to Santiago*, British art critic Brian Sewell offers, in a series of six, twenty-two minutes episodes, a condescension about place, people, and pilgrimage that ranges from the iconoclastic to the vitriolic. Seventy-two-year-old Sewell drives from London to Compostela stopping along the Way to pontificate about ecclesiastical architecture in between grumblings about the difficulties of travel. Frequently he makes reference to one purpose of his journey being to retrace the route he took forty years previously but pointedly he never once informs the viewer as to whether that trip, like the present one, was also by automobile. He seems confused about whether he is in fact a pilgrim, admitting several times to being a "cheat" but then absurdly identifying himself with those "fellow pilgrims" he encounters and briefly interviews – as frequently as not in a chiding or challenging way – who have been walking or cycling the pilgrimage routes across France and Spain. At times it becomes comical, with Sewell's voiceover going on about being a pilgrim while the filmed sequence shows him in his always nicely turned out clothes sitting in a French café eating a big bowl of lemon sorbet. In another scene, Sewell is again stating that he is beginning to feel like a real pilgrim as he rushes by the countryside in his Mercedes. The goal of his outing he unabashedly admits at one point is to have long, lazy lunches fuelled by copious alcohol before getting back in his car and rushing to the next place. In the end there are so many scenes of such egregious incongruity and inappropriateness that one wonders if it is all a big joke and he is taking the mickey out of the all-too-earnest pilgrims he encounters as well as ourselves, the all-too-serious viewers. The problem, however, is that he comes across as such a completely unpleasant individual that all the fun has been lost and one cannot help but be left with an abject distaste for the narrator.

And one's opinion of Sewell's demeanour is certainly not improved by his frequent architectural rants or grumblings about his various aches and pains from sitting in his Mercedes day after day as he flits past struggling pilgrims. It is impossible to feel empathy for him after listening to his repeated mocking comments about being sick of pilgrims, fed up with churches, bored with driving, angry with bad hotels, etc. When he does finally arrive in Compostela, after finally leaving the car and riding a horse for the last fifty kilometres so as – erroneously in his mind – to be considered a true pilgrim by the authorities, he admits to not understanding why tears come to many of the pilgrims around him when he feels nothing spiritual or "no hand of God hovering over" him. One cannot help at this point but talk back to the screen and offer the following simple words of revelatory insight: "Just walk a**hole!"

Even putting aside the issue of whether any pilgrimage can really be undertaken from a car, there is the question of the material that Sewell includes in the documentary that will leave veteran pilgrims puzzled and neophytes confused. Despite his frequently repeated goal to investigate the medieval mind in attempt to understand why people went on pilgrimages, in Paris he visits the modern Sacré-Coeur Basilica and the one-time royal and therefore private Sainte-Chapelle chapel but not the Tour de Saint Jacques where the pilgrims would have actually mustered. And while at Chartres Cathedral, he talks about the Day of Judgment carvings on the south side (incorrectly conflating their meaning with pilgrimage) yet does not mention the multiple representations of Sainte Jacques (Saint James): statues on the southern façade, the fresco in the crypt, or the brilliant stained glass windows in the nave and chancel. As well, while at the famous pilgrim gateway straddling the road in Pons, he dismisses the heralded carvings as being made by modern shopkeepers rather than their accepted ascription to early pilgrims. The whole thing is odd to say the least.

The film ends with Sewell on the beach of La Coruña misleading viewers with the statement that it is here rather than at Finisterre where one is supposed to, like him, burn one's clothes after completing the pilgrimage. From the title of the documentary I had hoped to encounter something along the lines of Pierre Mazeaud's classic autobiography of alpinism: *Naked Before the Mountain*. Instead, rather than presentation of a sensitive soul bared naked before God following an arduous physical exploit, the viewer is left with the image of flaccid buttocks bared naked as the narrator wades into the surf.

Within the Way Without, written and directed by Laurence Boulting, recounts the pilgrimages of three individuals from three countries at three times of the year. Scenes of the Camino are interspersed with scenes of the three pilgrims adjusting to their respective lives back at home while celebrating Christmas and enjoying their families as they each reflect back to their experiences along the Way. This is a lovingly rendered and beautiful documentary of homage and spiritual depth that offers many rewards. The powerful technique of cutting back and forth among the various pilgrimages so the viewer gets to see famous sites at different times of the year leaves a lasting impression of the permanence of pilgrimage. Spanning countries of origin and spanning seasons, pilgrims have for a thousand years shuffled toward Compostela, each preoccupied with integrating the interior and the exterior Ways – the eponymous "within" blended with "without".

The documentary contains many memorable images: close-ups of the sacred such as of the *Botafumeiro* sensuously emitting smoke as it swings back and forth in the Compostela cathedral or of the statue of Saint James high up on the baroque façade silhouetted by exploding fireworks on the millennium celebration, and close-ups of the profane such as of boots being pulled on and anoraks being zipped up; images of pilgrims back at home reliving their experiences while they unfold and hang up their *compostelas* or reread postcards they had sent themselves from the Camino; lingering shots of landscape panorama and architectural heritage; humorous or touching encounters with some of individuals along the Way; and of one pilgrim who hurls his boots into the ocean at Finisterre.

Only toward its conclusion does the film lose its appeal with the presentation of a series of unneeded and obviously staged if not outright scripted scenes that cross over from documentary to theatre, fact to fiction. These scenes are jarringly affected and leave a slightly uncomfortable feeling of mistrust about whether the whole production was like one of those television 'reality' shows. That criticism aside, the film works best when it presents voiceovers from the three pilgrims, for therein little gems of wisdom are shared: the Brazilian summer pilgrim writing her postcards to the "Me" she had left behind and recognises will never meet again; the Dutch winter pilgrim who has to go on pilgrimage lest he be left with eating "another bowl of cheap nuts and a life squandered while looking at the television"; and the Japanese spring pilgrim writing haiku poetry about a previous life of sleepwalking with eyes shut and heart closed. The film ends poignantly with one pilgrim unable to finish walking the Camino, another writing a book, and the third putting away his belongings and returning to Spain to help other pilgrims as a volunteer *hospitalero*.

Electronic

The Road to Compostela is a CD-ROM compiling many important medieval texts relating to the pilgrimage to the shrine of Saint James. Included are excerpts from the famous twelfth-century *Codex Calixtinus*, now held in the library of the Santiago Cathedral, in addition to passages from the travel diaries of medieval and Renaissance pilgrims. The package also contains a Gazetteer of historic sites on the Camino, a Dictionary of Saints encountered along the Way, a copious Bibliography of other historical documents, and a series of photographs, plans and maps (some interactive) of the modern route. Camino scholars benefit from the original source documents as Camino travellers do from the maps, particularly those of cities. Biographical details in the Dictionary of Saints are particularly interesting as are the other, rarely published books from the *Codex*. One travelogue, *The Itinerary of William Wey*, covers the 1456 trip of an Eton schoolmaster by boat from Plymouth to Coruña from where he walked to Compostela commenting upon the relics, indulgences, and the history of Saint James. Perhaps of more interest is the 1494 account of Nuremberg physician Hieronymus Münzer who travelled around Spain with a wonderful curiosity about science and an appreciation of architecture, collecting books as he went and making some of the first transcriptions of the *Codex* for non-Spanish readers. Though separated in time by only four decades, the two travelogues could not be more different. Whereas Wey's account seems firmly rooted in the antiquated medieval world, that of Münzer is characterised by a fresh and expansive Renaissance sensibility. He seems to have been just the sort of engaged and engaging travel companion whose company I would have enjoyed.

Pilgrim is an interactive computer video game based on an adventure story by Paulo Coelho with artwork by Moebius. The storyline is based on a knight returning from the Crusades with a Coptic manuscript which he leaves with a member of a secret order after he is ambushed and seriously injured. The manuscript is passed down to young Simon who is charged with carrying it along the road to Compostela to hand to another member of the order all the while being pursued by a multitude of enemies. Viewers have to navigate through various rooms and towns as in a game of Dungeons and Dragons. Questions need to be asked of the right characters in the right order and key objects need to be moved about from one place to another before one can continue. The difficulty in progressing from one stage to the next was completely beyond my own capabilities as someone who has never been interested in, much less played, such computer games. As a result, I sought out several teenage boys who in only a short time abandoned the enterprise as "a frustrating, old, sad, little game", unworthy of their attention. But perhaps they are more familiar with graphics and interactions that characterise recent computer games rather than those on this dated example.

The CD *Stone by Stone* by writer, pilgrim, and life coach Sue Kenney begins with instructions to the listener to relax before immediately lathering on such oft-repeated New Age baubles of insight as that we are all pilgrims each on our own journey, that we need to surrender to the Camino, and that since love is the essence of the soul, we have need for self-love. The CD does have admirable features such as the frequent changes in tonal reflection and emotion that ring through in Kenney's voice and a pleasant soundtrack of atmospheric music and background chants. And the overall theme of the sorrow stones, a well-known custom of catharsis on the Camino, is certainly interesting and meritorious of recounting. The problem is that that positive message is, as so often the case in Camino story-telling, drowned out by the trite, the overwrought, and the maudlin. So here we have statements about the need to give oneself to "the miracle of the Camino", and that "when the Camino ends, the journey begins", etc. The listener learns that the lesson Kenney has recognised from her own pilgrimage experiences is that her life purpose is to inspire people. By inference then, one assumes that the recording is her way of bringing this about. And therein lies the inherent problem in this and indeed most self-help productions, namely that the purveyors go beyond the simple desire of authors to retell interesting anecdotes in their presumption of an imagined position of sufficient self-import so as to qualify them to impart wisdom. Unfortunately this raises the bar much higher than that expected from a straightforward narrative where the author is mostly concerned about trying to understand his or her own problems rather than having the chutzpah to presume that they can help others. The result is that rarely do such pedagogies leave the discriminating reader, or in this case, listener, satisfied. As a case in point, though Kenney does offer some useful insights at the very end of *Stone by Stone*, by that time it comes out in too rushed a voice that ultimately seems to have too little to offer that is either particularly new or of paramount significance.

Althea Hayton's *Walk With Me: The Pilgrim Road to Santiago*, is quite simply one of the very best contemplations in any media of the modern pilgrimage experience. Three CDs present a series of thirty daily recordings of reflections made either in the quiet of an evening after the walk or *in situ* at identified locations where listeners can themselves perhaps remember the background sounds of a babbling brook, the hustle and bustle of a busy city square in front of a church, automobiles racing by overhead on a viaduct, or singing birds in a forest glade. Layered over this is Hayton's sonorous English-accented voice spoken with such emotion, sincerity, and depth of feeling that one cannot help but fall a little in love with it…and her in the process. Hayton searches for a theme to surface from each day's events and draws the listener in through the seduction of referring to making this recording in such and such a location that day particularly for "you" as if she is somehow operating under direct charge as one's own personal agent and reporting to each of us individually. It is beguiling and almost instantly believable. This is a recording not to be distractingly listened to during a long road trip but rather one needing an individual's full attention while being savoured over several peaceful winter nights in front of a fire accompanied perhaps by a bottle of Rioja wine.

Several recent books have attempted to break free of the limitations of the regurgitated daily narrative, either thematically (as I too have done in Part II of the present book) or by offering various life lessons. Hayton's attempt at the latter is transcendent and of a high quality absent in New Age self-help guides about the Camino. Following a brief overview of each day's activities or explanation of where she is at the particular time of the recording, she offers up stories, some about animals, trees, geometrical creatures, or archetypal pilgrims, told in the form of allegorical parables. One of my favourite such is inspired by some vineyards she had walked through one particular day. The lesson is that spiritual growth comes about through pruning. In other words, by getting smaller, by pruning out that which is not required. Stripped right down to the bare base of the trunk, only then can fruit be born aplenty. And likewise only then, metaphorically, through the wonderful process of simplification offered by a pilgrimage can we too, stripped down to the bare essentials of existence by pruning away the unneeded, become smaller and through the process, grow spiritually larger. Hayton provides other wise words about pilgrimage in general, in one case concerning the frequently voiced "call of the Camino." Here, she distinguishes between those who are either drawn to or are driven to the undertaking, the former process an exercise of internal free will, the latter, submitting to some external force.

Concluding each day's story – though once or twice instead of a story a poem or song is given – with a pause, Hayton then states "And now let's pray." A short, topical, and usually personally written little gem is presented that encapsulates both the day's activities and the previously recounted story.

And if all this were not enough, the collection also contains a thirty-page booklet of liner notes that, truth be told, is itself, even without the accompanying CDs, more insightful than most modern pilgrimage narratives of the Camino. Here each day's stage is entitled something like "Surrender", "Giving", "Regrets", "Inadequacy" and such, beneath which are four or five brief paragraphs of text summarising the day. Finally, this in turn is followed by two suggested daily self-help activities, an apropos Bible reading, and finally a recommended secular book to read for further insight on the topic.

During his 2004 pilgrimage from Le Puy to Compostela, musician Oliver Schroer carried his violin, as he writes in the liner notes to his album *Camino*, "like a wooden chalice, like my own precious relic, carefully packed in its reliquary of socks and underwear and waiting to work a miracle." Thankfully for all of us, he would periodically withdraw that relic and record playing it in churches along the Way. The haunting notes from Schroer's violin seem to rise up and hang there in the air, resonating and capturing the spacious essence present in both the grand cathedrals as well as, interestingly, also in the tiniest of chapels. Each musical recording was uncertain since Schroer never knew if he would be permitted to continue (he mentions being shut down after only thirty-three seconds in the church in Astorga). Interspersed between the violin solos are ambient sounds carefully selected to add to the immersion experience: pilgrims praying, children playing, passing conversations, songs from both parishioners and birds, ringing bells from village churches and cows in fields, and the atmospheric tramping of boots over gravel on the Camino itself. Accompanying photographs by walking companion Peter Coffman add to the package as do the few carefully selected words of liner notes of a sensitivity equal to the best of contemporary pilgrimage accounts. Following the "blissful daze of arriving" in Compostela, the group attend the pilgrim mass and hear the priest announce *Cuatro de Canada*, provoking the following reflection: "There was a time in our lives before the camino, and there is a time after it. These three words mark the transition." Sadly there was not to be a great deal of after time for Schroer. Bravely facing his treatment, which he referred to as "El Chemino", he expired from cancer not long after releasing his album. Reflecting that the recording was made while cells may have already been metastasising within his body when he was on pilgrimage makes the album all that more precious. In the end, we are left with this parting musical gift, Schroer's legacy to fellow pilgrims, captured in one brief instant during the Camino's millennium of history. Perhaps that is the true miracle.

Music

MY COLLECTION OF CAMINO-INSPIRED traditional music contains albums produced by two English-language groups. *Pilgrimage to Santiago* was recorded in a London church following the return of the Monteverdi choir from their trip to France and Spain. During their coach trip, the choir had sung in fourteen churches along the Way, such as those in the towns of Conques, San Juan de Ortega and Oviedo, in order for members to have the "experience of living inside the music." Such immersion is very much in the spirit of the group's mandate to match ancient music with localised architecture. Excerpts from member diaries shown in the liner notes remark that with every performance a feeling of camaraderie grew among members and that whenever pilgrims were present in the audience an extra special quality was added to the experience. Some pilgrims in fact became groupies and would get up in the middle of the night to walk to the next stop to catch the choir a second time.

All tracks on the album are unaccompanied vocal pieces covering a time-span from Gregorian origins to Renaissance a cappella. The tracks were compiled from a number of sources across Europe to demonstrate the interconnectedness of Spain via the Camino to the rest of the continent, in particular musical innovations from Rome, France, and Flanders. The selected polyphonic songs, for example, contain elements of both *conductus* (two voices moving together in union) and *organum* (two voices in parallel, the upper voice in melody against the long-held notes of the lower chanting voice) styles originating in France. A quarter of the tracks come from the *Codex Calixtinus* or *Liber Sancti Jacobi* (Book of Saint James), the collection of five books of sermons, accounts of miracles and legends, travel guide, liturgy, and texts and chants compiled in Cluny in the mid-twelfth century.

The remarkable voices on the recording are infused with a feeling of vast, echoing spaces of church vaults. Absence of instrumental accompaniment allows the listener to focus on the rising, falling, and holding of impossibly prolonged notes of the drone. Most of the songs are devotional pieces such as chants and antiphons that have an overall sombre feel. The album begins with the famous 'pilgrim song' from the *Codex*: *Dum Pater familias* [Before the Father] with its haunting refrain "*Herru Santiago! / Grot Santiago! / e ultreya e suseya / Deus adjuva nos*." Another selection from the *Codex*, translated in the liner notes from the original Latin sung on the recording, gives a wonderfully succinct indication of the pan-European breadth of the Camino in the twelfth century: "Armenians, Greeks, Apulians, / English, French, Dacians, Frisians, / all nations, tongues and tribes / journey there with gifts." A favourite track of mine for obvious reasons, whose words I would struggle to discern from the Latin while listening *en route* and which would be the first track I sought out after reading the Latinised form of my name on my *compostela* at the Santiago Cathedral pilgrim office, concludes with a prayer to Saint James, translated as "Strong protector of body and soul, / may you help us all, and with your holy staff / may you drive war from our shores, / but you yourself keep Robert wholly safe! [*ipse sed totum tege jam Robertum!*]"

The second group, Anonymous 4, was established to study and perform medieval chants and polyphony with higher female voices. *Miracles of Sant' Iago: Music from the Codex Calixtinus* was the first recording of liturgical music from the medieval source by an English-language group. The liner notes, as well as containing a photograph of the original document, inform that ninety percent of the music from the *Codex* is plainchant liturgical hymns, antiphons, responsories, and benedictions adapted from existing chants for the Divine Office and Mass for Saint James' Feast Day and relict Translation Day. Ten percent of the music is polyphonic, mostly for two voices, but also including the earliest preserved documents of such for three voices. The liner notes also mention that the notation in the *Codex* is notoriously ambiguous as to rhythm, metre, and oral alignments in the polyphonic sections. This of course allows for a wide interpretation by modern groups.

The recording is of four angelic voices which float and linger in haunting melody. Though these may be the most beautiful voices to have ever recorded Camino-inspired music, if one is historically minded, it is impossible not to miss hearing male voices as being more representative of liturgical chants. And despite the statement that the source material is "infectiously joyful and exuberant", the impression left by listening to the disc is, like that of the other English recording noted above, one of being very "churchy", which of course is to be expected given the liturgical intent of the music. As such, in both these recordings one searches in vain for a glimpse of the joyous and jostling pilgrims mentioned in the *Codex* sitting in their clusters of nationality in all-night vigil outside the Santiago cathedral, warming themselves over braziers, drinking copious quantities of local wine, and singing their joyous hearts out after successfully arriving at their destination. That said, there still are instances in the songs where the liturgical lyrics admirably recount the true spirit of the pilgrimage – prayers, relics, hope, healing, absolution, etc. – which, when attentively listened to at home with the liner notes in hand, reveal Latinised versions of the following: "[Galicia] rejoices to be visited / by all peoples / for the blessings of the holy / man, who must be revered." (from the *Codex*); "He whose body was entombed / is visited by multitudes / and by his body healing / is given in Galicia." (by the Bishop of Troyes); "O bright light of Galicia, / O friend of pilgrims, / James, you victor over vices: break the chains of our transgressions, / and lead us to salvation's gate." (again by the Bishop of Troyes); "Be the savior of your pilgrims, / help us, St. James! / Give us fallen ones / hope of heaven, / help us, St. James!" (by the patriarch of Jerusalem); "The sick pray to his sarcophagus / that they may regain their health. / All peoples, tongues and tribes go there / crying out: Come along! Let's go! / And they bring different gift-offerings / confessing their own crimes." (by Pope Calixtus); and also attributable to Calixtus, the following, seldom better expressed, distillation of the early pilgrimage:

> "To the tomb of blessed James / the sick come and are healed, / the blind are given light, the crippled raised up, / the demon-possessed are set free, / the sorrowful are consoled, / and, what is best of all, / the prayers of the faithful are heard. / There, foreign folk from every part of the world / hasten in great numbers, / bearing gifts of praise to the Lord, Alleluia!"

Medieval Pilgrimage to Santiago, by the Ensemble für Frühe Musik Augsburg, was the only German recording I carried on my iPod while on pilgrimage to Compostela. The liner notes make the interesting point that most songs of the pilgrims were idiosyncratic and ephemeral and have been lost – many not even surviving beyond the individual pilgrimage or spreading to other groups of pilgrims. As a result, the legacy is one of songs written for and about pilgrims rather than from them. "Even in this warped perspective," the liner notes continue, "numerous facets of the pan-European cult of St. James are nonetheless discernible." The recording contains selections from the *Codex* augmented by many songs that German pilgrims would have heard as they set out from home and walked along the busiest route, not as it is today, that from Le Puy, but rather that which traversed the Aquitaine, the region of the troubadours. The Ensemble organised the songs on the album into categories representing such a pilgrimage journey: "The Parting (Germany), "The Route" (Aquitaine), "The Arrival" (Spain), and "At the Destination" (Compostela). Subjects of the songs include procurement of necessary accoutrements, trusting to the will and mercy of God, infrastructure maintenance of the Camino, warnings about dishonest innkeepers and other dangers of the Way, and chants and prayers to Santa Maria, interesting in that it indicates the importance of Marian shrines even on the pilgrimage route to the relics of Saint James. There are also encouragements for pilgrims to continue onward to Finisterre, demonstrating the importance of that end-of-the-world location to the medieval mindset and that it has always been a destination in its own right and not just a modern, New Age epiphenomenon. Also of interest, is mention in several songs of the significance of witnessing the demonstrated grace and encouragement provided by pilgrims heading back home to those still making their way onward to Compostela. Sadly, this is something that is almost completely missing from today's Camino experience. The album is characterised by sombre, deep-voiced male chants interspersed with rousing music and occasional shouts of jubilation, which can easily be imagined, as I frequently did when listening to the recording when lying on my *refugio* bed just before sleep, as originating from pilgrims, recorded in situ as they crossed the fields of medieval Europe.

Recorded in the Irache Abbey on the Camino by the French group Ensemble Organum, *Compostela ad Vespers Sancti Jacobi* is designed to represent a Vespers Mass on July 24th, the day before the Feast Day of Saint James. The liner notes mention that before such medieval music can be performed by modern groups considerable research is needed on text and vocal styles, physical positioning of singers, in addition to inference about many things in the oral traditions that have been lost over time. One point the Ensemble is emphatic about is that the suppression of vitality, energy, and ornamentation that has occurred in many modern religious recordings of medieval songs has no historical basis. Their research argues that modern performers of Gregorian chants who use the plainchant format least their songs display non-spiritual materialism and sins of vanity and pride are basing their decisions on a tradition that is little more than a century old. Interestingly, the liner notes mention that the most famous pilgrim piece of music, the *Dum Pater familias*, is very different from the rest of the *Codex* and seems to have been added as a hasty afterthought to the original manuscript. The problem is that the rushed scribe failed to copy out a melody which results in each verse being somewhat different in rhythm. The Ensemble's decision was to perform this piece in polyphony with two parallel refrains, one in Latin, the other in various Germanic or Roman dialects, making their recording one of the most complex versions of the 'pilgrim song.' The all-male choir provides an authentic, resonating solemnity to the album. The deep background rumble of the drone almost sounds as if an organist has fallen asleep with his hand on the keyboard. One has to keep reminding oneself that it is all human voices. While on pilgrimage, it was often this particular recording that I would listen to at the end of the day when writing my journal, dreaming myself back in time to a scriptorium beside a Romanesque chapel from out of which the liturgy echoed.

Sur les Chemins de Saint-Jacques de Compostelle is likened by the Ensemble Amadis to a form of musical wayfaring. The recording is certainly one of the broadest available in terms of its source material, and with an alternating mix of male and female voices accompanied by replicated traditional instruments (zither, lyre, dulcimer, flute, pipe, trumpet, harp, vielle, bagpipes), it became one of my most listened to albums during my own wayfaring to Compostela. Liner notes remind readers that road-weary pilgrims, upon arriving at the Pórtico del Gloria, would be greeted by carvings of not only the Apostle but also of the accompanying twenty-four musician-kings. In contrast to the overly sombre tone of many Camino albums, this one is full of lively renditions of marching songs, troubadour ballads from Occitan France, period Galician, Catalan, and Spanish Sephardic songs, as well as pieces from King Alfonso X's *cantigas* collection (see below) and others intriguingly designed to instruct early pilgrims about the supremacy of Marian devotion and not to forget her shrines while on pilgrimage to that of the upstart Apostle in Compostela.

My very first Camino album, purchased the night before I took my first, life-transforming steps out of Le Puy Cathedral toward Compostela, and carried unheard on that initial journey to Moissac, is *Ultreia! Sur la Route de Saint-Jacaques-de-Compostelle* by Polyphonia Antigua. It is also one of the earliest modern recordings, dating from 1983, well before the modern revival of the pilgrimage, and to this day remains my most favourite Camino-themed album. Many tracks have a strong emphasis on instrumental music, some of which were recorded in the countryside to provide a more authentic pilgrimage feel to the music. The album is conceived as one liturgical drama from farewell laments, to joyous songs of jongleurs and jugglers heard at the end of each day, to the final *Te Deum* in the Santiago Cathedral. Overall there is a rough and raw 'garage band'-like vitality to the album that seems to wonderfully capture the exuberance one imagines of early pilgrims. Nowhere is this better displayed than in the repeated and varied renditions of *Dum Pater familias* that occur throughout the album. As mentioned previously, the absence of specific notes on tempo in the original *Codex* has meant that each group is free to interpret how the song is performed. In the present case, the well-known piece is performed as an up-tempo marching *Ultreia* song. During one rendition of the touchstone song, it progressively builds in the background to transition to another piece of more sombre liturgical music, as if the pilgrims were walking toward the priest reading the Mass. Soon the marching song dominates as the happy pilgrims shout out the refrain "*Ultreia! Suseia! Deus aia Nos!*" at the top of their lungs. Such joyous, cacophonic shouts are completely different from the polished polyphonies of most other Camino albums. Several other tracks contain brief talking sections as if pilgrims were offering personal instructions or encouragements to the listener. The feeling engendered is one of intimacy and total immersion. Even the more 'churchy' tracks on the album are rendered in a lively fashion with the reader and the singer of a Mass each alternating where the other left off as if in a medieval version of *Duelling Banjos*.

I have four Spanish albums in my collection of Camino-inspired music, one of which became the most frequently played recording during my pilgrimage whereas the other three were purchased in Compostela at the end of the journey. Interestingly, as a group, these albums are the most distinct of those in my collection in terms of their subject matter. Musica Antigua's *El Camino de Santiago en las Cantigas de Alfonso X el Sabio* can, despite the first four words of its title, be looked upon as a sort of counter-Camino album. This is because its source is the thirteenth-century songbook by the accomplished poet and historian King Alfonso X. The *cantigas* consist of a manuscript of over four hundred Galician-Portuguese poems composed in Mozarab style with corresponding musical notation and surrounded by lovely miniature drawings. Regarded as medieval Spain's most important lyrical work, King Alfonso's masterpiece recounts tales of miracles and praises of the Virgin Mary. Designed to attract Compostela-bound pilgrims to Villalcázar de Sirga, the *cantigas* repeatedly stress that the Lady can perform miracles where Saint James cannot. As a historical document the *cantigas* are also important in returning miracles to where they originated, such as that of the resurrection of the 'hanged pilgrim' back to Rocamadour in France from where it was conscripted by the Cluny-Camino cartel to Santo Domingo in Spain. Despite such counter-Camino propaganda, of all the albums on my iPod I listened to while on pilgrimage, this one, with its Spanish-aligned language and music, seemed most appropriate to the setting. The lively exchanges between female soloists and the mixed-gender choir, accompanied by incredibly spirited music, infuses the recording with a feeling of unbridled celebration.

Founded in Santiago de Compostela and named after a musical piece in the *Codex*, Resonet have been distinctive in producing three albums of pilgrimage songs from the fifteenth to eighteenth centuries. The matured and polished music of this period sounds very different from the *Codex*-inspired medieval music of other compilations, including those mentioned above. *Santiago! Music and Pilgrimage in Renaissance Europe* draws upon a wide range of pan-European sources which are performed exquisitely by crystalline voices. Lyrics suggest the Camino was already becoming romanticised at this time, containing expressions that would not be out of place in modern pilgrimage accounts or guidebooks: "I have walked a thousand steps for you / And I have done many foolish things, / And lived disorderly without any measure, / Therefore I am suffering from melancholy. / Oh! What will become of my life?"; "Saint Jacques' Way, / With greater faith than devotion, / My body departs alone / Leaving reason aside."; and "Anyone who is looking for consolation after misery / Must stand up and set off / On Saint Jacques' way, / two pairs of shoes he must have, / A plate and a bottle. / A wide hat he must have / And he must no set off without a coat, / his bag and his stick are his companions."

The liner notes in Resonet's *La Grande Chanson as Cancións dos Peregrinos de Santiago* state their thesis: "European culture – as well as its music, both popular and high – owes many of its features to the continuous coming together and exchange of influences that took place for almost a millennium around the Road to Santiago." The "Great Song of the Pilgrims" was compiled in 1718 and recounts the journey of French pilgrims from preparing for the journey to their return from Compostela. This particular recording was made in the convent church in Sarria on the Camino and is enriched by occasional interruptions by walkers-by, some of whom were no doubt bona fide pilgrims. Elements of eighteenth-century music were used whenever possible, including vocal techniques, rhythmical and melodic improvisations, and even a few old instruments. Excerpts from the Great Song include:

> When we left France / in eagerness / we left our sad and grieving / mother and father behind. / Our hearts craved so / to go to Santiago / that we forsook all pleasures / to make the trip…We carried our pumpkins, / and our staff, / in order to have courage in our journey, / and not be tired / during our pilgrimage…We carried on / through the fields, / and felt our courage drive away all evil…When we arrived at last in Compostela, / we were so happy. / We all run eagerly, / old and young, / to pay tribute to God…We could see pilgrims / from every corner of the world, / singing and praising / in every language…From Blaye we walked on diligently / to see our parents, / who thought us dead or almost. / They recognised us at once / because of our coats / and we gave them / plenty of presents from Santiago.

And from another contemporaneous songbook, the following advice in one song should be heeded just as much today as when it was written three centuries ago: "I humbly pray you / who are bound for Santiago, / not to hurry; / lead a gentle pace…Do not go laden, / but travel light, at least in the summertime, / For even a light load / can weight you down."

Les *Pellerines: La Mode du Pelrinage dans la France du Baroque* by Resonet originates from many sources and is organised into sections of "Farewell", "Departure", "Rest", "Dreams", "Prayer", "Joy", and "Gratitude." The liner notes inform that while pilgrimage was decreasing in popularity in the rest of Reformation Europe, it continued to linger on in France in a form completely transformed from its original inspirations. Under French Baroque sensibilities, pilgrimage became an abstracted journey to an imaginary poetic world. A far cry from Bunyan's allegory, the French version at this time, as shown in a famous enclosed painting, included in the liner notes was one of over-dressed dandies and décolletage-displaying females draped with pilgrim shells which, of course, also symbolise Venus, the goddess of love. The profane songs of courtly passion and drinking camaraderie on this album seem worlds away from the spirit of the Santiago pilgrimage…but then again…

On Confraternity...

CHAPTER 11

BULLETIN BONHOMIE

Purpose and methods

QUESTIONS CONCERNING AUTHENTICITY have always been part of the pilgrimage experience. Dante wrote, for example, that the only true pilgrims were those who had been to or were returning from the tomb of Saint James. Erasmus, in contrast, considered the granting of indulgences for pilgrimages to Walsingham and other shrines to be antithetical to true Christianity. Since near its inception, the *Bulletin* published by the British-based organisation, the Confraternity of Saint James (see Chapter 12), has provided a forum to allow members to articulate their views about what it means to be a pilgrim in our modern, overly secular society in the face of the growing popularity of the Camino as a tourist destination and of New Age esoterism as an alternative expression of spirituality.

One of the biggest debates concerned the nature of travel to Compostela. As far back as 1988, some Confraternity members were calling for more discrimination in the awarding of *compostelas* as statements began to emerge from the Secretariat of the Cathedral of Santiago de Compostela suggesting that the motives of mass-tourists and adventurists could pose a threat to "the vital spirit of the pilgrimage." Soon thereafter, the Secretariat started to break down their statistics into 'true pilgrims' who travelled by foot, bicycle, or horse and 'group pilgrims' who arrived by tour coach. Although many of the first Confraternity members travelled to Compostela as part of motorised tours, a gradual progression occurred such that by the early 1990s one of the long-time members, M. Marples, could write: "Traveling by coach in a large group can develop friendship and camaraderie. But even having a spiritual leader as well as a tour guide can never replace the experience of being reliant on the good will of whoever one meets along the way or the exhilaration of physically making the journey oneself." In another article, one Confraternity member, after completing a walk all the way from Le Puy, had nothing but condescension when referring to the superficial nature of tour coach 'pilgrims'.

Not everyone agreed, however, with the emerging definition of what constitutes a modern pilgrim. Confraternity Chairman, P. Quaife, began her 1994 report with the opinion that being a pilgrim is a state of the mind and heart and that she thought too much emphasis had been placed on walkers as being the only authentic pilgrims, before continuing on to describe a "pilgrimage" [my use of quotation marks] by mini-bus to several sites in Spain. But then, a few years later, L. Dennett, another early member and one of the first to write an account of her walk to Compostela, offered her opinion that regardless of the sincerity of those in motorised tour groups, they are "less likely to arrive at that acceptance of dependence and interdependence that is one of the Camino's gifts to the walker or cyclist in exchange for physical effort." Dennett, however, cautioned against prejudice toward recreationists and worrying about the overly dire warnings of the demise of the true pilgrimage experience, both of which ignore the fact that "the Camino has always been full of casual travelers and it seems to work its very considerable magic on a high proportion of them."

Concern about authenticity continued over the years, not without, one senses, a building frustration and growing fatigue about the whole issue. Anthropologist N. Frey, for example, offered the apt summary that all discussions about authenticity result in the Camino at times being "reduced to a competition for 'pilgrimness' (whatever that maybe) based on fulfilling or complying with an image of authenticity constructed in the last ten to fifteen years." Frey sums up the possibly nonsensical nature of the debate by reminding readers that "pilgrimage is both an inner and outer way and it is impossible to equate distance travelled with one's feet with the amount of inner terrain that one covers."

In a similar vein, P. Robins addressed the absurd fundamentalism that has crept into the debate in recent years wherein some are critical of those who deviate from the newly established 'official' route regardless of the fact that by doing so these individuals might actually be walking a more historically accurate route. Robins goes on to address the new 'rules' that determine in fundamentalists' opinions whether or not one can be regarded as being a 'real pilgrim': you must start in St.-Jean-Pied-de-Port, your *credentials* must be stamped each day, you must stay in *albergues*, etc. He makes the point that most medieval British pilgrims would have sailed to La Coruña and would not have been anywhere near the Camino Francés, much less Le Puy. And because the walking distance from La Coruña to Compostela is less than the hundred kilometres recognised today as demarcating a pilgrim by cathedral authorities, these medieval Britons would have been denied a *compostela* under the present regulations. Despite all the highfaluting, touchy-feely pontifications of many modern pilgrims about the importance of the journey and not the destination, the object for most medieval British pilgrims was first and foremost to reach Compostela, not to undertake a long walk when travel there and back by ship would get the job done with more surety. Robins extends the argument such that the modern, historically obsessed fundamentalist from Britain should in consequence walk to the nearest airport, take a plane to Lavacolla, and from there continue to Compostela on foot. "Doesn't all the talk of real and authentic miss the point?" he asks, "The most important thing about a pilgrimage is surely not whether it's 'real' or 'authentic' but whether it is meaningful." Amen.

The *Bulletin* has also contained several thought-provoking articles on the spirituality of pilgrimage. In 1995 and 1996, for example, anthropologist B. Haab explored the Way as an inner journey antithetical to the social structure of everyday life. An interest in the transformative or liminal nature of pilgrimage led her to ponder the adoption of St.-Jean-Pied-de-Port as the modern place of commencement, with the trip over the Pyrenees not only being a geographical transition but also a conceptual separation threshold between the external, profane world and the internal, sacred world. Further, for Haab, it is no accident that the Camino progresses from east to west, thereby following the daily birth and death of the sun, since death itself is a transition from the earthly to the spiritual worlds. This suggests the intriguing idea that whereas Jerusalem in the Middle Ages was regarded as the centre of the world, Compostela, by contrast, perched as it is on the western rim of Europe, is the gateway to the next world, one which we all will face once freed of our mortal coils. Indeed, Haab believed, the Camino can be regarded as a of shaman-like initiatory experience based on geographic stages: over the Pyrenees to Burgos representing preparation for the letting go of one's previous life; across the *meseta* to León mimicking death and the abandonment of the old; along the Way to Rabanal symbolising crossing the major threshold; on up to O'Cebreiro where one prepares to receive the Holy at Compostela; and continuing on to Finisterre being the time of recapitulation wherein "the very last trial of the Way is the interpretation of one's experience into one's everyday life."

INCIDENTS AND ANECDOTES

One of the major roles of the *Bulletin* is to provide a forum giving voice to the encapsulated experiences of common pilgrims, those for whom either lack of ego or presence of good judgment will never produce a full-fledged, step-by-step account of their complete pilgrimage undertaking. For the most part, these anecdotes comprise factual rather than reflective recollections of a particular event that the writers (sometimes mistakenly) believe to be novel or worthy of general interest. In reality, whereas a good number of the more recent recountings are quite pedestrian and offer little of distinction relative to the dozens of full-length treatments that exist today, it is the earlier accounts of intrepid pilgrims from the 1980s, when walking to Compostela was a real adventure, that are a joy to read. How different things were back then. In these gems of time-travel we learn, for example, that it was possible to walk for months without encountering more than one or two other pilgrims, and when one arrived at Compostela one could look forward to being treated like a visiting dignitary rather than like a nuisance or a number as often seems to be the case today. This was a time when there were no guidebooks, no yellow arrows, no maps and no *refugios*. Yet there is also much in these early accounts that resonates with pilgrims today: the seemingly miraculous chance encounters with someone who knows someone who knows of you, the feelings of fear, trepidation, disappointment, and self-doubt, and the simple acts of kindness from locals, all expressed with a freshness as if the writers were describing the excavation of a long-forgotten archaeological site or the discovery of a lost anthropological tribe in the very heart of Europe. Perhaps it is feelings of nostalgia or more accurately jealously on my part for having missed partaking in such adventures of three decades ago, but it seems that these early pilgrims, often so steadfastly English in their attitudes, appear on the whole to be a much more interesting bunch than many of today's pilgrims, at least as assessed from comparisons between their respective accounts in the *Bulletin*. It is fun to go back and read of donkeys, penny-farthings, caravans, and ship voyages, intermixed with bird counts, wine lists, raw legends, and hand-drawn, crude maps. Of interest too, is the fact that many of those walking in the early days of the Camino's rebirth began in England or northern France, it only being in the early nineties that St.-Jean-Pied-de-Port began to become established, for reasons that I personally find bizarre and baffling, as the new 'traditional' starting point.

Not all modern accounts are boringly repetitive; some certainly do reveal interesting, occasionally moving stories, skilfully told. One such example, by J. Banett, offers a wise lesson about prejudice and humility. One morning Banett encounters an old local in tattered clothes who insists that they enter a nearby bar for a coffee. When the local orders a beer, Banett feels his worst assumptions being confirmed. He is shocked when minutes later, just as he is about to pick up the bill, the fellow insists upon paying for both of them since giving is simply what one does for pilgrims. Banett is thus jarred into confronting his own feelings of superiority, the dictum about judging a book by its cover, and the true nature of charity. What need did this kind, old "trail angel" have to walk the Camino since he already had well learned its most valuable lesson? "I had failed to see in him that to which I myself aspired. If I could not even recognise my purpose in its real incarnation, how then could I ever obtain it? Approaching Frómista in the mid-morning, I suddenly realised that I still had a long way to go that day." It is the continued publication of such personal stories where the *Bulletin* perhaps shines brightest.

Depth and breadth

An objective of the Confraternity of Saint James is "to undertake and promote research into the history of the pilgrimage in Britain and to foster further studies of related history, art, architecture, and music." At times, this had led the *Bulletin* to resemble a scholarly journal in its purveyance of historical information germane to pilgrimage studies. Over the years, articles have broached an incredible potpourri of subjects, including St. Roch as a patron saint of pilgrimage, the protective orders of knights and monks, a depiction of St. Edmund in Burgos cathedral, details about the discovery of the remains of the 'Worcester pilgrim,' the presence of Vikings at Compostela in the tenth century, musical instruments portrayed in the Pórtico de la Gloria, the itinerary of the fifteen-century pilgrim William Wey, the power of saintly relics, medieval sea routes for English pilgrims, the role of Cluniac monasteries in fostering the cult of Saint James, symbolism of the scallop shells, medieval kingship on the Iberian peninsula, early pilgrim food and medicine, history of hospitality along the Camino, and an intriguing and ongoing series about the discovery, author search, and eventual publication of a long-forgotten thesis from the early 1960s about medieval English pilgrims.

One particularly fascinating and iconoclastic article by P. Henderson focused on the early history of Santiago de Compostela. Herein we learn that "the name Compostela is derived from the Latin *compositum*, meaning burial ground, and not from the more picturesque *campus stellarum* or field of stars, which is the popularly attributed derivation." Being a burial ground it is no surprise that many Roman graves were scattered around the early town site, including underneath where the central nave of the cathedral would be built. What is most interesting is that several of the fifth to seventh-century skeletons were interred with scallop shells, demonstrating their regard as talisman in early Christian times long before Saint James became associated with the site [In England, as I recently found out, one can view a scallop-decorated Roman coffin at the Lullingstone villa, incidentally, one the oldest Christian churches in the world]. And as for that saint's affiliation with Spain, Henderson states that it is tenuous at best and possibly based on nothing more than a scribal mistranslation of the word *Hierosolyma* for Jerusalem, where James was martyred, to *Hispania* for Spain. And further, as others have suggested, a case can be made that the tomb found in the ninth century by Bishop Teodomiro at what was clearly a sacred and visited site in earlier times, is much more likely to be that of Priscillian, bishop of Lusitania, whose body was carried to Galicia for burial – sound familiar?! – than that of the disciple Jacob. It is hard not to smile then with the realisation that for over two millennia, millions of pilgrims have been dutifully slogging their way, not to the tomb of the first martyred Christian Apostle but rather to the tomb of the first executed Christian heretic!

From its inception, the *Bulletin* has also encouraged discussion about other pilgrimage monuments and destinations. Thus, articles exist on the hundreds of Saint James statues, paintings, and churches scattered across the United Kingdom, including the relic of the hand of the Apostle himself which was reputed to have been at Reading Abbey, theories on the various routes English pilgrims might have taken to reach the Channel ports for debarking to Compostela, including establishing a new pilgrim way from Reading to Southampton, sites related to Saint James in the New World, and other pilgrimage routes such as that from Winchester to Canterbury, the ancient route to Finisterre, or those to the many shrines in England and France.

PRACTICALITIES AND RECIPROCITY

THE *BULLETIN* HAS ALWAYS PLAYED an invaluable role in providing a forum for veteran pilgrims to share helpful advice to neophytes planning their own journeys. In consequence, many pages are devoted to offering insights about locations along the Way (e.g. waymarking difficulties, good or bad accommodation, coping in Spanish hospitals), combined with hints on preparation (e.g. training regimes, the best type of gear), and suggestions on undertaking the pilgrimage (e.g. useful guidebooks, foot care, reasonable daily distances, hints on lightening the load, protecting valuables from thieves). Another role of the *Bulletin* is in notifying members about the Confraternity's upcoming lectures, its most recently published guidebooks, and its growing slide library that is available to anyone interested in promoting the Camino, in addition to providing information and germane news about other pilgrim organisations. In recent years as the Camino exceeds its summertime carrying capacity the *Bulletin* has promoted alternative pilgrimage routes in Spain and France as well as encouraged walking the Camino Francés at different times of the year. With respect to the latter, even had I not been a weather-hardy Canadian and my birthday not been in late December which was the inspiration behind when I opted to walk to Compostela, I, as a contemplative person, would have been swayed by the following advice from experienced pilgrimage guidebook author Alison Raju, as conveyed in the *Bulletin*: "If peace, quiet and silence are what you want, if time to observe, reflect and think about things or just to look, listen and walk along by yourself is what you need or prefer, then winter, suitably prepared for, could be a very good time to make your pilgrimage."

For many, the most important take-home memory they have of walking the Way is of witnessing and participating in sharing and giving, often in marked contrast to the selfishness (e.g. narrow preoccupation with job and family) and narcissism (e.g. Facebook fixation) that can easily dominate lives back home. No wonder then that there is often a deeply felt yearning to want to "give something back" to the Camino. The Confraternity, through the *Bulletin*, has done an incredible service in fostering and encouraging a growing movement of volunteerism. By showcasing testimonials of those whom have worked as wardens at established *refugios* or as builders helping to restore the Confraternity's own hostels, members can at first vicariously, and then hopefully later if inspired, actually themselves contribute to the Camino as a living, growing evocation of global *communitas*.

Rants and Reviews

Veteran pilgrims are an opinionated lot, filled – at times it seems almost to the point of bursting – with criticisms about what is wrong and who is to blame for the many imagined errors or sins committed on the Camino. Ignoring the old adage that one sure, early sign of approaching madness is to engage in writing letters to newspaper editors, many pilgrims have used the *Bulletin* to vent their deep-felt frustrations. Sometimes self-indulgent, occasionally illuminating, always entertaining, these missives tackle a broad range of topics. Easy targets of rage include deafening snorers, uncontrollable flatulence emitters, late-night loud talkers, early-morning plastic bag rustlers or door slammers, and of course the legion of those considered not to be 'true pilgrims.' In the early 1990s, the explosion of cyclists due to the popularity of mountain bikes led to frequent calls to limit or outright ban such pedalling 'pilgrims' from taking up spaces in *refugios* that should go to "tired, cold and wet walkers" who by consequence are deemed more worthy. In another example, P. Wren touches upon another bugbear common to many whom are taken aback by the lack of special attention given to walking pilgrims in the cathedral of Santiago in Compostela: "It was as if all these non-walkers were intruding into both the space and territory of the true pilgrims. This holy and sacred place…was being invaded by those who had not earned the right to be there. With the Mass finished I went and sat on the front row of the Cathedral and seethed with inner anger. How dare these tourists play at being pilgrims?" Somewhat ashamed of being so judgmental, Wren goes on to temper his rant and realise that his problem is due to his own prejudice and that "there are many different ways of authentically being a pilgrim as there are many different ways of authentically being a Christian."

Other Confraternity members have been drawn to criticise the physical changes that have occurred to the Camino over the years. The glut of waymarking and gentrification of *refugios*, leading it is presumed, though never explicitly stated, to the ease with which it is now possible to undertake the journey to Compostela, which has led many to question at what point does (or did) the Camino become a tourist route, thereby destroying the experience of pilgrimage? In other words, when did the sacred Way become a secular walk? Implicit here, of course, is the idea that true pilgrims must suffer a bit otherwise the enterprise is invalid, or at the very least, substandard. Another easy target of scorn was the "destruction" in the early 1990s of the hillside of Monte de Gozo by the Spanish government through their construction of a thirty-thousand-seat auditorium for the Pope, ugly buildings to accommodate three thousand 'pilgrims,' a campsite for another five thousand more, four-lane access to the highway and parking for two thousand cars (cars on the Camino?!), and the accompanying restaurants and supermarkets. The fact that all this development occurred at a UNESCO World Heritage site and the premier European Cultural Itinerary was particularly galling. "It is sad," wrote one protesting member, "to think that future generations of pilgrims will not experience that lifting of the heart on a green hill near Santiago as their destination – so long awaited – finally comes into view."

Book reviews in the *Bulletin* did not begin auspiciously. In 1984, the reviewer of *Holy Days and Holidays: The Medieval Pilgrimage to Compostela* displayed those Old World traits of British snobbery that many, Americans in particular, find so annoying. The reviewer questioned the legitimacy of the co-authors' capabilities for no better reason than that they were from North America and thus could never possibly understand or identify with the emotional intensity and significance of pilgrimage as could Europeans. Bosh! Subsequent reviews, although less biased in nature, are rarely of the professional quality found in scholarly journals. But that was never the intent. Instead, reviews have been from lay-readers commenting on their personal enjoyment of particular books, most frequently pilgrim travelogues, presented for the most part free of opinions concerning the relative merit of those works to the wider corpus of literature on the Camino. Many reviews, in consequence, although interesting in their bold honesty, are often lacking in any real critical appraisal, the multitudinous poor quality offerings garnering the same generous words of praise as the few gems that truly do merit accolade.

That said, some reviews have been insightful in that they allow critics to springboard into areas of commentary about pilgrimage in general and the Camino in particular, occasionally accomplished with considerable skill of penmanship. In one such example, M. Shearer begins her critique of Edward Stanton's *Road of Stars to Santiago* (in my mind, one of the best journalised accounts) by stating that although she likes reading such books she is apprehensive about whether they offer anything new, bemoaning "hearing, yet again, about Charlemagne and Roncesvalles, or the chickens in Santa Domingo, or the dates of construction of Burgos Cathedral, [that] have long since failed to interest." "Never mind the facts. Tell me the feeling," she charges before praising Stanton's innocent enthusiasm, self-examination, and sensitivity before taking issue with his aversion to hardship. Part of the function of the Camino, Shearer believes, is to embrace that hardship so as to "arrest us out of the security of home and its binding web of relations and expectations, and allow the discovery of a wider self and the achievement of simplicity."

There is often a traditional religious slant to the criticism. One book annoys its reviewer by being too flippant, clever, and mocking in tone. Other books are criticised because the authors went out of their way to avoid entering any churches along the Way and thus were not 'true pilgrims.' Another book is dismissed due to the basic belief and flowery prose used by the author to describe his New Age belief in ley-lines that he imagines underlie the Camino. Reciprocally, another reviewer comments favourably on a book based on its author's upfront declaration that her work contains no references to ley-lines or mythical companions of the psyche.

Interestingly, the two biggest selling books about the Camino generate different opinions from their respective reviewers. In her review of *The Camino*, veteran guidebook author A. Raju thinks it disingenuous of Shirley MacLaine to complain about being harassed by the press after she had broadly announced her plans to friends and associates, and is also critical about the lack of content for MacLaine's strange, visionary experiences. In contrast, J. Rix concludes an uncritical and simplistic three-page review of Paulo Coelho's *The Pilgrimage* with a recommendation of it being ideal bedside reading as the chapters are short and exercises only a few sentences long. "Then settle down," she states, "shut your eyes, and as you drift off to sleep, continue reading between the lines." As the reader will find elsewhere in these present pages (Chapter 9), I am of the opinion that the only thing of merit to be found between Coelho's lines is the gift of empty, word-free space.

It is heartening to note that in later years, reviewers in the *Bulletin* seem to have become more discriminating. R. Billingham is correct in stating that due to the plethora of books now available, "any new account of personal pilgrimage to Santiago needs special qualities in order to command our attention." Two reviews of unusual works make this point. S. Willson champions Althea Wilson's deeply reflective audio-book *Walk With Me* (discussed in Chapter 9) for its spontaneity and quiet reflection that carries the listener forward: "Hayton's calm voice brings the camino to life; reassures us, encourages and challenges us to imagine, to dream, to confront painful issues and to grow during our own inner journeys." And S. Nilsen is enthusiastic in her praise of the intriguing conceit behind Julie Kirkpatrick's *The Camino Letters: 26 Tasks on the Way to Finisterre* (discussed in Part I) in terms of it being a beautifully written, heartfelt, and honest book that uses the Camino as a landscape to construct letters that explore the author's relationships, life-choice directions, and memories.

On Zeitgeist...

CHAPTER 12

SHELL SHOCKED AND STAR STRUCK

"The Santiago pilgrimage has been decreed dead or dying by numerous observers over the past several hundred years, but the Spanish cultus has been revived repeatedly through the centuries."

– Nolan, M. and S., *Christian Pilgrimage in Modern Western Europe*

Slouching towards Santiago

THE MODERN RESURGENCE AND GROWTH in popularity of the Santiago pilgrimage has been remarkable. In 1970, when I first learned of the pilgrimage from my National Geographic Society *School Bulletin* (described in Part I's Pre-script), there were fewer than 500 *compostelas* issued by the Pilgrim Office of the Santiago cathedral. It was not until the mid-eighties that numbers had climbed to 2,000 annual pilgrims. By the early-nineties, annual numbers were still below 10,000 with the exception of the Holy Year of 1993 when nearly 100,000 walked the last hundred kilometres to Compostela to be officially registered. Numbers grew throughout the decade reaching 30,000 in 1998 and peaking at about 150,000 in the Holy Year of 1999, the year in which I had first thought of undertaking the pilgrimage as my own millennium project. The first half-decade of this century saw a continuing rise in numbers of annual pilgrims from 50,000 to 80,000, with another peak to over 175,000 for the Holy Year of 2004. In 2005, the year I walked my first steps from the cathedral in Le Puy, 90,000 pilgrims arrived at the Pilgrim Office in Compostela to receive their certificates. By 2009, the numbers had swelled to nearly 150,000 annual arrivals. The 2010 Holy Year saw more than a quarter million pilgrims walk at least the last hundred kilometres to the Apostle's shrine, with numbers settling down to a still staggering 187,000 for 2011.

Statistics reveal that in recent years more than half the arriving pilgrims do so during the summer holiday months of July and August. Adding the abutting months of June and September brings the proportion to seventy-five percent. Less than three percent undertake the pilgrimage during the winter months of December to February.

It is interesting to see how one fits into this grand flow of humanity. More than 110,000 pilgrims arrived at Compostela in 2007. When I walked the Camino during December of that year, 796 pilgrims were received at the Pilgrim Office. Like me, 70% of these were men, 94% arrived on foot, 66% were between the ages of thirty and sixty, 61% stated their motivations as being a combination of "religious and cultural", 4% were from Canada (i.e. another 31 beside myself), 7% stated their profession as being "professors", and 76% walked the Camino Francés, with 8–10% starting out between Pamplona and Estella.

The grandfather of the English language societies focused on the pilgrimage to Compostela is the British Confraternity of Saint James, which, despite its oddly antiquated and vaguely sinister, Dan Brown-esque sounding appellation, is an extremely friendly and most helpful organisation for past, present, and future Camino pilgrims from around the world, and who now total more than two thousand members. Like all such societies, its purpose is to advance, promote, and educate about the Camino, something it does by funding scholarly research and providing useful information on its website and through its own guidebooks about the history and practicalities of the Jacobean pilgrimage. Through publication of its bimonthly *Bulletin* (see Chapter 11), the Confraternity endeavours to bring together its community of members and keep them informed about current and future events. In addition to historical, practical, and newsworthy information, the website contains order forms to obtain a *credential*, notes on the Confraternity's two managed *refugios*, information about alternative routes to Compostela, an online shop for purchasing books, badges, postcards, posters, calendars, t-shirts, and mugs, a photo gallery, links to other, similar organisations around the world, and a very engaging members' discussion forum on a broad range of topics.

Other, less established organisations follow a similar mandate. The Australian Friends of the Camino website lists local meetings and contains simple descriptions of various routes with links to other sites. The website of Irish Society of the Friends of St. James (founded in 1992) contains information on the historical background and practical tips in addition to news and events, a photo gallery, and a handful of pilgrimage accounts from members, as well as links to other sites. The Confraternity of St. James of South Africa was founded by eighty-five members in 2006 and grew four-fold by 2010. As well as containing the usual features as the Irish and Australian societies do, the South African website also contains frequently asked questions, a library from which members can borrow books, a future planned online shop, an order form to obtain a *credential,* and an attractive online publication, *Amigos*, that is published three times a year. The Canadian Company of Pilgrims, which grew out of an earlier organisation that had been established in 1994, now boasts over five hundred members and has issued more than two thousand *credentials*. In addition to the aforementioned features shared by the other societies, the Canadian organisation's website contains articles about *hospitalero* training, the traditional pilgrim blessing, notes on various *refugios*, Camino statistics, recipes, music, memorials, information about the various local chapters, and poetry, songs, and blogs from its members. The website of the American Pilgrims on the Camino contains all this and more and is the most modern and useful of all the non-British sites. Essays are unpretentious and on interesting and unusual topics (e.g. "Ode to a Bedbug"); the online newsletter *La Concha* is among the best; the listing of books and music albums is very comprehensive; and the resource links are useful (e.g. to Spanish weather and transportation, Camino 'apps,' and various webcam sites).

In medieval times, first-time pilgrims set out from their villages across northern Europe in complete ignorance of what they would encounter, unless they had had the opportunity to grill a neighbour who might have been to the shrine in Compostela. All they would know is that they had to trend toward the south and then veer off, following the sun westward. For safety reasons, it would be advised that they make their way to the cities of Tours, Vezélay, Le Puy or Arles, where they could meet up with other pilgrims, some of whom would be veterans returning home and able share knowledge about the route they would face ahead. Remember that most of these villagers would have never strayed beyond the borders of their townships unless they had visited markets in the surrounding region. For them, undertaking the pilgrimage to Compostela was very much a great leap of faith into the unknown.

In contrast, today's wannabe pilgrims can access a plethora of material from internet sources. A major difference between pilgrims of today and those of yesteryear it is that preparedness has replaced adventure, assuredness has replaced uncertainty, and information has replaced speculation. Dozens of websites exist from which it is possible to obtain detailed maps or satellite photos of the entire route, real-time webcams from key Camino locations, link up with other pilgrims without having to travel to the aforementioned French rendezvous cities, join various fora to obtain advice from veterans, purchase Camino memorabilia, engage in computer-game-like virtual fly-throughs of ecclesiastical buildings, book accommodation in hotels for those averse to roughing it in *refugios*, view *sellos* (pilgrim stamps) available on the Camino to determine which ones you might want to collect, follow the daily blogs of pilgrims as they slouch forward, and acquire a suite of Camino apps for smart phones and tablet computers that some will carry along the Way. Soon it may be possible to undertake the complete pilgrimage digitally, step-by-step from the comfort of your office chair as in Google street-view. And lest one become too self-righteous and critical of these modern or future techno-geeks, reflect on how little different this really is from some of our medieval forefathers who would perambulate about symbolic labyrinths in their local cathedrals as vicarious pilgrimages or, if wealthy, hire surrogates to undertake the journey in their stead. The following four websites represent some of the most interesting ones about pilgrimage in general and the Camino in particular.

From the largely commercial website *Mundicamino* one can sign up for *hospitalero* training workshops, rent bicycles, arrange to have your luggage ferried each day, as well as purchase guide books, hiking gear, and all kinds of souvenir merchandise such as, but by no means limited to, pens, pins, pendants, key rings, fridge magnets, crosses, rosaries, pottery, replica stained glass windows, jewellery, spoons, calendars, and crystal pyramids carved with scallop shells no less! Other sites are much more scholarly.

The website *The Journey of Heaven and Earth* is an obvious labour of love (or obsession) containing a remarkable amount of information about the history of the Santiago pilgrimage with a particular focus on the Romanesque art and architecture along the routes through France and Spain. The amount of clearly laid out and easily accessible information is truly humbling. Scholarly articles cover topics such as the cult of saints, eschatology, medieval faith, iconography of scallop shells, influence of the Cluny Abbey, legends of the Camino, the *Codex*, Charlemagne, *Matamoros* symbolism, monasticism, the *Reconquesta*, *chansons de geste*, and many specific locations along the routes through France and Spain. Accompanying the always informative and succinct text are many photographs and several videos. This is the best privately run, historically based website.

The Christianity and Culture research group at York University in England have produced a marvellously comprehensive educational website about pilgrimage writ large: the history, the motivations, and the destinations. Readers can obtain information about the varied meanings, old and new, of pilgrimage as a universal practice, a New Age faddism, and as a secular holiday. Covering the social anthropology of pilgrimage from the early Christian tradition to today, one learns about moral, place-based, and interior inspirations for the practice. From this, it is interesting to situate one's own feelings in a conceptual venn diagram of personal motivation.

Peregrinations is the official publication of the International Society for the Study of Pilgrimage Art. It is published as an open-access journal and contains peer-reviewed articles on a vast range of subjects about architectural theory and practice, sculpture of the pilgrimage routes, and medieval art history. An exhaustive photo database of thousands of pilgrimage sites is available to be shared by scholars for teaching purposes. Other features include notices on upcoming conferences and exhibitions, links to other online journals and organisations, and recent newsworthy archaeological discoveries. Viewers know they have found a Camino-friendly website from the first glimpse of the twinned scallop shells on either side of sectional title mastheads. Further digging through online back issues reveals articles about the Emperor Charles V as Santiago *Matamoros*, wayfaring music inspired by the Jacobean pilgrimage, use of fossilised scallop shells in the Middle Ages, sculpted capitals in religious buildings on the Camino, and photo-essays on Puente la Reina and the Pórtico de la Gloria, for example.

Anthropology, Ethnography, and Geography

Ellen Feinberg's doctoral thesis, *Strangers and Pilgrims on the Camino de Santiago in Spain: The Perpetuation and Recreation of Meaningful Performance*, is an important milestone in modern pilgrimage studies. In Chapter 2, Feinberg grapples with the hoary and problematic questions about what actually constitutes a pilgrimage and who can justifiably call themselves a pilgrim. Can excursionists be pilgrims? Is a spiritual attitude enough or does a pilgrim require religious fervour? Are true pilgrims only those who walk? Through many interviews with locals, she concludes that there is a blurring between pilgrims and tourists and that motives may trump methods; in other words, undertaking a pilgrimage by car but with the right spirit is a more genuine experience than a superficial hike.

In Chapter 4, Feinberg provides an intriguing snapshot of the Compostela pilgrimage at the start of its modern revival. It is interesting to learn, for example, that the official Compostela document was reinstated in 1965 on the condition that the individual had walked the last three hundred kilometres of the Camino, a distance it is worth noting which is three times longer than that required to receive the certificate today. The majority of pilgrims thirty years ago were students and teachers, with only three percent being retirees. It is unsettling to learn that General Franco took an active role in promoting the pilgrimage and had a personal devotion to San Iago to whom he would often pray to help quash his rebel foes. In this, he was of course simply following the long-established tradition of close relationships between the Spanish State, Church, Military, and Santiago, however distasteful this may be for many international pilgrims. Feinberg is struck by the egregious ignorance of most of the pilgrims she interviews concerning the historic rituals along the Way – remember that this was a time before guidebooks, *refugios*, confraternities, etc. – and the fact that unlike their medieval precursors, most are too pressed for time to take any detours.

Also, Feinberg is saddened by the lack of interest shown in the pre-Christian initiation path, stating that "the monks of Cluny succeeded in detouring the ancient route of the stars, transforming the Camino into an itinerary of idiots and tourists." The present Camino de Santiago is but "a misleading copy" of "the true route" as shown in the ancient board game, *Juego de la Oca,* in which the true Camino is displayed as sixty-three numbered squares arranged as a spiral, marked with inns, bridges, and dangers, leading the pilgrim into the centre, with thirteen goose markers on the board that represent the thirteen stages of the original Camino.

Criticism continues in Chapter 5 with Feinberg bemoaning the spiritual ambivalence of pilgrims she encounters, many of whom do not enter a single church based on the nonsensical pretence that that is what tourists do. The idea of "walking in the footsteps" of previous pilgrims is a myth, she informs, since the reality is that the modern waymarked route rarely coincides with the historical one. Also, Feinberg exposes the fallacy of Roncesvalles or St.-Jean-Pied-de-Port being the traditional starting point, something that has obviously not been a concern to the tens of thousands of pilgrims who have since commenced their walks at these locations for no better reason than that other people have previously done the same. Feinberg concludes on a positive note, identifying the core of pilgrimage being personal revitalisation, pilgrims having "participated in a movement in which the past becomes idealised and history becomes mythologised; in which individuals can – through their own creative actions, by constructing and enacting their own traditions – build a meaningful spiritual realm in an increasingly secularised, rationalised, disenchanted world."

In Chapter 6, Feinberg considers how individuals shape and are shaped by their participation in the ritual process of pilgrimage as a rite of passage moving from separation, through the liminal transition of the act itself, to the reintegration once back at home. Interestingly, she contests the frequently voiced belief that it is the desire for *communitas* or shared bonding that is the primary motivation of pilgrims, instead positing that pilgrimage is always a personal experience, having more in common with a vision quest than a unifying community ritual.

Adapted from her doctoral thesis, *Pilgrim Stories: On and Off the Road to Santiago*, by Nancy Frey, has become one of the most popular scholarly texts about the Camino experience. By conducting hundreds of field interviews of pilgrims as they made their way to Compostela, Frey, through astute questioning, is able to capture a realistic glimpse of the underpinnings of modern pilgrimage in an age of increasing secularisation. She believes that by undertaking such a task, pilgrims are subversively making a conscious statement about their society and its accepted values, including an appreciation of nature and physical effort, a rejection (even if only temporarily) of materialism, an interest in nostalgia and history, a search for inner meanings, an examination of personal spirituality, and a desire for paradoxically both more meaningful relationships as well as more solitude.

Frey's book is structured around the various stages one progresses through while on pilgrimage. In the chapter "Journey Shaping" she succinctly summarises the diversity of aspirations, ranging from the impulsive to the realisation of a long-held desire, from the fulfilment of a promise, to the hope for change and a fresh beginning. In the chapter "Learning New" Frey explores the metaphysical realignment that often transpires on a pilgrimage, wherein time expands while distance contracts. The Camino, many of those interviewed state, is a reminder of the transience of life, an act where one feels connected to a living history and a union with the surroundings as a sort of outdoor liturgy.

In the chapter "Landscapes of Discovery" Frey summarises many elements common to the stories pilgrims tell of their experiences: the commonplace doubts, despair, fatigue and pain suffered along the Way, the cult of authenticity that engenders an antisocial dismissal of those on bicycles as "decaffeinated" or watered-down pilgrims, feelings of fraud or of "cheating" if one does not walk every single metre of the Camino, the unfamiliar and strangely off-putting nature of Spanish Catholicism, and the irony that today's glut of waymarking limits the opportunity to get lost and thereby be a means in which to find oneself. A wonderful and heartbreaking story is retold of a dog in bad shape who befriended a group of pilgrims near the start of the Camino and stayed with them until, upon reaching Santiago, when after visiting the cathedral, the group retired to a nearby park at which time the dog, sensing that the journey was over, laid down beside them and died. Learning of Camino stories such as this, is it really any wonder that many pilgrims have bestowed the route with such exalted, near deification, status?

In other chapters, Frey reviews the mixed feelings of elation, ambivalence, superiority, disillusionment, and pride that characterise those finding themselves standing rooted in place in front of the cathedral in Compostela, the forward imperative which has dictated their lives for so many weeks or months, suddenly being abandoned. The anxiety is palatable, pilgrim to tourist in a heartbeat, self-doubt bubbling up as to whether the experience has really changed one for the better as all know it is supposed to if one believes the epiphanies offered up in any number of Camino narratives. And for the emotionally unsettled and those with more time, there is always the lure of continuing on to Finisterre. For those partaking, this is a real geographic endpoint where one might be able to achieve that peace of mind that seems so lacking when standing in the square in front of the cathedral filled as it is with crowds milling about ignorant of the significance of what has transpired within the pilgrim. Finisterre, the location where every act assumes a symbolic significance, such as the story recounted of a pilgrim throwing his walking staff into the sea only to have it wash back to shore several hours later, to lie there beckoning at his feet, the Universe seemingly in collusion in telling this individual that his journey is far from over.

Today, pilgrimage is a one-way journey. The last chapter in Frey's book is significant in that it addresses an issue that has seldom been examined: the challenges pilgrims face upon returning home. Most pilgrimage accounts end in Compostela with the experience treated as a "frozen memory" when the reality is that though that location may be the goal, it is really not the end of the pilgrimage. For some pilgrims, returning home is a positive time characterised by a strengthening of faith or a newly discovered purpose. Other pilgrims, however, become disoriented due to an inability to articulate the experience or through a possible reneging on promises made to change their lives. For some, the solution to such difficulties is to succumb to the pilgrimage bug and to go back time and again to the Camino. Frey cautions, however, that the Camino, like any beneficial drug, can be overdosed on, the danger being when the experience becomes habitual rather than stimulating. One solution that many find rewarding is to return to the Camino, not as a pilgrim but as a *hospitalero*, providing the opportunity to give something back in gratitude.

Place-Making and Meaning-Making in the Pilgrimage to Santiago de Compostela, the recent doctoral thesis by Cecilia Gossen, explores how the Camino resides in the collective mindscapes of participants. Anchoring her work in a rich tradition of social and conceptual geography, Gossen reminds us that places are human constructs built of embodied experiences. They are locations made socially meaningful by the palimpsest layering of history and accumulated attachment to a piece of the world. For Gossen, the Jacobean pilgrimage route can be just such a place through fostering physical, social, and religious engagement.

In the simplest form, referring to the pilgrimage route as "the Camino" and naming towns as being of or "del Camino" helps to create the journey as a tangible place. It is the interactions with art, architecture, historical events, memories, place names, and institutions, in addition to landscapes, that imbue the Camino with being a unique and cherished *place* rather than merely a long walk through a non-special space. These elements of the materiality of the pilgrimage create, Gossen proposes, a "Camino Identity" which leads to the development of a strong bond among participants. This affirmation of belonging, in turn, does much to reinforce the sense of place of the Camino.

The Camino Identity then is a territorial ideology that links people to place. Being the object of repeated activity and encounters through time, the Camino is a place of thick meaning. Such places are of course recognised as being culturally significant. They are public spaces. Elsewhere Gossen has referred the Camino as Europe's "Main Street" or "High Street." And likewise, I have myself referred to pilgrimage routes as being "memory roads."

Gossen ends her thesis by considering what the role of pilgrimage might be in today's world. One of humankind's most basic desires is the need to belong. For some anthropologists, this has historically been a role played by organised religion wherein adherents belong to a community that offers a shared way to deal with pain and loss related to the idiosyncrasies and vulnerability of life itself. It is no accident that in an age when participation in organised religion is in marked decline, the Camino pilgrimage has reciprocally grown in popularity. As a result, the most important reason, Gossen believes, for the resurgence in the Camino pilgrimage today, is in constructing a world of meaning in which pilgrims feel a common purpose by being part of a community in which they as individuals are recognised, accepted, and valued. The Camino Identity therefore fills a niche left vacant by the decline in church attendance; in other words, it addresses one of modern society's most keenly felt losses, that of the loss of community.

It comes as no surprise then that Gossen's review of hundreds of pilgrim diaries in the Confraternity of Saint James' library revealed that for the majority it was the Camino itself that was the main element of the pilgrimage experience and not arrival at the cathedral in Compostela. Extending these findings leads one to wonder if the more accurate titular name for today's pilgrimage should really be "the Camino pilgrimage" rather than "the pilgrimage to Santiago de Compostela" given that the Way-as-*place* is more significant in the minds of many compared to either those mere spaces of the destination city or its cathedral.

BUILDING A CAMINO REFERENCE LIBRARY

OVER A PERIOD OF THREE YEARS during and after the First World War, Georgiana Goddard King, professor of art history at Bryn Mawr College, travelled the Camino by motorcar, donkey cart, horse buggy, and omnibus, punctuated here and there by little bits of walking. Although ostensibly designed to show the relationship and depth of Spain's debt to the medieval architecture of the rest of Europe and to document the historical roots of the cult of Saint James, King's three-volume, fourteen-hundred-page magnum opus is most interesting to lay readers for its wonderful descriptions of conditions along the Way at a time when the Camino had been largely forgotten. And though her writing style is somewhat affected and dated, her words can still resonate for today's Camino pilgrims:

> Mystics can tell how journeys to such shrines are made: *The way is opened before you, and closed behind you.* Simple, that: believe it nor not, it happens. So with Compostela: to those grey granite hills, ringed round with higher, the blind longings are drawn, the restless feet are guided. It is not a place to live, *triste*, grey, quite dead; nor even a place to love, not beautiful, not sympathetic; but when you are away, it draws you. In the spring, when frost is out of the ground, and ships are sailing, week by week, you cannot get it out of your head: as you smell the brown fresh-turned clods, it works in your blood.

King was the first American scholar to recount the Santiago pilgrimage in travelogue form. And she encounters a Spain in the early decades of the twentieth century that was unspoiled (both physically and politically) and was, in her eyes, unquestionably romantic (no doubt, if one may be critical, perhaps a touch overly so):

> Here tawny Spain, lost to the world's debate, rejoicing in the abundance of corn and vine, salutes the coy dawn with the tinkling bells of mule-trains, and wakes the early moonlight with pipe and guitar. Translucent grapes, flushed peaches, freckled pears, with white and powdery bread, strong and limpid wine that glitters like jewels in the reddened glass, — these transmute into something venerable and sacramental the ancient sun-burnt mirth. On every hand the land is green…The cool well-water is abundant, wholesome, and delicious. The town plants poplars and sycamores in multiplied rows along the roadside, till *camino* becomes *paseo*, turning the dusty track into a place of solace and refreshment. Women are handsome here, babies clean, men devout. Only of late a narrow line of railway has pushed down from Haro, and the spell of the sleepy centuries is not yet rent. It is strange in a world of trippers and tourists to find a happy land so abounding in its own kindly life, and a church so richly undespoiled, still intact of dealers and restorers.

Putting aside the obvious point that if given half a chance, many of the villagers might have quickly traded places with King to set up new lives in the imagined promised land of America, there is no denying that the march of time has erased much of the sense of place that had once characterised the Camino. But not completely, however. Today, one can still encounter scenes, seemingly anachronistic, just like the following:

> Every town has these little churches, that stay open after dark for a few veiled, whispering women. They have a special feeling, like the scent of dried leaves, like the taste of night air, like the hushed Friday evening of the return from Calvary in Ribalta's painting. To Spanish women they are very comfortable. The subdued glow of light, the warm smell, the rustling human figures, offer something of the attraction of hearth, without the *ennui* of home. The great point is that in church one is never bored; that prayers lull, like the nursery rocking-chair, while a solemn little child, not more than seven years old, goes lighting the candles and ringing the bell with anxious care, pounding in his soft shoes from one end of the church to the other. It will be hard to break women of the habit, at winter nightfall, while men are in the cafes, of going to church.

And in this, of course, King was prescient.

In addition to admiring the Gallegan rural way of life, King expresses her enchantment at Villafranca but openly dislikes both Ponferrada and Sarria and is harshly critical of the way the Spanish treat their animals. She is no fan of the liturgy and the way mass is conducted, imagining the Santiago cathedral in years past to have been like the fun-park of Coney Island. The idiosyncratic amalgam of history and opinions in the book continues to a fascinating, though odd, conclusion wherein Saint James, in a flurry of syncretism, is likened to various Asian gods. King also offers up the intriguing medieval belief that the Milky Way is composed of illuminated souls on their pilgrimage to visit the lonely Saint in his grave and the much older pagan belief that following the stars was a journey across the Bridge of Death toward a Western Paradise of souls. Clearly there is much more to the Camino than it simply being a political ploy created by Cluny for financial gain or by the Spanish as part of their *Reconquesta* efforts.

Folklorist and writer Walter Starkie set out in the Holy Year of 1954 to travel by bus, hitched rides, and walking from southern France to Compostela, repeating the route he had previously travelled decades earlier, recording the journey in the classic *The Road to Santiago*. Following a lengthy introduction to the Jacobean cult and pilgrimage (which would have been quite new to readers in the middle of the twentieth century), Starkie details a linear recounting of his wanderings toward Compostela. His encounters with locals and eccentrics are engaging and wonderfully characteristic of a time when pilgrims were almost non-existent and Spain was in the midst of General Franco's dictatorship. Once, Starkie finds himself travelling with a troupe of players as if in a time-warp to the Middle Ages, but the reverie is broken when they begin complaining about the newfangled cinemas that are ruining their business. On another occasion he meets a sad, elderly man dressed in shabby apparel who is without money and sleeps outside while continually walking barefoot on expiatory pilgrimages throughout Europe for his sins which he somehow imagines to have contributed to the destruction of his entire family in the war. Upon arriving at Compostela Starkie joins several pilgrims whom he had previously met and all play an impromptu concert of pieces from the *Codex Callxtinus* in front of the Pórtico de la Gloria. Later he dodges past government officials and works his way into the cathedral to hear Franco go on about Spain's crusading spirit on behalf of the Church during the Empire as well as the recent Civil War. Outside, he has a discussion with a local priest who does not want to hear about Henry VIII's walk to Walsingham but who would rather discuss "the most beautiful English record of a soul's pilgrimage", the *Vision of Thurkill* and its relationship to Compostela. Starkie finishes with a flourish, comparing the nobility of the old, decrepit pilgrim whom he meets again at the cathedral with the "pilgrimages without tears" of the pampered, superficial tourists whom in his mind are the complete antithesis to the original idea of religious wayfaring. His concluding words are some of the most beautiful to be written in the shadow of the Pórtico de la Gloria:

> Nevertheless, even today, there are still in every country a number of lonely pilgrims who forsake the rapid-moving superficial pilgrimages and make the long journey guided by the myriads of wandering souls in the star-dust of the Milky Way – that galaxy which, as Dante tells us, the common people call 'the Way of St. James.' When, however, those lonely waifs and strays turn their faces homeward after praying at the tomb in Compostella and reaching the misty lands of the Dark Star where the ebbing and flowing tide murmurs at the foot of the World's End, their mental plight resembles that of the monk in ancient times who lingered in the wood listening entranced to the divine song of the bird in the tree. When the bird

ceased, he heard the monastery bell calling him to prayer, but all the world had changed and none of the monks recognized him, for the bird's entrancing song had lasted a hundred years.

In the early 1970s, journalist and writer Edwin Mullins set out to Compostela by car and on foot on what he referred to as a journey through history, peopled by ghosts, to heaven, with art and architecture as signposts along the Way. The resulting book, *The Pilgrimage to Santiago*, has seldom been equalled in the four decades since, in terms of its seamless blending of historical lessons with personal travelogue. From the start, Mullins announces his interests: "How amazing and ironical it is that this legend, so improbable, so flawed, so disputable, should have trodden a path through the history of western Europe that is flagged by some of the brightest achievements of our civilisation. The road to Santiago is a monument to the creative strength of crude blind faith." But not only that, for as Mullins shows, the pilgrimage was essentially a propaganda creation of the great abbey at Cluny, invented to capitalise on gullible pilgrims steeped in reverence, in wonder, and in hope. Such unvarnished interpretations of history do not interfere with his writing of some of the most heartfelt appreciations of the architecture of the Santiago pilgrimage routes, as for example, on the famous doorway carving of the prophet Jeremiah at Moissac – "Is there anything in European sculpture which combines such refined elegance with such pure feeling, or which more cogently expresses the passionate nature of the medieval religious experience;" on the Last Judgment in the tympanum at Conques – "the most powerful feeling of the pilgrimage itself" apart from Compostela; on the carvings of Christ as a pilgrim on the road to Emmaus in the monastery of Santo Domingo de Silos – "among the most radiantly beautiful places on Earth…there are few artistic achievements of mankind that have moved me so deeply;" and on Santiago de Compostela itself – that "rain-washed city of granite and dreams."

In 1998, soon after I had moved to Cambridge, Massachusetts to begin a new professorship, I discovered the Globe Corner Travel Bookstore, one of those now sadly, increasingly rare places that cater to bibliophiles. In those halcyon days when one could actually browse, physically rather than electronically, through arrays of books, the opportunity always existed for serendipitous purchases. And so it was with this visit when, while taking a break from shopping for New England travel guides, I wandered a few aisles over to the section on Spain and my eye caught the front-facing cover of William Melczer's *The Pilgrim's Guide to Santiago de Compostela*. In an epiphany, suddenly remembering my childhood interest in the pilgrimage (see Part I, Pre-script), I immediately made the decision to walk the Camino as my millennium project in several years time. Scooping up Melczer's book in addition to the travel narratives of Lee Hoinacki (see Part I) and Edward Stanton (*The Road of Stars to Santiago* – another extremely good early account), I hurried home to begin my planning, little knowing that the books acquired that day would remain some of my favourite in my soon-to-be-expanding pilgrimage library.

Melczer was one of the leading scholars of the Santiago pilgrimage and his book contains the first English translation of Book Five of the *Liber Sancti Jacobi*, otherwise known as the *Codex Calixtinus*. Where Melczer's book is remarkable is that the 48-page medieval pilgrimage guide is bracketed by his 81-page introduction and a 94-page section of more than six hundred scholarly notes, followed in turn by a 42-page hagiographical register and a 27-page gazetteer. There remains no better introduction to the history of the Santiago pilgrimage than this, Melczer's commentary on the world's first travel guide. I will highlight only a single section from this comprehensive tome. In a section of the Introduction dealing with the motivations for pilgrimage, Melczer stresses how much of a completely life-altering occurrence this must have been for the peasant masses of the early and central Middle Ages who lived their entire lives from cradle to coffin within the limited confines of a single hamlet or village:

> With such a disconsolate prospect the pilgrimage to Santiago de Compostela must have appeared as the one luminous exception, the one great adventure, the one almost-miraculous opening to distant lands, unheard-of customs, the marvels of the world – no matter how perilous the journey would turn out. It is only partly appropriate to associate such a motivation with the modern notion of tourism. It was much more than that. For the majority of the eleventh- and twelfth-century pilgrims to Santiago, those six to nine months spent on the road in strange lands and among strange people meant the only occasion to cast a glimpse upon the broader existence, to measure for once the world and its wonders, to see, once in their lives, the mountains and the sea.

I defy anyone, retaining even the smallest vestigial shred of a spirit of adventure, not to be moved by reading those words of Melczer that describe what has been called by others, the *pelegrino curioso*. He picks up and continues the thread a few paragraphs later:

Most significantly, no matter from where the pilgrims came and what the ultimate declared goal of their pilgrimage was to be, all of them, from saint to sinner, felt the invigorating air of a new world gradually unfolding before their incredulous and astonished eyes in all its unpredictable complexity and savagery, but also in its surprising beauty and magnificence. This was a lesson that none of them would henceforth forget.

Pilgrimage then, from the early get-go, can be characterised just as much as a secular push outward from the familiarity of home as it can a spiritual pull toward the "cloud of unknowing" of Compostela. Importantly too, it was from Melczer that I first learned that the Santiago pilgrimage had as much or more to do with France as it did with Spain. For an historical purist like myself, the decision became an obvious one: I would have to start my own pilgrimage farther 'upstream' in France rather than partway through at the non-historical St.-Jean-Pied-de-Port. And so for the two years before I planned to walk to Compostela to mark my fiftieth birthday, I traversed 1,200-kilometres over sections of the four French 'feeder routes.' And the single book that I consulted more than any other during that time as well as leading up to finally heading out on the Camino Francés, was the collaborative work *The Roads to Santiago de Compostela*. Translated from the original French, this work has the perfect mix, similar to *National Geographic* magazine, of text and colour photographs, maps and images. Sections cover the history of James the Greater from Galilee to Galicia, medieval Spain, background documents of the pilgrimage, major sites along the four French roads feeding into the European Isthmus, evolution of perceptions about the pilgrimage, and finally the Camino Francés. If there is a single Camino-related book that I could not do without while marooned on that archetypal desert isle this would be this one. Today, nearly half a decade after I last set foot on a road leading to or from Compostela, there is not a month that goes by without me taking down this book from the shelf and day dreaming about steps as yet to taken along various unwalked sections of these pilgrimage roads.

Pretty picture books are often lacking learned text of a caliber to match the quality of their photographs. One exception is Kathleen Ashley and Marilyn Deegan's *Being a Pilgrim: Art and Ritual on the Medieval Routes to Santiago*. Whereas other coffee-table books present haunting images of atmospheric landscapes or empathy engendering images of struggling pilgrims, here the emphasis is on close-ups of stained glass windows, religious paintings, and pieces of statuary that are among the most remarkable that have ever been published. The text is scholarly yet accessible to lay readers and is arranged thematically rather than geographically, thus making for an intriguing introduction to the visual legacy of the Jacobean pilgrimage routes. This is the single pilgrimage book that I keep out, upon a coffee-table for visiting guests to browse through.

In 2000, I attended a reading by two authors of their recently published book in a church hall located near my Harvard University office. Recovering from a 'love's labour's lost' episode that had forced me cancel my planned millennium pilgrimage that very summer (see Chapter 7), I sat captivated by David Gitlitz and Linda Kay Davidson's reading from *The Pilgrimage Road to Santiago: The Complete Cultural Handbook*, and vowed (again) to undertake the walk at some future date. During the present writing project, only a single book was permanently removed from my pilgrimage library bookshelf and placed within arm-reach on my home writing desk. For the pilgrimage scholar as well as the intellectual pilgrim, there is no single book that is more invaluable for its comprehensive covering of the art, architecture, history, folklore, and hagiography of the Spanish Camino than this particular tome (one is left wishing for similar detailed and useful books about for the four French 'feeder routes'). Hundreds of times I would dip into this (re)source well of information while writing the present pages. Earlier, because I could not imagine being without the book while walking the Camino, I had carried a reduced-sized and double-sided photocopy of the complete text (four book pages per single sheet of lightweight paper) with me, leaving behind the pages covering sections I had just walked in *refugios* scattered along the Way.

Truth be told, for many Camino pilgrims it is immersion into Spain itself – its customs, its people, its food, its history, its landscape – that is the basis for their interest, Saint James and the Camino functioning as convenient means toward such ends. In any "best travel books ever" compilation there is likely to be only a single work about the Santiago pilgrimage that is so accoladed: *Roads to Santiago: A Modern-Day Pilgrimage Through Spain* by Dutch author and poet Cees Nooteboom. The result of an admitted forty-year affair of the body, soul, and heart, this book is one of the most remarkable love letters that has ever been composed to a place and its people (in my limited reading, only Joseph Brodsky's *Watermark* about Venice comes close to capturing such heartfelt emotion). For Nooteboom, the Spanish character and landscape "correspond to the essence I am, to conscious and unconscious things in my being, to what I am about." And it is the *meseta* where he considers true Spain begins and to which he is most attracted, imagining it to be reflective of how he himself looks on the inside. Spain, Nooteboom believes, has never really been part of Europe. And it is specifically because of that, with its vast expanses being empty of people as nowhere else on the continent, thereby resulting in the preservation of a different passage of time, that makes the place so special, so precious. Spain, in sharp contrast to his birth country of Holland, is "the last refuge from the fullness of Europe."

Nooteboom begins by bemoaning the fact that journeys today no longer take years to complete, and that those undertaking modern trips always know exactly where they are going. Not for him. His pilgrimage to the Apostle's shrine is one giant circumlocution about the entire country by automobile over a period of twenty-years in which he becomes diverted from the detours he takes on his detours from the linear Camino: "My goal was Santiago, but the roads frayed like a rope, the years piled up, I drifted off course and became increasingly immersed in a Spain that is changing and a landscape that it constant." Along the Way, Nooteboom offers up a series of priceless, erudite digressions about the soul of Spain and how it has become linked to that of his own. Although he had of course physically visited Compostela several times before, he did not consider his pilgrimage complete until he was able to write about it. And so, once more he sets off toward that magnetic yet elusive city:

> I am about to undertake the journey one more time, and even now I know that I will be side-tracked, a tour being synonymous with a detour in my experience, the eternal, self-contrived labyrinth of the traveler who cannot resist the temptation of side roads and country lanes, of a branch road off a main road, of the sign pointing to a village with a name you have never heard before, of the silhouette of a castle in the distance with only a track leading to it, of the vistas that may lie in store for you on the other side of that hill or mountain range.

Roads to Santiago remains one of the ultimate expressions in all of travel literature of the singular importance of the journey over the destination.

The Pilgrimage Disease: Diagnosis Caminophilia!

Earlier I made the analogy that the Camino of today is rather like Venice of the eighteenth and nineteenth centuries, in that travellers to both have often felt compelled to write about their experiences which they imagine to be much more unique and therefore worthy of note than is often the case.

Judith Martin, in *No Vulgar Hotel: The Desire and Pursuit of Venice*, coined the expression "Venetophiles" to describe the fixation that some feel toward the famous lagoon city. Likewise, the obsessive behaviour displayed by some veterans in relation to the Camino pilgrimage can be likened to a form of landscape stalking. I offer the following list of observable symptoms to what might be referred to as 'Caminophilia':

- Creating a special pilgrimage shrine-like area in your guest or sun room at home in which to concentrate and display all your Camino related paraphernalia.
- Frequently checking the weather forecast for northern Spain on the computer or in your weekend newspaper.
- Marking the Feast Days of various saints found along the Way on your refrigerator calendar and calling in 'sick' to work year after year on July 25th in order to celebrate Saint James' Day.
- Developing a predatory 'search image' and acquisition zeal for anything remotely related to the Camino or northern Spain.
- Displaying your framed *compostela* on the wall of your office or home in a place of greater prominence than any of your university degrees or professional certificates.
- Resolving to always walk to and from church.
- Trying to use your pilgrim passport to obtain cheaper rates in hotels, motels and B & Bs when travelling to other countries far from Spain and France.
- Writing and self-publishing your pilgrimage diary even if you have not strung together more words than those in your signature on cheques since leaving school four decades ago.
- Saving insignia-emblazoned bags from Santiago de Compostela shops to reuse at home.
- Buying and consuming wine only from those specific regions of Spain or France through which you have walked.
- Proudly continuing to display a scallop shell on your daypack years after returning from the Camino.
- Visiting hitherto ignored museums close to home to gaze at medieval Spanish paintings.
- Purging your portable music player of all music of a date more recent than the fourteenth century.
- Speaking Spanish or French to anyone at any time when back at home for no logical reason.
- Trying to convince your priest that the single best solution to declining church attendance would be to remove the relic from beneath the altar and instead display it in a grand, faux jewel-incrusted reliquary in order to attract visiting pilgrims.
- Insisting that everyone start referring to you by the Latinised version of your name as shown on your *compostela*.
- Changing your hallway night-light covers and all your bathroom soap-bowls to those shaped as scallop shells.

Consulting your guidebooks each day when back at home after walking one section of the Way in order to vicariously travel the rest of the journey in real time with fellow pilgrims you met whom are continuing onward to Compostela.

Dutifully loitering about in front of the replica of the Pórtico de la Gloria at the Victoria and Albert Museum in London so as to inform visitors about how it differs in slight details from the real one you walked to in Compostela.

Repeatedly rearranging your library of Camino literature in different ways to reflect date of publication, country of author, or judged quality.

Volunteering to work in a *refugio* during your next summer vacation.

Joining all English-language Camino confraternities regardless of whether or not you originate from, have family connections in, or have ever been to Canada, Australia, New Zealand or South Africa.

Searching out cookbooks and visiting restaurants specialising in Spanish cuisine.

Dressing up year after year as a medieval pilgrim for Halloween costume parties.

Nailing up replica yellow-and-blue stylised shell or yellow arrow waymarking signs around your property and house.

Finding yourself, if you live on the eastern coast of North America, visiting beaches and staring nostalgically eastward back toward Finisterre.

Consuming Coquilles Saint Jacques or *pulpe* at least once a month.

Travelling distances from your small town to the city in order to view, for the third time, Martin Sheen's recent movie *The Way*.

Seriously considering switching religious denomination to be able to attend a church dedicated to Saint James located in your neighbourhood.

Launching into mini-lectures to your friends and family about Romanesque architecture, medieval pilgrim apparel, the *Reconquesta*, scallop shell symbolism, and the like, often at the most non sequitur of times and completely oblivious to any ensuing eye-rolling.

Retaining your pilgrim garb and especially your boots long after they should have consigned to the rubbish bin as if they were holy relics that had somehow absorbed the spirit of the Camino.

Booking your next flight to Spain or France for another pilgrimage months in advance but within a only few days after returning home from your last pilgrimage.

Finding yourself exclusively dating Spanish men or women in order to practise your language skills.

Reading your own daily journal entries in real time on recurring anniversaries of your own pilgrimage.

Engaging in long-winded punditry about what separates a 'true' pilgrim from a religious tourist and becoming protective of the word 'pilgrimage' and hyper-critical of its ascription to anything other than a destination that is walked to.

- Checking out used car advertisements in newspapers and websites to see if anyone nearby might be selling an old El Camino.
- Experiencing nightmares in which Tony Blair or George W. Bush appear dressed as Saint James the Moorslayer.
- Suggesting to your church planning committee, regardless of denomination, that the altar would benefit from the presence of an enormous gilded Baroque *retablo*.
- Seriously considering sending off your troublesome teenage son or daughter to the monasteries in Samos or de las Huelgas in Burgos.
- Restricting your family's playing of board games to only the Game of the Goose.
- Wishing that the judges on those reality courtroom television shows so popular in the United States would sentence guilty individuals to penitential pilgrimages rather than menial fines.
- Building a backyard *bodega* wine cellar or *polloza* stone hut that would make Bilbo proud.
- Having your name legally changed to 'King,' 'Roy,' or "Kaiser' upon returning home because you were the first in your company of pilgrims to ascend Monte de Gozo.
- Driving to Saskatchewan or Kansas for the next family holiday just because it reminds you of the *meseta*.
- Naming your next born offspring, James…regardless of gender.
- Thinking you should write a book like this one no matter how unqualified you may be for such a task.

And thus, if any five of the aforementioned symptoms accurately describes your situation, this is indication that you have progressed from being merely an enthusiastic pilgrim to being one suffering from Caminophilia. For treatment, intervention by friends and family might be needed…or a return to the Camino Francés, required.

The modern cultural phenomenon

In the scholarly tome *Christian Pilgrimage in Modern Western Europe*, Mary Lee and Sidney Nolan build a convincing case for the continued popularity of pilgrimage as a contemporary European phenomenon. The authors investigate more than six thousand active shrines scattered over the continent that are visited by millions of pilgrims, providing analyses of shrine distribution, visitation timing, typology of visitation and shrine, motivation, devotional subjects, methods of veneration, and ethnography of the visitors. Examining the copious maps, tables, and statistics, one cannot but be struck by the incredible range of the modern pilgrimage experience. Also of interest is the fact that, even with the modern ease of far ranging travel, the vast majority of the documented pilgrimage visitations are, just as they always have been, to small, humble, local shrines. In contrast, one major difference in today's pilgrimages compared to those in medieval times is the shift in subject focus of the devotional journeying. Whereas in the past, pilgrims sought proximity to the physical remains or relics of saints, the bulk of today's religious pilgrims visit sites of Marian apparition (Lourdes, Fatima, Knock, etc.). The Nolans' research was conducted throughout the Eighties and can thus no longer be referred to as 'modern' since this was the period immediately predating the meteoric rise in popularity of pedestrianised peregrinations during the last two decades. This explains why the authors could write at the time, when referring to Saint Foy in Conques, that "the Medieval pilgrimage to this saint is virtually extinct." Today, tens of thousands of pilgrims walk through Conques along one of the major feeder routes to Santiago de Compostela.

With the title of Ian Bradley's recent *Pilgrimage: A Spiritual and Cultural Journey*, comes the formal realisation that modern pilgrimage is both a religious and secular phenomena. The book provides a wealth of information about the blossoming of walking pilgrimages that are, on the surface, "so striking and unexpected in an age that is usually described as secular or post-Christian." For example, about a hundred thousand people climb Croagh Patrick each year. The year 1997 saw the establishment of St. Cuthbert's Way from Melrose to Lindisfarne and St Olav's Way from Oslo to Trondheim, and recently, the Italians have provided five million euros to waymark and improve the *Via Francigena* which runs from Canterbury to Rome. Thousands of pilgrims now walk these revitalised pilgrim paths each year. Pilgrimage renewal is not restricted to only predominantly Catholic countries. In Britain, for example, thousands of pilgrims undertake annual walks to St. Cedd's Chapel in Bradswell, to St Ninian's cave at Whithorn, and to the shrine at Walsingham. Then there are the celebratory events such as the 1997 pilgrimage from Canterbury to Iona to celebrate the 1,400th anniversary of the arrival of Augustine to Kent and the death of Columba, and the 1998 pilgrimage from Glastonbury to Canterbury to mark the millennium of the death of Dunston who began as abbott of the former and finished his life as archbishop of the latter. Indeed, there is now an organisation, the *Cammini d'Europa*, headquartered in Rome and backed by the European Commission and Council of Europe, that was established to "promote and develop Europe's historic pilgrimage routes…as a way to encourage cultural links and tourism...[and] the widespread desire to recover and celebrate Europe's spiritual roots and soul."When the European ministers of culture met in 1987 – no accident that this gathering took place in Compostela – they hoped that their citizens travelling the newly established cultural routes (many of which were ancient pilgrimage ways) would help to build a new pax-Europa society "founded on tolerance, respect for others, freedom and solidarity."

Bradley's book is arranged as a timeline of western pilgrimage from its Biblical roots, through its Celtic, Medieval, and post-Reformation developmental periods, to its contemporary expression as a cultural phenomenon. Punctuating the text are gorgeous photographs of Europe's most popular shrines, including those destinations to which modern-day pilgrims walk (e.g. Rome, Compostela, Nidaros, Assisi, Croagh Patrick, Iona, and Lindisfarne). The revival of pilgrimage is part of "the recovery of a sense of the sacredness of place and landscape in an increasingly fragile and urbanised world, the growing emphasis on physical well-being and exercise, and the widespread desire to rediscover and connect with roots, traditions and history", Bradley writes. Looking at the beautiful images in the book, one can see why in our anxious age of self-doubt and listlessness, where most people have no special desires, only preferences, that the very act of pilgrimage and the viewing of landscapes along the way can be so therapeutic to so many. No more miracles need be sought by many of today's pilgrims upon their return home beyond that of an enrichment of spirit and a revitalisation of life purpose.

The recent reanimated popularity of pilgrimage has been paralleled by publication of a suite of books designed to inspire and nurture the aspirations of would-be pilgrims. In this regard, I have found myself drawn repeatedly to several overviews of the cultural phenomena. As an antidote to the puzzled expressions and voiced bafflement often raised from friends and family when one gushes on about the manifest benefits accruing from walking to Compostela, these books help readers recognise their inherent solidarity with a rising tide of humanity through shared participation in a growing global trend. And for those readers of an adventurous spirit, these books are ultimately just as depressing as they are simultaneously inspiring, for one soon comes to realise that no single life can ever be of sufficient duration to enable venturing along all the wonderfully evocative pilgrim pathways.

In *Sacred Tracks; 2000 Years of Christian Pilgrimage*, James Harpur reminds us that in pre-Reformation Europe pilgrimage was just as much a part of the fabric of religion as was the "hypnotic tolling of the church bell." The interesting irony is that whereas attendance in those churches is today at an all time low, pilgrimage is now stronger in some parts of Europe than it has been since the end of the Middle Ages. Accompanied by powerful photographs, readers are guided through the history of Christian pilgrimage from the early paths to the catacombs of Rome, Christ's imagined footsteps in the Holy Land, to the cells of the desert fathers and Celtic saints, to the well-travelled medieval roads to Jerusalem, Rome, and Santiago de Compostela, and finally to the modern ways to Lourdes, Croagh Patrick, Fatima, Iona, Walsingham, and Taize. For early pilgrims, arriving at a shrine after a long and arduous journey was the opportunity to be granted a glimpse on earth of what heaven had in store. For today's pilgrims, however, the significance of travelling has often superseded the importance of arriving. Of particular interest to Camino veterans is the title page image of a backpacked pilgrim striding toward the distant baroque towers of the Compostela cathedral, and also the estimation that at the height of its popularity in the late eleventh and twelfth centuries, up to half a million pilgrims a year walked to the Santiago shrine. Indeed the pilgrimage to Saint James was so predominant that Dante, writing in *La Vita Nuova* in 1292, actually defined a "pilgrim" as specifically being someone who had journeyed to Compostela.

Jennifer Westwood, in *Sacred Journeys: An Illustrated Guide to Pilgrimages Around the World*, expands the subject with two dozen detailed case studies of locations such as Mecca, Benares, Mount Kailash, Shikohu Island, Chaco Canyon, and the Western Wall, in addition to secular sites. Pilgrimage in the modern age, Westwood tells us, by its very nature, stands slightly to one side of organised religion and is rapidly attracting the interest of anthropologists, sociologists, and geographers. Because many of our traditional support systems are either weakened or have disappeared, individuals today, as in no other time in history, have never felt so truly alone. We collectively suffer from the modern Western malaise, Westwood states, of alienation from ourselves, from each other, and from the rest of creation. Today's pilgrims, recoiling from a despoiled world in thrall to technology, seek the simple spiritual solidarity of *communitas* offered by a journey as a rite of passage involving a liminal crossing of a threshold connecting present to past, inner to outer worlds. Pilgrims, when they reach their destination, find a spiritual reservoir from which they can withdraw but also reciprocally into which their very presence there serves to replenish at the same time. "To be a pilgrim is not to perform an individual act of devotion, but to engage in humankind's dialogue with the divine; not in time, but eternity." Bracketing the richly illustrated case studies, Westwood guides the reader through a series of chapters that describe the various stages of pilgrimage: longing, getting ready, setting out, the sacred way, adventures and difficulties, midway (doubt and hope about going on or turning back), drawing near (anticipation), arrival (excitement and preparation), climax (encounter with the unknown), reflection and redirection, and coming home. Interestingly, the Camino case study recounting the pilgrimage from Belgium to Compostela was made by several juvenile delinquents who had been sentenced in a revival of the medieval custom to undertake the journey as a form of penance. The book ends with brief introductions to a further forty places of pilgrimage around the world.

At any time today there are thousands – possibly *tens* of thousands – of aspiring pilgrims around the Western world nervous and uncertain about how to proceed on such a daunting enterprise. Racked with self-doubt fostered by a society that has done little to encourage a spirit of adventure and exploration, many individuals today are simply afraid to leave behind their comfortable, easy, surprise-fee lives for the challenge of an independent pilgrimage to Compostela. This has led to a minor growth industry in self-help books designed to encourage the house-bound to venture forth for what might become one of the most important undertakings of their otherwise sedentary, domesticated lives.

Edward Sellner has produced a useful little book with *Pilgrimage*, part of a series that explores spiritual practice (topics of other books include meditation, fasting, and journaling). Blending together a sensitivity to variable religious traditions (in particular early Celtic Christianity) with an obvious passion for nature, the book is laid out as a pilgrimage manual that provides a catholic (in the true sense of the word) and at times idiosyncratic introduction to the history and motivations of pilgrimage present in many faiths. This is followed by a pragmatic "How to do it" section in which Sellner lays out and discusses what he considers to be the seven common elements of pilgrimage: longing, motivation, timing, surrender, synchronicity, ritual, and storytelling. The book concludes with a series of interesting, though occasionally puzzling and eclectic, listings of famous pilgrims, famous holy places, and the best pilgrimage books and films.

Of somewhat similar intent, Sarah York's *Pilgrim Heart: The Inner Journey Home*, unfortunately comes across as a jumbled potpourri of not terribly interesting personal musings that conflate and confuse pilgrimage with mindful travel. The sequential stages of pilgrimage are immersed in a barrage of tangential snippets from many traditions. The lack of structural focus in the book may be understandable when one reads that the author is an ordained Unitarian Universalist minister, an American humanist organisation that some consider to not be a religion due to its lack of formal creed, belief system, and theology. In short, this is the type of book to appeal to Camino pilgrims enthusiastically steeped in the New Ageism of Shirley MacLaine and Paulo Coelho.

By using phrases such as "attentive travel", "soulful journeys", and "awakened wonder", Phil Cousineau, in *The Art of Pilgrimage: The Seeker's Guide to Making Travel Sacred,* shows that the distinction between tourism and pilgrimage, which have always been overlapping, has become even more blurred in recent times. He believes that the two distinguishing traits of pilgrimage are the necessity for spiritual longing behind the undertaking, and the purpose of the journey being one of self-improvement in order to make one's life more meaningful. This latter can only happen by enduring and overcoming difficulties, and for that reason alone, true pilgrimage by definition needs to be rigorous. True pilgrimage then, even in modern times, will not come easy and may be regarded as a foolhardy task. For as Cousineau reminds us, it is perhaps no accident that in the Tarot, the card of the Fool is represented by a pilgrim, with the Fool's Journey, just like pilgrimage itself, being the metaphor for life. Cousineau's book is chock-a-block full of fascinating pilgrimage minutiae and inspiring anecdotes from the famous and the unknown. He also provides a guide for pilgrim travellers to progress through the stages of the longing, the call, departing, the way, the labyrinth, arrival, and what he intriguingly calls "bringing back the boon."

Like ripened apples bobbing to the surface of my consciousness, it is with only minimal effort that I can resurrect vibrant, searing memories gathered from a lifetime of travel of witnessing the devotional practice of the faithful:

- the angled, late afternoon light in Durham Cathedral causing a spontaneous outburst of carol singing from a group of angelic-voiced schoolboys
- the bloodied feet of those slogging up the sharp scree slopes of Croagh Patrick, shoes draped defiantly around their necks as proud talismans of their pain
- the robed priest mouthing a prayer into the howling wind as he looks out over the landscape from the summit of the wounded mountain of La

Verna, site of Saint Francis' stigmata

- those queuing up in silent reverence to visit the tomb of recently deceased Pope John Paul II in the Vatican
- the happy villagers decorating a Derbyshire holy well with flowers, repeating an ancient ritual of thanksgiving
- the shocked silence of those standing in front of the martyrdom site in Canterbury Cathedral
- those crying and crossing themselves when seeing the collection of miraculously unneeded crutches and leg-braces leaning against the walls of the Basilica Saint Anne de Beaupré outside Quebec City
- the loving gazes and delicate caresses bestowed by the aesthetically enraptured upon the magnificent carved capitals in the cloisters of Moissac and Santillana del Mar along pilgrimage routes to Compostela
- the Bible-totting faithful slowly making their way along the *Via Dolorosa* in Jerusalem or singing on the presumed site of the Sermon on the Mount overlooking the Sea of Galilee, shimmering in the distant heat
- those shivering after emerging from the pool at Holywell, hopeful of being healed
- the pained yet ecstatic expressions of those ascending the steps to Saint Joseph's Oratory in Montreal on their knees
- the hundreds of the white-robed believers gathering silently in the early morning darkness in the town of Axum to await the arrival of the Arc of the Covenant
- Etc., etc., etc.

And those are just the Christian sites. In my mental rolodex reside an equal number of similarly powerful memories garnered from watching pilgrims at Buddhist, Shinto, Islamic, and Jewish sacred sites, not to mention the humbled and awestruck whom I've witnessed visiting many sacred landscapes around the world. And then there are those famous pilgrimages which I have only seen on a television screen: the millions who do the *Hajj* to Mecca each year, the largest annually recurring pilgrimage, and the *tens* of millions who venture into the Ganges during the various *Kumbh Mela* pilgrimages taking place every six to one hundred and forty-four years in what have become the largest gatherings in all of human history.

One would not be wrong to imagine that at times it seems as if pilgrimage has taken over the entire world. Indeed, it has even been stated that the planet is itself but a pilgrim moving on its celestial way through the cosmos…the Milky Way, itself a sometimes moniker for the Way to Santiago de Compostela, otherwise known as the Camino Francés.

Ultreia! to us all.

ACKNOWLEDGMENTS

The writing of this manuscript was supported by Marilyn France and an operating grant from Dalhousie University's Faculty of Agriculture. The latter might at first seem strange before learning that one etymological root of the English word "pilgrimage" is from the Latin "*per ager*" or "through [the] fields." Titles used for Chapter 6 and for the third section in Chapter 7 are cribbed from phrases in J. Hitt (2005) and E. Mullins (2001), respectively. C. Gossen is thanked for providing a copy of her thesis dissertation, as are H. Taylor and C. Cozens for designing and facilitating production of the book.

BIBLIOGRAPHY

Amadis Ensemble. 1998. *Sur les chemins de Saint-Jacques de Composelle*. Editions Jade.

Amadis Ensemble. 2001. *The chants of Camino de Santiago*. Editions Jade.

Amawalker. 2009. 101 books on the Camino – Pilgrim stories, guides, cultural, children's books. www.amawalker.blogspot.com

Anonymous 4. 1995. *Miracles of Sant'Iago: Music from the Codex Calixtinus*. Harmonia Mundi USA.

Ashley, K. and M. Deegan. 2009. *Being a pilgrim: Art and ritual on the medieval routes to Santiago*. Lund Humphries.

Atman. 2008. *Walking in grace*. Trafford Publishing.

Aviva, E. 2001. *Dead end on the Camino*. Pilgrims Process.

Aviva, E. 2004. *The journey: A novel of pilgrimage and spiritual quest*. Pilgrims Process.

Badone, E. and S.R. Roseman. (Eds.) 2004. *Intersecting journeys: The anthropology of pilgrimage and tourism*. Univ. Illinois Press.

Barral, A. and R. Yzquierdo. 2004. *Santiago cathedral: A guide to its art treasures*. Edilesa Guides.

Boers, A. 2007. *The way is made by walking: A pilgrimage along the Camino Santiago*. Intervarsity Press.

Boulting, L. 2010. *Within the way without*. Confraternity of Saint James.

Bradley, I. 2009. *Pilgrimage: A spiritual and cultural journey*. Lion Hudson.

Brierley, J. 2003. *A pilgrim's guide to the Camino Francés*. Camino Guides.

Brierley, J. 2003. *A pilgrim's guide to the Camino Fisterra*. Camino Guides.

Brown, M.K. 2008. *A pilgrimage story*. Trafford Publishing.

Buñuel, L. (Dir.) 1969. *The Milky Way*. Janus Films.

Bussac, E. 2005. *Sculteurs au Moyen Age: The fantastic world of Romanesque capitals*. Editions L'Instant Durable.

Chaput, S. 2004. *Santiago*. Turnstone Press.

Chat, M.M. 2012. *Thoreau and the aquatic cats of Concord: A love story*. Green Frigate Books.

Christmas, J. 2007. *What the psychic told the pilgrim*. Greystone Books.

Clem, Jim and Eleanor. 2004. *Buen Camino*. Page-Free Publishing Inc.

Coelho, P. 1987. *The pilgrimage*. HarperSanFrancisco.

Coelho, P. and Moebius. *Pilgrim adventure game*. Arxel Tribe.

Cohen, E. 1992. Pilgrimage and tourism: Convergence and divergence. *In* Morinis, A. (Ed.) *Sacred journeys: The anthropology of pilgrimage*. Greenwood Press.

Confraternity of Saint James. 2008. *Roads to Santiago: A spiritual journey*. Confraternity of Saint James.

Cousineau, P. 1998. *The art of pilgrimage: The seeker's guide to making travel sacred*. Conari Press.

Curry, N. 1992. *Walking to Santiago*. Enitharmon Press.

Curtsinger, E.C. 2005. *Ten thousand ways to Santiago: A pilgrimage novel.* Xlibris.

Dennett, L. 1987. *A hug for the apostle*: MacMillian.

Dickenson, D. 2010. *Death of a pilgrim.* Soho Press.

Edilesa. 2002. *The road to Santiago.* Edilesa.

Dutey, G. and R. Gastineau. 2004. *Compostelle: A spiritual journey.* Editions Austrevue.

Egan, K. 2004. *Fumbling: A pilgrimage tale of love, grief, and spiritual renewal on the Camino de Santiago.* Random House.

Ensemble Organum. 2004. *Compostela ad vespers Sancti Jacobi.* Sound Arts AG.

Estevez, E. (Dir.) 2011. *The Way.*

Feinberg, E. 1985. *Strangers and pilgrims on the Camino de Santiago in Spain: The perpetuation and recreation of meaningful performance.* Ph.D. Thesis. Univ.

Feinberg, E. 1989. *Following the Milky Way: A pilgrimage across Spain.* Iowa State Univ. Press.

Fladmark, J.M. (Ed.) 1998. *In search of heritage as pilgrim or tourist?* Donhead Publ.

France, R.L. 2003. *Profitably soaked: Thoreau's engagement with water.* Green Frigate Books.

France, R.L. 2003. *Deep immersion: The experience of water.* Green Frigate Books.

France, R.L. (Ed.) 2007. *Ultreia! Onward! Progress of the pilgrim.* Green Frigate Books.

France, R.L. 2012. *Veniceland Atlantis: The bleak future of the world's favourite city.* Libri Publishing.

Gardiner, J. 2006. *Pilgrimage to Santiago.* Ontevderdi Productions.

Frey, N.L. 1998. *Pilgrim stories: On and off the road to Santiago.* Univ. California Press.

Gitlitz, D.M. and L.K. Davidson. 2000. *The pilgrimage road to Santiago: The Complete cultural handbook.* St. Martin's Griffin.

Goodwin, J.B. 1970. *Beacon of faith led medieval travelers.* National Geographic School Bulletin 14: 218-221.

Gonzlaez, A. 2006. *"San Isidoro" in Leon: Romanesque paintwork in the Pantheon of Kings.* Edilesa.

Gossen, C.E. 2012. *Place-making and meaning-making in the pilgrimage to Santiago de Compostela.* Ph.D. Thesis. University of Calgary.

Harman, L.D. 2009. *We are never alone: Healing Lessons From the Camino.* Ursus.

Harper, J. 2002. *Sacred tracks: 2000 years of Christian pilgrimage.* University of California Press.

Hayton, A. 2006. *Walk with me: The pilgrim road to Santiago.* Verulam Productions.

Hoinacki, L. 1997. *El Camino: Walking to Santiago de Compostela.* Pennsylvania State Univ. Press.

Italica Press. 1998. *The road to Compostela for the Macintosh and Windows.* Italica Press.

Jacobs, M. 2002. *The road to Santiago.* Pallas Athene.

Jecks, M. 2003. *The templar's penance.* Headline Book Publishing.

Kenney, S. 2003. *Stone by stone: Inspirational storytelling: a pilgrim's journey to self-love.* Rosy Dragon Productions.

Kenney, S. 2004. *Sue Kenney's my Camino.* White Knight Publications.

Kenney, S. 2006. *Las peregrinas: The women who walk*. Limited Screening Edition.

King, G.G. 2008. *The way of Saint James. Vols. I, II and III*. Pilgrims' Process.

Kirkpatrick, J. 2010. *The Camino letters: 26 tasks on the way to Finisterre*. Pyxis Press.

Kuh, M. 1969. Pilgrimage to Compostela. p. 172-200 in *The age of chivalry*. National Geographic Society.

Lack, K. 2003. *The Cockleshell pilgrim: A medieval journey to Compostela*. Society for Promoting Christian Knowledge.

Lassell, L.L. 2005. *Walking home on the Camino de Santiago*. Pilgrims Process.

Lodge, D. 1995. *Therapy*. Penguin.

Lozono, M.B. 2004. *A practical guide for pilgrims: The road to Santiago de Compostela*. Everest.

Luard, N. 1998. *The field of the star: A pilgrim's journey to Santiago de Compostela*. Michael Joseph Ltd.

Mahoney, R. 2003. *The Singular pilgrim: Travels on sacred ground*. Houghton Mifflin.

Martin, V. 2001. *Salvation: Scenes from the life of St. Francis*. Alfred A. Knopf.

McWatt, T. 2009. *Step closer*. HarperCollins.

Melczer, W. 1993. *The pilgrims' guide to Santiago de Compostela*. Italica Press.

Melville, M. 2002. *Peregrina: A woman's journey on the Camino*. Reed Press.

Metras, M. 2006. *Walking life: Meditations on the pilgrimage of life*. Self-published, Lulu.

Mitchell, J.H. 1995. *Walking toward Walden: A pilgrimage in search of place*. Addison-Wesley.

Mullins, E. 2006. *Cluny: In search of God's last empire*. Bluebridge.

Musica Antigua. 2004. El *Camino de Santiago en las cantigas de Alfonso X el Sabo*.

Myers, P. 2009. *Rooster in the Cathedral: Reflections of a pilgrim while walking to Santiago*. Shoreline.

National Geographic Society. 1969. *The age of chivalry*. National Geographic Society.

Nelson, H. 1998. *Trust and tears: Poems of pilgrimage*. Private publication.

Newman, S. 1996. *Strong as death*. Tom Doherty Associates.

Nolan, M. and S. 1989. *Christian pilgrimage in modern Western Europe*. Univ. North Carolina Press.

Nooteboom, C. 1992. *Roads to Santiago; A modern-day pilgrimage through Spain*. Harcourt Inc.

O'Marie, C.A. 1993. *Murder makes a pilgrimage*. St. Martin's Press.

Polyphonia Antiqua. 1983. *Ultreia! Sur la route de saint-Jacques de-Compostelle*, Pierre Verany.

Post, P. 1994. The modern pilgrim: A study of contemporary pilgrims' accounts. *Ethnologia Europaea* 24: 85-100.

Raju, A. 2003. *The way of St. James: Le Puy to the Pyrenees*. Cicerone.

Reilly, B. 1997. *Secret of Santiago: A novel of medieval Spain*. Combined Books.

Reilly, B. 2001. *Journey to Compostela*. Combined Books.

Resonet. 2000. *Les pellerines*. Clave Records.

Resonet. 2001. *Santiago*. Clave Records.

Resonet. 2003. *La grande chanson*. Clave Records.

Roux, J. (and others). 2004. *The roads to Santiago de Compostela*. MSM In Situ Themes.

Rudolph, C. 2004. *Pilgrimage to the end of the world: The road to Santiago de Compostela*. Univ. Chicago Press.

Rupp, J. 2005. *Walk in a relaxed manner: Life lessons from the Camino*. Orbis Books.

Samartin, C. 2008. *Tarnished beauty*. Washington Square Press.

Santiago, R. (Ed.) 2008. *Al final del Camino*. Warner Brothers.

Santz, M.J.H. 2006. *Guides Santa María la Real de Huelas*, Burgos. Reales Siticos de Espana.

Saunders, T. 2007. *Pilgrimage to heresy: Don't believe what they tell you*. iUniverse.

Schroer, O. 2008. *Camino*. Boreal Records.

Sellner, E.C. 2004. *Pilgrimage: Exploring a great spiritual practice*. Sorin Books.

Serreau, C. 2007. *Saint Jacques…la mecque (Start walking)*. Métropole.

Sewall, B. 2004. *The naked pilgrim: The road to Santiago*. WAGtv.

Sewall, L. 1999. *Sight and sensibility: The ecopsychology of perception*. Tarcher.

Shea, M. 2008. *The Way, Camino de Santiago*. Overlander Media.

Sing, S.S. 1981. *A pilgrim in Assisi: Searching for Francis today*. St. Anthony Messenger Press.

Smith, C. (Ed.) 2000. *Before and after the end of time: Architecture and the year 1000*. Harvard Design School.

Stanton, E.F. 1994. *Road of stars to Santiago*. Univ. Press Kentucky.

Starkie, W. 1957. *The road to Santiago*. E.P. Dutton and Company.

Temple, F. 1994. *The Ramsay scallop*. HarperTrophy.

Temple, K. 2003. *Peregrina: On pilgrimage to Santiago de Compostela*. StringTown Press.

Thatcher, G. 2008. *A journey of days*. General Store Publishing House.

Tomar, R. 2004. [Ed.] *Romanesque: Architecture, sculpture, painting*. Ullman and Konemann.

Turner, V and E. 1978. *Image and pilgrimage in Christian culture*. Columbia University Press.

Vincenot, H. 1996. *The prophet of Compostela: A novel of apprenticeship and initiation*. Inner Traditions International.

Wallis, M.W. 2003. *Among the pilgrims: Journeys to Santiago de Compostela*. Trafford Publishing.

Ward, R. 2007. *All the good pilgrims: Tales of the Camino de Santiago*. Thomas Allen Publishers.

Wegen, A.J. 2003. *Medieval pilgrimage to Santiago*. Christophorus.

Westwood, J. 1997. *Sacred journeys: An illustrated guide to pilgrimages around the world*. Henry Holt and Company.

Whyte, D. 2012. *Pilgrim*. Many Rivers Press.

Wiegman, N.A. 2009. *Walking the way: A medieval quest*. WingSpan Press.

York, S. 2001. *Pilgrim heart: The inner journey home*. Jossy-Bass.

INDEX

A

accidents 31–2, 33–4, 108
accommodation see *albergues*
albergues
  beds 158–60
  meals 155–8
  overcrowding 162
  routines 144–8
American Association of Retired Persons (AARP) 133
American Pilgrims on the Camino 255–6
Anonymous 4
  Miracles of Sant'Iago: Music from the Codex Calixtinus 233–4
architecture
  bridges
    Ponte Maceira 94
    Puente de los Peregrinos 90–1
    Puente del Passo Honoroso 93
    Rio Odrilla causeway 92–3
  capitals 115
  cathedrals
    cathedral of St James 18, 47, 48, 74, 104–7
    cathedral of St Mary, Burgos 119, 126
    Santa María de León 47, 100–1
  churches 47–8
    Basilica de San Isidoro, León 102–3
    Iglesia de San Miguel, Estella 98–9
    San Marcos, León 97
    San Martín, Frómista 99–100
  landscapes 117
  monuments 108–12
  sculpture 94–8
    church of San Pedro de la Rúa 94–5
    Iglesia de Santiago 96
    Santa Maria de Cañas, monastry 95
    Urraca López de Haro, tomb 95–6
  structures 86–90
    Monasterio de las Huelgas 87
    Palacio de los Reyes de Navarra 87
    pallozas 72–3
    San Anton monastery and hospice 88–9
    Templar castle, Ponferrada 89–90
art
  The Artist's Journey: The Perfumed Pilgrim Tackles the Camino de Santiago (2010) 212–13
  A Painting Pilgrim: A Journey to Santiago de Compostela 212
  Santiago El Grande (1957) 213–14
Arzua 76, 87
Ashley, Kathleen
  Being a Pilgrim: Art and Ritual on the Medieval Routes to Santiago (2009) 268–9
Astorga 87, 157
Atapuerca 133
Atapuerca Mountains 67
Atman
  on danger 32
  emotional experiences 49
  on happiness 40, 41
  interactions with others 49
  on landscape 45
  on physical hardship 34
  on relaxation 39
  on solitude 45
  Walking in Grace (2008) 15, 21
  on wayfinding 31
Australian Friends of the Camino 255
authenticity debate 25–6, 242–4, 258–9
Aviva, Elyn *see also* Feinberg, Ellen
  Dead End on the Camino (2001) 178
  The Journey: A Novel of Pilgrimage and Spiritual Quest (2004) 189–90

B

Barranco Mataburros 66
Basilica de San Isidoro, León 102–3
Panteón de los Reyes 103
beds 158–60
Belorado 87, 155
Bethsaida, Galilee 137
Boers, Arthur Paul
  on church-based spirituality 23
  on excitement of experience 38
  on faith 24
  on physical hardship 34
  on the pilgrim experience 25–6
  on spirituality 22
  on walking 44–5
  The Way is Made by Walking (2007) 15, 21
  on wayfinding 30–1
Boulting, Laurence
  Within the Way Without (2010) 227–8
Brabbs, Derry
  The Roads to Santiago (2008) 209
Bradley, Ian
  Pilgrimage: A Spiritual and Cultural Journey (2009) 274–5
bridges
  Ponte Maceira 94
  Puenta la Reina 60
  Puente de los Peregrinos 90–1
  Puente del Passo Honoroso 93
  Puente la Reina 86
  Rio Odrilla causeway 92–3
Brown, Margaret K.
  A Pilgrimage Story (2008) 194
Bulletin
  depth and breadth 246–7
  incidents and anecdotes 244–6
  pilgrim authenticity debate 242–4
  practicalities and reciprocity 247–8
  rants and reviews 248–51
Buñuel, Luis
  The Milky Way (1969) 191, 220–2
Bunyan, John
  Pilgrim's Progress 175
Burgos 64, 67, 68, 87

cathedral of St Mary 119, 126
Monasterio de las Huelgas 87
pilgrim mural 134

C

Cabo Fisterra *see* Finisterre
cairns 139
Calle del Agua 72
Camino, the 44–5
  author's own interest 11–13
  connectivity to the past 18–20, 48–9
  dangers 30–2, 108
  emotional experiences
    excitement 38
    happiness 40–2
    playfulness 40
  historicity 18–20
  landscape 21, 45–7
    coasts
    communities
    hills
    the *meseta* 45–6, 64–5
    woods
  literature review 13–16
  personal and societal reflections 21
  physical experiences
    hardships 30–2
    relaxation 39
    walking 44–5
    wayfinding 30–2
  pilgrim community 51–2
  post-pilgrimage experiences 51
  solo or collective endeavour 49–53 *see also* companionship
  spirituality 22–4
  wayfinding 69–70
  weather 30
Camino Francés
  communities 71–5
  landscape
    coasts 79–84
    fields 60–5
    hills 65–70
    woods 75–8
  terrain 133
  'the therapy route' 56–7
'Caminophilia' 25, 271–3
Canadian Company of Pilgrims 255
capitals 115
Carrión de los Condes 166

Hotel Monasterio San Zoilo 121, 127
Iglesia de Santiago 96
Castañeda 141
Castilla y León 61
Castle of the Marquesses 71
Castrojeriz 87, 92, 120, 149, 155
  church of Santiago de los Caballeros 135
Cathedral of the Assumption of the Virgin Mary of Santander 173
cathedrals
  cathedral of St James 47, 104–7
    archivolt 104–5
    pilgrim mass 131
    pilgrims' disppointment with 48, 105–6
    Pórtico de la Gloria 47, 104, 107
    Puerta de las Platerías 106
    Santiago *Peregrino* 74, 104
    tomb of Saint James 18, 130
    tympanum 104, 106
  cathedral of St Mary, Burgos 119, 126
  Cathedral of the Assumption of the Virgin Mary of Santander 173
  Santa María de León 47, 100–1
CD-ROMs
  The Road to Compostela 228–9
  Stone by Stone 229–30
  Walk With Me: The Pilgrim Road to Santiago (CD-ROM) 230–1, 251
Chaput, Simon
  Santiago (2004) 200–3
Christ in Majesty 115
Christian Reconquest of Spain 126
Christianism 126
Christmas, Jane
  on architecture 48
  on companionship 45
  on dangers 32
  on hardship 35–6
  on landscape 46–7
  on the pilgrim community 52–3

on the pilgrim experience 26–7
on prayer 23
on relaxation 39
on Santiago de Compostela 48
on urban development 48
on wayfinding 31
on weather 30
What the Psychic Told the Pilgrim (2007) 15, 18, 21
churches
  architecture 47–8
  Basilica de San Isidoro, León 102–3
  church-based spirituality 22–3
  contemporary shortcomings 23
  Iglesia de San Miguel, Estella 98–9
  Iglesia de Santiago, Carrión de los Condes 96
  San Lorenzo, Sahagún 146
  San Marcos, León 97
  San Martín, Frómista 99–100
  San Nicholás church, Portomarín 97–8
  San Pedro de la Rúa, Estella 94–5
  San Salvador church, Sarria 73
  Santa Maria de la Asuncion, Rabanal 128
  Santiago de los Caballeros, Castrojeriz 135
Cirauqui 92
Cluny Abbey 117, 126, 136, 257
coach tours 242
coasts 79–84
Codex Calixtinus 12, 229, 267
Coelho, Paulo
  The Pilgrimage: A Contemporary Quest for Ancient Wisdom (1997) 192–3
Coffman, Peter 232
Colegio Mayor de Fonseca 74
Columbrianos 150
commercialism 48, 73
community *see* pilgrimages
companionship 41, 45, 49–53, 75
  en route 149–54
  local people 169–70

meals 155–8, 165
Compostilla 150
computer games 229
Confraternity of Saint James 242, 246, 254–5 *see also* Bulletin
Confraternity of St. James of Africa 255
Cousineau, Phil
  The Art of Pilgrimage: The Seeker's Guide to Making Travel Sacred (1998) 171, 278–9
Cruz de Fierro 18, 139, 140
Cuesta de Mostilares 149
Curry, Neil
  Walking to Santiago (1993) 203–4
Curtsinger, E.C.
  Ten thousand Ways to Santiago: A Pilgrimage Novel (2005) 194–5

D

Dali, Salvador
  Santiago El Grande (1957) 213–14
Dante 242
Davidson, Linda Kay
  The Pilgrimage Road to Santiago: The Complete Cultural Handbook (2000) 269
death 135–6
Deegan, Marilyn
  Being a Pilgrim: Art and Ritual on the Medieval Routes to Santiago (2009) 268–9
Dennett, Laurie
  on architecture 47, 48
  on connectivity to the past 48, 277–8
  on dangers 32–3
  on happiness 40–1, 41
  A Hug for the Apostle (1987) 15, 21
  interactions with others 49–50
  on landscape 45
  on the *meseta* 46
  on physical hardship 33–4
  on pilgrim authenticity 242–3
  on playfulness 40
  on relaxation 39
  on walking 44
  on weather 30

Dickinson, David
  Death of a Pilgrim (2010) 178–80
documentaries
  Las Peregrinsa: The Women Who Walk (2006) 222–3
  Naked Pilgrim: The Road to Santiago (2004) 225–7
  The Way: One Man's Spiritual Journey Along the Camino de Santiago (2008) 223–5
  Within the Way Without (2010) 227–8
Doña Mencía Condestables 119
Dutey, Guy
  Compostelle: A Spiritual Journey (2004) 205

E

El Acebo 68
"*El baño de las nueve olas*" 83
Eleanor Plantagenet 87
electronic media
  Pilgrim (computer game) 229
  The Road to Compostela (CD-ROM) 228–9
  Stone by Stone (CD-ROM) 229–30
  websites 256–8
emigration 110–11
Ensemble Amadis
  Sur les Chemins de Saint-Jacques de Compostelle 236
Ensemble für Frühe Musik Augsburg
  Medieval Pilgrimage to Santiago 234–5
Ensemble Organum
  Compostela ad Vespers Sancti Jacobi 235–6
epiphanies 23
Erasmus 242
esoteric literature
  The Journey: A Novel of Pilgrimage and Spiritual Quest (2004) 189–90
  The Pilgrimage: A Contemporary Quest for Ancient Wisdom (1997) 192–3
  Pilgrimage to Heresy: Don't Believe Everything They Tell You (2007) 191–2
  The Prophet of Compostela:

  A Novel of Apprenticeship (1995) 190–1
  Walking Home on the Camino de Santiago (2005) 189
Espalion 174
Estella
  church of San Pedro de la Rúa 94–5
  Iglesia de San Miguel 98–9
  Palacio de los Reyes de Navarra 87
  pilgrim memorial 108
Estevez, Emilio
  The Way (2010) 217–19
Eunate 47
excitement 38 *see also* playfulness

F

faith 22–4, 125
Feinberg, Ellen *see also* Aviva, Elyn
  Strangers and Pilgrims on the Camino de Santiago 258–9
Ferragut 87
fiction
  crime 177–82
    Dead End on the Camino (2001) 178
    Death of a Pilgrim (2010) 178–80
    Murder Makes a Pilgrimage (2003) 181–2
    Strong as Death (2008) 180–1
    The Templar's Penance (2003) 182
  history
    Journey to Compostela: A Novel of Medieval Pilgrimage and Peril, 185–7
    The Ramsay Scallop (1994) 183
    Secret of Santiago: A Novel of Medieval Spain (1996) 184–5
    Walking the Way: A Medieval Quest (2009) 183–4
fields 75–8
films
  Al Final del Camino (2009) 217–19

The Milky Way (1969)
    191, 220–2
Saint Jacques…La Mecque
    (2005) 214–17
The Way (2010) 217–19
Finisterre 80, 81, 82, 111–12,
    115, 132
Fladmark, J.M.
    *In Search of Heritage as
    Pilgrim or Tourist?* (1998)
    173
Fogg Museum 115–16
Foncebadón 139
food 155–8, 165
forests 78
France, Anatole
    My Friend's Book (1885)
    57
France, Robert 115
    *Ultreia! Onward! Progress of
    the Pilgrim* (2007) 206
Frey, Nancy 243
    *Pilgrim Stories: On and Off
    the Road to Santiago*
    (1998) 143, 259–60
Frómista 47, 165, 166
    church of San Martin 99–
    100

G

Galilee 137, 138
Gautama Buddha 171
Gitlitz, David
    *The Pilgrimage Road to
    Santiago: The Complete
    Cultural Handbook*
    (2000) 269
Gonzar 77, 161
Gossen, Cecilia 14, 15
    *Place-Making and Meaning-
    Making in the Pilgrimage
    to Santiago de Compostela*
    (2012) 213, 261–2
gothic architecture 47
    cathedral of St Mary,
    Burgos 126
    San Anton monastery and
    hospice 88–9
    Santa María de León
    cathedral 100–1

H

Haab, B. 244
happiness 40–2
hardships
    emotional 35–6
    physical 33–5

Harman, Lesley D.
    emotional experiences 49
    interactions with others
    50
    on the *meseta* 46
    on the pilgrim experience
    27
    on spirituality 24
    on walking 44
    on wayfinding 31
    *We Are Never Alone:
    Healing Lessons From the
    Camino* (2009) 15
Harpur, James
    *Sacred Tracks; 2000 Years
    of Christian Pilgrimage*
    275–6
Hayton, Althea
    *Walk With Me: The Pilgrim
    Road to Santiago* (CD-
    ROM) 230–1, 251
health 33, 134
Henderson, P. 246
Herrerías 69
hills 65–70
historical fiction
    *Cockleshell Pilgrim: A
    Medieval Journey to
    Compostela* (2003) 187–9
    The Ramsay Scallop (1994)
    183
    *Secret of Santiago: A Novel
    of Medieval Spain* (1996)
    184–5
    *Walking the Way: A
    Medieval Quest* (2009)
    183–4
historicity 18–20
Hoare, Mark
    *A Painting Pilgrim: A
    Journey to Santiago de
    Compostela* (2003) 212
Hoinacki, Lee
    on dangers 32
    *El Camino: Walking to
    Santiago de Compostela*
    (1997) 15, 21
    on excitement of
    experience 38
    on happiness 40, 41–2
    on historicity 19–20
    interactions with others
    50
    on landscape 45, 46
    on monuments 47–8
    on physical hardship 33
    on the pilgrim experience
    24–5
    on relaxation 39

on solitude 45
on spirituality 22, 23
on walking 44
on wayfinding 31
on weather 30
Hontanas 64
Hospital de Órbigo 93
hostels *see albergues*
Hotel de los Reyes Católicos
    162–4
Hotel Monasterio San Zoilo,
    Carrión 121, 127–8

I

Iglesia de San Francisco 71,
    72
Iglesia de San Miguel, Estella
    98–9
Iglesia de Santiago 96
illness 33, 134
injury 33–5
innukshucks 67
International Society for the
    Study of Pilgrimage Art
    257–8
Irish Society of the Friends
    of St. James 255
Isabel de Azofra 159
Isidoro (archbishop) 102–3

J

Jean-Pied-de-Port 114
Jecks, Michael
    The Templar's Penance
    (2003) 182
Journey of Heaven and Earth
    website 257
joy 40–2

K

Keller, Pablo
    *The Pilgrim Route to
    Santiago* (1987) 210–11
Kenney, Sue 24, 25
    on architecture 48–9
    on dangers 32
    on excitement of
    experience 38
    on happiness 40
    interactions with others
    50
    on landscape 45
    on landscape and
    spirituality 46
    *Las Peregrinsa: The Women
    Who Walk* (2006) 222–3

My Camino 15
  on physical hardship 34
  on playfulness 40
  on relaxation 39
  Stone by Stone (CD-ROM) 229–30
  on walking 44
  on wayfinding 31
Kimpton, Mary Catherine 108
King, Georgiana Goddard
  The Way of St James (2008) 262–4
Kingsley Porter, Arthur 116
Kirkpatrick, Julie
  The Camino Letters: 26 Tasks on the Way to Finisterre (2010) 15, 21, 251
  on dangers 32
  on excitement of experience 38
  on happiness 41, 42
  on landscape 46
  on landscape and spirituality 46
  on the pilgrim experience 27
  on playfulness 40
  on solitude 45

L

La Rioja 61
la ruta de la terapia 56–7
Lack, Katherine
  Cockleshell Pilgrim: A Medieval Journey to Compostela (2003) 187–9
landscape 45–7
  architecture 117
  coasts 79–84
  fields 60–5
  forests 78
  hills 65–70
language barriers 50
Laswell, Linda L.
  Walking Home on the Camino de Santiago (2005) 189
Le Puy 173
León 64, 87
  Basilica de San Isidoro 102–3
  Panteón de los Reyes 103
  pilgrim hospital and monastery 108
  San Marcos church 97
  Santa María de León

  Cathedral 47, 100–1
literature
  art
    The Artist's Journey: The Perfumed Pilgrim Tackles the Camino de Santiago (2010) 212–13
    A Painting Pilgrim: A Journey to Santiago de Compostela 212
  compilations
    Roads to Santiago: A Spiritual Companion (2007) 206
    Ultreia! Onward! Progress of the Pilgrim (2007) 206
  contemporary literature
    A Pilgrimage Story (2008) 194
    Santiago (2004) 200–3
    Step Closer (2009) 198–200
    Tarnished Beauty: A Novel (2009) 194–6
    Ten thousand Ways to Santiago: A Pilgrimage Novel (2005) 194
    Therapy (1995) 196–8
    Walking Life: Meditations on the Pilgrimage of Life (2007) 205
  crime fiction 177–82
    Dead End on the Camino (2001) 178
    Death of a Pilgrim (2010) 178–80
    Murder Makes a Pilgrimage (2003) 181–2
    Strong as Death (2008) 180–1
    The Templar's Penance (2003) 182
  history
    Cockleshell Pilgrim: A Medieval Journey to Compostela (2003) 187–9
    Journey to Compostela: A Novel of Medieval Pilgrimage and Peril (2001) 185–7
    The Ramsay Scallop (1994) 183
    Secret of Santiago: A Novel of Medieval

    Spain (1996) 184–5
    Walking the Way: A Medieval Quest (2009) 183–4
  new ageism/esoteric
    The Journey: A Novel of Pilgrimage and Spiritual Quest (2004) 189–90
    The Pilgrimage: A Contemporary Quest for Ancient Wisdom (1997) 192–3
    Pilgrimage to Heresy: Don't Believe Everything They Tell You (2007) 191–2
    The Prophet of Compostela: A Novel of Apprenticeship (1995) 190–1
    Walking Home on the Camino De Santiago (2005) 189
  photography 208–14
    Being a Pilgrim: Art and Ritual on the Medieval Routes to Santiago (2009) 268–9
    Camino Footsteps: Reflections on a Journey to Santiago de Compostela (2008) 209
    The Pilgrim Route to Santiago (1987) 210–11
    The Road to Santiago (1998) 209–10
    The Roads to Santiago (2008) 209
    Santiago: Saint of Two Worlds (1991) 211
  pilgrim accounts 13–16
  poetry
    Compostelle: A Spiritual Journey (2004) 205
    Peregrina 204
    Trust and Tears: Poems of Pilgrimage (1998) 204
    Walking to Santiago (1993) 203–4
  reviews 249–51
local people
  anger 165–6
  bureaucrats 168–9
  companionship 169–70
  kindness 166–7

pilgrims 164–5, 169–70
Lodge, David
  Therapy (1995) 56, 196–8
Logroño 87, 125
loneliness 35 *see also* solitude
Luard, Nicholas
  To Santiago de Compostela: A journey of remembrance (1998) 173

M

Maiestas Domini 115
Mansilla de las Mulas 64, 136, 156
maps 69–70 *see also* wayfinding
Martin, Judith 271
Mateo 105–6
McWatt, Tessa
  Step Closer (2009) 198–200
meals 155–8, 165
Melczer, William
  The Pilgrim's Guide to Santiago de Compostela (1993) 59, 266–8
Melville, Marilyn 25
  on dangers 32
  on excitement of experience 38
  on happiness 40, 41
  Peregrina: A Woman's Journey on the Camino (2002) 15, 21
  on physical hardship 35
  on playfulness 40
memorials 108
Mencia de Mendoza 119
meseta 45–6, 64–5
Metras, Michael
  Walking Life: Meditations on the Pilgrimage of Life (2007) 205
monasteries
  Monasterio de Irache 65
  Monasterio de las Huelgas 87
  San Anton monastery and hospice 88–9
  San Zoilo monastery, Carrión 121
  Santa Maria de Cañas 95
Monasterio de Irache 65
Monasterio de las Huelgas 87
Monte del Gozo 109–10, 153
Monte Irago 68, 139
monuments 108–12
  emigration 110–11

pilgrim memorial, Estella 108
statues 108–9, 110–11, 122, 133–4
Mount of Joy of Compostela 48, 109–10
Mullins, Edward
  The Pilgrimage to Santiago (2001) 85, 266
Mundicamino website 257
Munios 79
music 41–2, 127–8, 232–3
  Camino (Schroer, Oliver) 231–2
  Compostela ad Vespers Sancti Jacobi 235–6
  El Camino de Santiago en las Cantigas de Alfonso X el Sabio 237–8
  La Grande Chanson as Canciós dos Peregrinos de Santiago 238–9
  Les Pellerines: La Mode du Pelrinage dans la France du Baroque 238–9
  Medieval Pilgrimage to Santiago 234–5
  Miracles of Sant'Iago: Music from the Codex Calixtinus 233–4
  Pilgrimage to Santiago 232–3
  Santiago! Music and Pilgrimage in Renaissance Europe 238
  Sur les Chemins de Saint-Jacques de Compostelle 236
  Ultreia! Sur la Route de Saint-Jacaques-de-Compostelle 237
Musica Antigua
  El Camino de Santiago en las Cantigas de Alfonso X el Sabio 237–8
Muxía 79, 117, 162
Myers, Joan
  Santiago: Saint of Two Worlds (1991) 211
Myers, Paul
  on architecture 47, 48
  on happiness 41–2
  interactions with others 50–1
  on physical hardship 34
  on the pilgrim experience 27
  on playfulness 40
  on relaxation 39

Rooster in the Cathedral; Reflections of a Pilgrim While Walking to Santiago (2009) 15, 21
  on Santiago de Compostela 48
  on spirituality 22, 23
  on walking 44
  on wayfinding 31
  on weather 30

N

Nájera 87
Navarrete 125, 144, 164–5
Negreira 110
Nelson, Howard
  Trust and Tears: Poems of Pilgrimage (1998) 204
new ageism 24, 50
pilgrim literature
  The Journey: A Novel of Pilgrimage and Spiritual Quest (2004) 189–90
  The Pilgrimage: A Contemporary Quest for Ancient Wisdom (1997) 192–3
  Pilgrimage to Heresy: Don't Believe Everything They Tell You (2007) 191–2
  The Prophet of Compostela: A Novel of Apprenticeship (1995) 190–1
  Walking Home on the Camino De Santiago (2005) 189
Newman, Sharon
  Strong as Death (2008) 180–1
Nolan, M. and S.
  Christian Pilgrimage in Modern Western Europe (1989) 253, 273–4
Nooteboom, Cees
  Roads to Santiago: A Modern-Day Pilgrimage Through Spain (1992) 269–70
Nuestra Señora de los Angeles 159

O

O Cebreiro 35
Obanos 60, 86

O'Cebreiro 69–70, 71, 72, 87, 141, 148, 157, 160
Olveiroa 154, 169
O'Marie, Sister Carol Anne
  Murder Makes a Pilgrimage (2003) 181–2

P

Palacio de los Reyes de Navarra 87
Palas de Rei 47
Panteón de los Reyes, León 103
Pedrafita 70
Peregrinations 257–8
photography
  Being a Pilgrim: Art and Ritual on the Medieval Routes to Santiago (2009) 268–9
  Camino Footsteps: Reflections on a Journey to Santiago de Compostela (2008) 209
  The Pilgrim Route to Santiago (1987) 210–11
  The Road to Santiago (1998) 209–10
  The Roads to Santiago (2008) 209
  Santiago: Saint of Two Worlds (1991) 211
Pieros 71
pilgrim accounts *see also* literature
  ascribing meaning and significance 24–6
  dangers 30–2
  excitement 38
  experiential categories 13–14
  happiness 40–2
  hardships 33–6
  historicity 18–20
  incidents and anecdotes 244–6
  interactions with others 49–53
  landscape 45–7
  literature review 13–16
  personal and societal concerns 21
  phenomenological analysis framework 14–15
  playfulness 40
  rants and reviews 248–51
  relaxation 39
  secularism 22–3
  spirituality 22–4
  unexpected emotions 49
  walking 44–5
  wayfinding 30–2
  weather 30
pilgrim mass 131
pilgrim passports 167–9
pilgrimages
  authenticity debate 25–6, 242–4, 258–9
  'Caminophilia' 271–3
  connectivity to the past 18–20, 48–9
  as cultural construct 24–5
  as cultural phenomenon 273–5
  healing aspects 25
  incidents and anecdotes 244–6
  the pilgrim community 51–2, 144
    beds 158–60
    companionship 41, 45, 49–53, 75, 149–54, 169–70
    meals 155–8
    routines 144–8
  popularity growth 254, 273–5
  post-pilgrimage experiences 51
  repeat pilgrims 174–5
  rituals
    burning belongings 118–19
    groin-washing in Rio Lavacolla 152
    kissing the statue of St James 130
    pilgrim mass 131
    rock transport 137–42
    twig fence crosses 125
  solo or collective endeavour 45, 49–53
  spiritual motivations 22–4
  starting off 114–15
  walking 44–5
plains *see* meseta
playfulness 40 *see also* excitement
Plaza de Obradoiro 74, 137
poetry 203–6
  Compostelle: A Spiritual Journey (2004) 205
  Peregrina 204
  Trust and Tears: Poems of Pilgrimage (1998) 204
  Walking to Santiago (1993) 203–4
Polyphonia Antigua
  Ultreia! Sur la Route de Saint-Jacaques-de-Compostelle 237
Ponferrada 69, 150
  Templar castle 89–90
Ponte Maceira 94
Porter, Kingsley 104
Pórtico de la Gloria 47, 104, 107
Portomarín 151, 161
  San Nicholás church 97–8
Post, Paul 13–14, 15
prayer 22–3
Priscillian 18
Puenta la Reina 60
Puente de los Peregrinos 90–1
Puente del Passo Honoroso, 90–1
Puente del Passo Honoroso 93
Puente la Reina 86
Puerta de las Platerias 106
Puerta del Perdón 72
Pyrenees 35

Q

Quaife, P. 242

R

Rabanal 68, 127, 146–7
  Monte Irago 139
Reconquista 126
reference books 262–70
Reilly, Bernard
  Journey to Compostela: A Novel of Medieval Pilgrimage and Peril (2001) 185–7
  Secret of Santiago: A Novel of Medieval Spain (1996) 184–5
relaxation 39, 80–1
Renaissance architecture
  San Marcos church, León 97
repeat pilgrims 174–5
Resonet
  La Grande Chanson as Canciöns dos Peregrinos de Santiago 238–9
  Les Pellerines: La Mode du Pelrinage dans la France du Baroque 238–9
  Santiago! Music and Pilgrimage in Renaissance

Europe 238
retablo 126
Rio Lavacolla 152
Rio Odrilla 92–3
Rio Sil 150
Rio Tambre
  Ponte Maceira 94
Rio Ucieza 166
rituals 141
  burning belongings 118–19
  groin-washing in Rio Lavacolla 152
  kissing the statue of St James 130
  rock transport 137–42
Robberstad, Knud Helge
  The Road to Santiago (1998) 209–10
Robins, P. 243
Roland 87
Roman architecture
  Rio Odrilla causeway 92–3
  Via Traiana 92
Romanesque architecture 47
  Basilica de San Isidoro, León 102–3
  Palacio de los Reyes de Navarra 87
  Puente de los Peregrinos 90–1
  San Martín church, Frómista 99–100
  San Salvador church, Sarria 73
  sculpture
    Apostles Matthias, Jude, and Simon 116
    capitals 115
    church of San Pedro de la Rúa, Estella 94–5
    Iglesia de San Miguel, Estella 98–9
    Iglesia de Santiago 96
    Pórtico de la Gloria 47, 104, 107
    tympanum 104

S

Sahagún 64, 87
  church of San Lorenzo 146
Saint James *see also* cathedrals
  birthplace 137
  remoteness 23
  secular attitudes towards 18–19, 130
  slayer of Moors 126, 130
  tomb 18, 130
Samartin, Cecilia
  Tarnished Beauty: A Novel (2009) 194–6
Samos
  pilgrim statue 122
San Anton
  monastry and hospice 88–9
San Juan de Ortega 75
San Lorenzo, Sahagún 146
San Marcos
  pilgrim hospital and monastery 108
San Marcos church, León 97
San Martín church, Frómista 47, 99–100
San Nicholás church, Portomarín 97–8
San Pedro de la Rúa church, Estella 94–5
San Salvador church, Sarria 73
San Zoilo monastery 121
Santa Domingo 87
Santa María church, Eunate 47
Santa Maria de Cañas 95
Santa María de León Cathedral 47, 100–1
Santander 173
Santiago, Robert
  Al Final del Camino (2009) 219–20
Santiago de Compostela 74, 87, 104–7
  cathedral of St James 47
  archivolt 104–5
  pilgrim mass 131
  pilgrims' disappointment with 48, 105–6
  Pórtico de la Gloria 47, 104, 107
  Puerta de las Platerias 106
  Santiago *Peregrino* 74, 104
  tomb of Saint James 18, 130
  tympanum 104, 106
  early history 246–7
  Hotel de los Reyes Católicos 162–4
  Mount of Joy 48, 109–10
  museum 123
  piazza 116–17
  Plaza de Obradoiro 74, 137
Santiago de los Caballeros, Castrojeriz
  carvings 135
Santiago *Matamoros* 126, 130
  see also Saint James
Santiago *Peregrino* 74, 104
Santillana del Mar 173
Santo Domingo de la Calzada 60, 61, 159
Sarria 73, 76, 87, 151
  San Salvador church 73
Saunders, Tracey
  Pilgrimage to Heresy: Don't Believe Everything They Tell You (2007) 191–2
Schroer, Oliver
  Camino (2006) 231–2
sculpture
  Apostles Matthias, Jude, and Simon 116
  Cecilia Gossen 213
  church of San Pedro de la Rúa 94–5
  Maiestas Domini 115
  Pórtico de la Gloria 47, 104, 107
  San Marcos church, León 97
sepulchres
  Doña Mencía Condestables 119
statues 108–9
  Atapuerca 133–4
  emigrant experience 110–11
  pilgrim statue, Samos 122
Urraca López de Haro, tomb 95–6
secularism 22–3
self-help books 277–8
Sellner, Edward
  Pilgrimage (2004) 277
Sewell, Brian
  Naked Pilgrim: The Road to Santiago (2004) 225–7
Shaver, Marcia
  The Artist's Journey: The Perfumed Pilgrim Tackles the Camino de Santiago (2010) 212–13
Shea, Mark
  The Way: One Man's Spiritual Journey Along the Camino de Santiago (2008) 223–5
Shearer, M. 250
Sierra de Atapuerca 67

social concerns 21
societies
   American Pilgrims on the Camino 255–6
   Australian Friends of the Camino 255
   Confraternity of Saint James 254–5
   Confraternity of St. James of Africa 255
   Irish Society of the Friends of St. James 255
solitude 45, 50–1, 75, 153–4
song 41–2, 126, 135–6
   Compostela ad Vespers Sancti Jacobi 235–6
   El Camino de Santiago en las Cantigas de Alfonso X el Sabio 237–8
   La Grande Chanson as Canciòns dos Peregrinos de Santiago 238–9
   Les Pellerines: La Mode du Pelrinage dans la France du Baroque 238–9
   Medieval Pilgrimage to Santiago 234–5
   Miracles of Sant'Iago: Music from the Codex Calixtinus 233–4
   Pilgrimage to Santiago 232–3
   Santiago! Music and Pilgrimage in Renaissance Europe 238
   Sur les Chemins de Saint-Jacques de Compostelle 236
   Ultreia! Sur la Route de Saint-Jacaques-de-Compostelle 237
spirituality 22–4
   and landscape 46
   and walking 44–5
Stanton, Professor Edward
   Road of Stars to Santiago (1994) 56, 250, 267
Starkie, Walter
   The Road to Santiago: Pilgrims of St. James (1957) 113, 264–6
statues 108–9
   Atapuerca 133–4
   emigrant experience 110–11
   pilgrim statue, Samos 122
St.-Jean-Pied-de-Port 173
stones 137–42
Sutton, Robert 187

T

Tardajos 62
Tate, Brian and Marcus
   The Pilgrim Route to Santiago (1987) 210–11
Templar castle, Ponferrada 89–90
Temple, Francis
   The Ramsay Scallop (1994) 183
Temple, Karen
   Peregrina 204
Thatcher, Guy
   on happiness 41, 42
   interactions with others 51
   A Journey of Days (2008) 15
   on physical hardship 34
   on the pilgrim experience 27
   on relaxation 39
   on spirituality 23–4
Thoreau, Henry David 14–15, 138, 139, 140
Tricastela 141, 160

U

urban development 48, 109
Urraca López de Haro 95

V

Via Traiana 92
Viana 66
Victoria and Albert Museum 107
Villafranca del Bierzo 69, 71
Villamayor de Monjardin 65
Vincenot, Henri
   The Prophet of Compostela: A Novel of Apprenticeship (1995) 190–1

W

Walden Pond 138, 139, 140
walking 44–5
Wallis, Mary Victoria
   Among the Pilgrims: Journeys to Santiago de Compostela (2003) 15, 18, 19
   on architecture 47
   on connectivity to the past 18–19, 20
   on excitement 38
   on faith 24
   on happiness 42
   on the *meseta* 46
   on the pilgrim experience 25
   on playfulness 40
   post-pilgrimage experiences 51
   on spirituality 22–4
   on walking 44
   on weather 30
Ward, Robert
   All the Good Pilgrims: Tales of the Camino de Santiago (2007) 15, 18
   emotional experiences 49
   on excitement of experience 38
   on landscape 46
   on physical hardship 34–5
   on the pilgrim community 51–2
   on the pilgrim experience 26
   on spirituality 23
   on weather 30
wayfinding 30–2, 69, 78
weather 30
websites 256–8
Wells, Kim and Malcolm
   Camino Footsteps: Reflections on a Journey to Santiago de Compostela (2008) 209
Westwood, Jennifer
   Sacred Journeys: An Illustrated Guide to Pilgrimages Around the World (1997) 276–7
Whyte, David
   Pilgrim 113
Wiegman, Neal A.
   Walking the Way: A Medieval Quest (2009) 183–4
woods 60–5
Wren, P. 248–9

Y

York, Sarah
   Pilgrim Heart: The Inner Journey Home (2001) 277–8

CPSIA information can be obtained
at www.ICGtesting.com
Printed in the USA
LVHW070948290422
717554LV00015B/394